MAKING FACES

MAKING FACES

Memoirs of a Caricaturist

Aline Fruhauf

Edited by Erwin Vollmer
Foreword by Marchal E. Landgren

JOHN DANIEL AND COMPANY
Publishers
Santa Barbara · 1990

Frontispiece. Aline Fruhauf, Self-Portrait, 1933.

This is a reprint of the hardbound edition published by Seven Locks Press.

Copyright ©1987 by Erwin Vollmer
Printed in the United States of America

LIBRARY OF CONGRESS CATALOGING-IN-PUBLICATION DATA
Fruhauf, Aline, 1909–1978.
    Making faces: memoirs of a caricaturist / Aline Fruhauf
        p.   c.m.
    ISBN 0-936784-85-7: $10.95
    1. Fruhauf, Aline, 1909-1978. 2. Cartoonists—United
States—Biography. I. Title.
NC1429.F79A2   1990
741.5'092—dc20   90-2793
[B]   CIP

John Daniel and Company, Publishers
Post Office Box 21922, Santa Barbara, California 93121

John Daniel & Company books are distributed to the trade by
National Book Network, 4720 Boston Way, Lanham, Maryland 20706

CONTENTS

ILLUSTRATIONS

Arnold Schonberg

MUSICAL AMERICA
for January 14, 1928

ACKNOWLEDGMENTS

Marchal Landgren, scholar in the arts and mentor to Aline Fruhauf, was supposed to edit this book. He wrote the sensitive foreword that follows, and in fact gave the manuscript its first comprehensive editing. But he was ill with cancer, and in 1982 he was in the hospital for the last time. I received a short, poignant letter from him. It began, "The news from here is not good," and ended, "Don't try to telephone—I have no voice."

As Aline's husband and companion for the last forty-four years of her life, I could not accept that the book remain unpublished; I became, *faute de mieux*, editor. And as such, my first duty is to record the role of this gentle man who gave Aline so much help and encouragement, almost from the time she started writing her story.

Relative to this, I must thank Michael Botwinick, director of the Corcoran Gallery of Art, who made it possible for me to use in this book material Marchal originally prepared for the brochure on Aline's retrospective show at the gallery in 1977.

Jerry Fried, a friend from California, was perhaps the memoirs' first reader. He stopped by for a weekend in the mid-1970s and sat for hours on our front porch, chuckling over Aline's first sheaf of manuscript. The next week he sent her a seven-page, single-spaced critique, full of useful advice. He was a professional writer, and I think his letter gave her the assurance she needed to continue.

Another friend who assisted materially in the latter stage of preparation is Martha Johnson, owner of the Francis Scott

Key Bookstore in Georgetown, who saw to it that a well-typed, presentable package of manuscript with pictures was assembled and sent to publishers.

And in the final stages of preparation for publication I have several to thank. Wendy Wick Reaves, curator of prints at the National Portrait Gallery, was often available when I needed advice on illustrations and matters of editorial sense and sensibility. Betty and Douglas Duffy, owners of the Bethesda Art Gallery, gave me similar help. Bettie Roos, Keiko Moore, and Jem Hom supplied me with much out-of-the-way information. Lifelong friends Prentiss Taylor and Grant Arnold helped me revive memories and gave permission for quotations. And finally, special thanks to Abby Wasserman and Mark Esterman, whose suggestions led me to Seven Locks Press. There Calvin Kytle, president, and his wife, Elizabeth, gave me warm welcome and sure guidance in the unfamiliar world of publishing.

The works of artists are like thistle seeds in the wind: once bought, begged, borrowed, or burgled, they are dispersed in all directions. The larger part of Aline's drawings are scattered in places difficult to trace or summarize, but there are four appreciable collections very representative of her work.

The Museum of the City of New York has fifty-one pieces, including watercolors, lithographs, woodcuts, and drawings. The collection is heavily weighted toward the dance and theater, including (among others) dancers Mary Wigman, Charles Weidman, Martha Graham, and Doris Humphrey; actors Katharine Cornell, Lillian Gish, Basil Rathbone, and R.E. Jones; authors Clifford Odets, Alexander Woollcott, George Kaufman, Noel Coward, and J.P. McAvoy; a mime, Angna Enters; puppeteer Remo Bufano; and composer George Gershwin.

The National Portrait Gallery in Washington has at least seventy pieces, mostly watercolors and ink drawings. The collection favors dress designers (Lilly Daché, Tom Brigance, Pola Stout, inter alia) and artists (Orozco, Eilshemius, Adolph Dehn, Zorach). Writers, including Aldous Huxley, Samuel Behrman, and Edith Hamilton, are well represented. And finally, a miscellaneous group includes financier Otto Kahn, lawyer Clarence Darrow, and congressman Maury Maverick.

Georgetown University has eighteen portrait-caricatures from an exhibit, "The Face of Music in Washington," which had been on display at the Baltimore Museum. These are done in encaustic, a medium Aline experimented with in the 1950s. Included are a number of musicians and music-related personalities such as Robert Evett, Paul Callaway, Elmira Bier, and Paul Hume.

The University of Wyoming has a collection of sixty-four lithographs and woodcuts representing a wide variety of Fruhauf subjects and interests, including personalities such as writer Edith Hamilton, a few scenic pieces (*The Bridge at Widewater* and *The New Hope Canal*), and even a few imaginary ones, such as a legendary "Cape Cod Horse."

The term *Family Collection* in this book refers to illustrations of which the originals are owned by myself or my daughters, Susan Forthman and Deborah Vollmer. Other illustrations are credited to institutions or individuals who own original works and have given permission, in some instances upon payment of usage fees, for reproduction in this book.

E.V.

Marchal E. Landgren,
unpublished draw-
ing, ca. 1933.

xiv

FOREWORD

by Marchal E. Landgren

During the period between the two world wars, when Aline Fruhauf reached her majority and began her career as a caricaturist, there was, at least in America, a wave of humanism that found expression in the art and literature of the time. The paintings of modern life by The Eight and their successors, and the novels of Willa Cather, Theodore Dreiser, Sinclair Lewis, Scott Fitzgerald, Thomas Wolfe, John Steinbeck, and William Faulkner were essentially essays in humanism. As to the caricaturists, a backward glance immediately conjures up the magical names of Art Young, William Gropper, Ralph Barton, Miguel Covarrubias, Constantin Alajalov, Peggy Bacon, and Will Cotton. And, related to the caricature, were the splendid masks of the illustrator W.T. Benda and the puppeteer Remo Bufano.

It is not surprising that the art of caricature flourished during this wave of humanism. Caricature in the fine arts, as the historians of art agree, was born of the humanistic outlook of the Renaissance in Italy. The word *caricature** itself differentiates the art from the merely comic, and the first exponents of the art, Agostino (1557–1602) and Annibale

---

*From the Italian verb, *caricare*, to load. The "loading" added by an artist to a drawing may be, but is not necessarily, comic. According to one authority the word *Caricatura* came into vogue only in the second half of the seventeenth century, although the practice of the art evolved much earlier (Bohun Lynch, *A History of Caricature*, Boston: Little, Brown & Co., 1927).

(1560–1609) Carracci and Giovanni Lorenzo Bernini (1598–1680), built their work on Renaissance studies of physiognomy and anatomy.

In a kindred spirit Aline Fruhauf, too, always worked from life, starting each portrait with sketches aimed at revealing basic structure and facial expression. Her caricatures are direct responses to the individuals they portray, tempered, of course, by her own turn of mind, which, more often than not, was friendly and whimsical. Because she worked from life, she did not cast her subjects in an arbitrarily chosen mold; they, more than she, determined the outcome of her work. If the portrait "spoke" to her, she accepted it.

But her response to her subjects, her fascination with their faces, would have been only a private and largely unexpressed joy had she not been gifted with an exceptional talent and, most especially, prodigious powers of observation. And how acutely, how precisely, she observed! Note, for instance, her recollection of her chance meeting when she was a child of nine with Sarah Bernhardt on the boardwalk at Long Beach, New York.

Her rouged mouth was the shape of the masks of Comedy and Tragedy, somewhere in between. Her gray-green eyes were luminous and like a lion's, with thick tarry lashes; her nostrils were imperious and sharply defined. Her clothing was all silk and velvet in shades of dark red and purple. A pouf of red hair showed under her ruched hat. Cream-colored lace cascaded at her wrists and throat.

The words are those of the adult, but the observation is the child's.

I say Aline always worked from life. There was one exception—her portrayal from photographs of the Supreme Court during the Roosevelt administration—but even here her skill and observation enlivened and humanized in a peculiarly faithful way what the nation otherwise remembers stereotypically as "the nine old men." The work gave her great difficulty until she realized that Justice Brandeis "bore a structural resemblance to her friend Remo Bufano" and that Justice Sutherland reminded her of her paternal grandfather. Not insignificantly, Justice Cardozo later wrote a friend, "Brandeis and Sutherland are, I think, the best."

Aline's criterion that the image "talk back" to her pre-cluded the development of a stereotype for her work. So did her use of various mediums—pen and ink, dry brush, lithography, watercolor, oil, encaustic, and the woodcut—each of which has its distinct potentials and its limits. Working from life meant the development not only of a style that reflected her friendly nature—Ravel called her his "amiable caricaturist"—but also of a style, although identifiable, that was devoid of mannerism. Though there is virtually no pretension, and little self-consciousness, in her work, she nevertheless well understood the historical importance of caricature as an art form. As a consequence, as you will see in the faces and figures on the pages that follow, she has left us with a uniquely personal, very human, and extraordinarily valuable record of a time when the individual mattered—when people were both the object of our politics and the primary subject of our art.

Marchal Landgren was guest curator of the retrospective exhibition of Aline Fruhauf's work held at the Corcoran Gallery of Art, Washington, D.C., from September 24 through November 6, 1977. His comments here are adapted from his notes for the catalog of that exhibition.

Aline Fruhauf, Studio
Mother, ca. 1948.

EDITOR'S PREFACE

A book, like any other receptacle of human thought, must have its own inclusionary rule: what goes into it and what does not. I think that for Aline this book's subtitle, *Memoirs of a Caricaturist*, was the sufficient guide. It is as if she had been asked, as I have heard her asked by friends, how she became a caricaturist and what it was like to be one.

Her answer is simple, direct, and conversational in tone. She tells how, as a young child, she became intrigued with people's faces, how she tried to catch their uniqueness in little drawings, and how, as she grew up, this near-obsession merged under other influences into a general appreciation of pictorial arts, ending with the selection of one—caricature—as her own means of expression. I see the memoirs as the story of that child in development and later life, a longitudinal segment of her inner life shielded from everything else going on in the world. Never mind the Great Depression, world wars, politics, domestic matters . . .

Aline and I met in Woodstock, New York, in 1932. Her development up to that time is the subject of the first half of her memoirs; my own, more briefly, is as follows.

I had been graduated from Dartmouth College three years before and had gone to New York City to find a job. Work of any kind was scarce. I had hoped to continue my education in biological science through a fellowship or other academic work, but I could not find anything along these lines and had to settle for a number of bread-and-butter jobs.

For a young person like myself, life in the city was always exciting in some aspects, but my clerical job boring. Sometime early in 1931 I chanced to meet Grant Arnold, an old friend from high school who had become an artist and lithographer. He told me about Woodstock, a small town in the Adirondacks where artists like himself could get away during the summer and work in a country environment. After my year in the doldrums of the city, Grant's description glowed with promise. I managed to get away one weekend, sampled Woodstock, and returned to New York enthralled.

The following year I was back in Woodstock, sharing a cabin with a news reporter who was at the time "between jobs." Kenneth Jones and I had resolved to beat the depression by writing a best-seller novel.

This involved a life-style that was interesting, if only for the change from city routines. We did do some writing and at length produced a manuscript. Most of the time, however, we were busy with other things.

One day when I was at the town center I stopped to see Grant Arnold, whose shop was in the basement of a building occupied by the Woodstock Artists Association.

Grant was at his press, pulling prints. Near him, watching intently with serious brown eyes, was a slim young woman in a gray artist's smock. Grant introduced us. The brown eyes shifted momentarily to me, then back to the press. Obviously it was her print that was being squeezed off the stone onto damp white paper. I joined in the watch and we began to chat casually. (No bells rang; no one cried, *Mark this moment, you will think of it hereafter!*)

Knowing how memories important to us revise themselves over the years—fifty plus in this instance—I checked against the only remaining source of verification. Grant answered promptly with a letter dated February 23, 1986, from which I quote:

> *You did meet Aline in my shop. I was printing a lithograph for her. Jenny was there and invited you and Aline for lunch the next day. You both came, and after lunch we all walked up to the top of Overlook Mountain. It was 1932 when you and Jones were writing "Rusty Chains."*. . .

Another excerpt captures the ambiance of Woodstock in that day in its lighter moments:

One of my recollections is the time you and Jones took Jenny

and me to a farmhouse for something to eat. You and Jones
ordered a pitcher of home brew. After a few drinks, Jenny and
I left & somehow much later you came to the "Canal Boat"
[the Arnold's cabin] with six bottles of beer that you gave us.
Early the next morning, I was awakened by the home brew
blowing off its cap, splashing the beer all out. I took the other
bottles outside, where, one by one, they blew their tops.

I also remember that you and Jones boiled 50 pounds
of potatoes that became your staple food while you were
writing.

Blown beer tops notwithstanding, the Woodstock in which
Aline and I met was a far cry from the later, psychedelic
Woodstock. The depression was casting its shadow on every
activity, and the prevailing mood was one of "life is real, life
is earnest." Most of the artists I knew were sober, talent-
driven people. A few were flamboyantly bohemian, but most
chose a frugal life-style that gave them ample time for work
as well as play.

That summer Aline and I saw each other only a few more
times. In the autumn we went our separate ways and returned to New York, after promising to see each other again.

In retrospect, I think that our Woodstock experience con-
ditioned our future relationship more than might appear. On
the surface it seemed we had only formed a good friendship,
but there was more. In spite of great differences in
background, and maybe in part because of them, we had established a mutual credibility, each as a serious person with
ideals of self and career. This might not have happened so
readily in a more conventional setting.

But Woodstock was not to remain the backdrop of our
future. Rather, it would be New York, at least that part of it
lying between the Harlem River to the north and the Battery
to the south—the island of Manhattan, spine and soul of the city.
This was Aline's stamping ground from the time she put on
her first pair of patent leather shoes, and it became mine
from adolescence on, through the lure of good jobs and
cultural glamor.

Back in town, Aline and I began to see each other now and
then. Our meetings were casual and our amusements inexpensive and tame, such as lunch in Central Park or a ride on

an open-deck bus to the Cloisters. Sometimes Aline got complimentary tickets for a show or concert where one of her targeted subjects was playing. She had many friends in Manhattan, and occasionally there would be a party at one of their homes or at the Fruhauf apartment. All such gatherings were backdrop for long conversations, which became more frequent as the year wore on.

So far as romance was concerned, we both showed a forbearance appropriate to the times and our situation. I was acutely aware of and embarrassed by the low state of my funds and prospects, and Aline was understanding about this. She, according to her friends, was supposedly being cautious because of a recent, failed love affair. Moreover, I believe she was more shy and inexperienced than her demeanor suggested.

But youth will be served; if the restaurant is closed a picnic lunch will do. Early in 1933 I wrote Aline that I was planning a weekend in Woodstock, and she decided to join me there. Asked by a confidante whether this implied an escalation in our friendship, Aline replied (she told me later), "I hope so!" By summer's end we were fully committed to one another and planning eventual marriage.

The obstacle, of course, was economic. Aline had no problem so long as she remained with her parents, but she wanted her independence. Between us, we did not have enough income to set up a household. My salary was actually smaller than it had been two years before, and her return for drawings published came in sporadic dribbles.

But this state of suspension could not last. A few months later we decided to wait no longer for "better days" to come; we had a feeling they were beginning to pass us by. In February 1934 we went to City Hall, where an amiable judge certified us to be man and wife. It was a ceremony as simple as checking into a hotel, and it cost much less (two dollars, I think). We rented a one-room kitchen apartment on Jones Street in the Village and settled in cozily. *Small*, we thought even then, was beautiful.

Our life-style was correspondingly simple. I had been on my own through college and five depression years, and I was by now advanced in the art of getting along on a wardrobe of one suit and a pair of shoes. For all her sheltered upbringing, Aline slipped into this way of life contentedly.

She shopped daily among the pushcarts of Bleecker Street, where a dollar would bring several days' supply of fresh vegetables. More remarkably, for one who had not had to cook at home, she found a talent for cooking simple, delicious meals and did not seem to mind using it. Our budgeting was radically simple: almost daily we divided the cash we had, according to what we planned to do over the next few days.

Like many people seemingly bogged down in an unsatisfactory situation in life, we devised or were drawn into ventures a bit short on realism. Once, anticipating the end of Prohibition, we hit upon the idea of a cook-with-wine book. So far as we could find, there was no such book in the libraries. Aline collected recipes and illustrated them with cute drawings while I wrote an essay on wines, based on books of old vintage. A publisher actually considered the manuscript, treated us to a duck-with-orange dinner made with one of our recipes, and prepared an attractive "dummy." The enterprise died when another publisher announced a similar book by one of the real mavens of haute cuisine.

In spite of the new demands on her time, Aline maintained a steady program in her art. It was during this period (1934–36) that she did her series of New York judges. Even more important for her experience and morale was the opening of work on the Federal Art Project. It was an exhilarating experience for her: for the first time in her life she was on a regular payroll, getting paid for what she loved to do, and she was frequently in the company of artists who comprised a veritable Who's Who of American arts. My friend Grant Arnold was among them, a master printer of his and other artists' work. Aline made a number of fine lithographs, which were eventually to be scattered across the country in schools, libraries, and other public buildings.

Nothing so congenial to my ambitions had come my way, but in late 1936 a series of opportunities began that soon got me back into academics. First, there was an opening—thanks again to federal funds—for a laboratory assistant to work with a prominent bacteriologist in tuberculosis research. Bacteriology was not my first love in biology, but this was "hands-on" science and I took the job happily. We moved to the East Side to be close to the hospital where the work was under way.

A few months later I got wind of something new and exciting: a new class of antibacterial agents—sulfonamides—had been discovered in Germany, and an American firm was setting up a small research unit on Long Island to study their effectiveness. I applied for the bacteriologist's slot and was accepted. Aline and I moved to Huntington.

But my run of good luck was not over. Over the years I had continued to put out feelers for work in colleges and universities. I now learned my application for a teaching fellowship at New York University had been accepted and I was to report at Washington Square the following autumn. It was one of the best of fellowships, offering a salary, research money, free tuition, and a choice of study program. I accepted, and we moved back to Greenwich Village.

I admire the way Aline treats chronology in the memoirs: minimally. She deals with time in great unequal swatches pinned down only sparingly by dates. I think this is the way we do see our lives in retrospect: in periods of time, long or short, each with its own peculiar mood and circumstances.

One such "swatch" of time, as my memory shapes it, is the period from 1937, when we returned to the Village, to 1943, when I entered the Navy. During this time we had a stable household and an apartment with good space for a studio, all within walking distance of my place of work. We set up interlocking routines that gave Aline plenty of studio time and myself the freedom to cope with a complicated schedule of teaching, research, and study.

Although we did not have much time for social life, we tried to keep Saturday evenings free for recreation and visits with friends and relatives. Aline had always been gregarious, and she had many friends of long or recent standing. I had a few old friends and some new ones from among my colleagues. We were close in the Village to friends like the Bufanos, who gave parties featuring spaghetti, good wine, and good conversation. Occasionally we entertained. I remember in particular two evenings: one in which Zorach recited "Horatio at the Bridge" in a heavy, self-mimicking accent, and another in which Stuart Davis talked about art in a monologue which fascinated the company. I

understood little of it, but he was a man of convincing presence and he made it sound very rational. The salient event of the period, of course, was the arrival of our first child, Susan, on Christmas Eve of 1938. She was examined and admired by grandparents and friends, but it was Aline's Japanese picture framer who gave the review we always remembered. He walked around Susan in her crib as he would a work of art and finally pronounced solemnly, "*Ver*-ee successful baby!"

Successful baby could have spelt havoc for Aline's program, but for the services of a retired woman who was glad to be part-time nurse for a small wage. This arrangement was facilitated by the fact that Aline had just begun to receive a small income from her father's estate. Mrs. Ray stayed with us as friend and nurse as long as we were in New York, and Aline worked contentedly in what was now a studio-nursery.

She had had a show of caricatures of dancers at the Brooklyn Museum in 1936 and of caricatures of artists at the ACA Gallery in 1938. Now she turned her sights on the dress designers of the city, producing a series of portraits in watercolor. Several appeared in *Vogue*, and all appeared in an exhibit entitled "American Dress and Designers" at the Norlyst Gallery in 1943.

I attended that exhibit in a navy blue uniform, which helped me keep my dignity while my friend from Brooklyn College bubbled about pretending to be a Mexican painter. My costume was legitimate. Since receiving my doctorate in physiology I had continued to teach premedical biology, and this exempted me from the draft. Now, after much soul-searching and with Aline's full agreement, I applied for and received a commission in the Navy.

Our plan was that, once indoctrination was complete and I was assigned to a base, I would find a home nearby for our little family. My role in the Navy was to be largely one of research and was not expected to include duty overseas. And so it came about; but it would be almost nine months before we would be reunited.

My first assignment was to the naval air base at Pensacola. There I had my first introduction to semitropical weather and cockroaches, loop-the-loops in a "yellow peril" trainer plane, and work in a low pressure chamber. Grapevine information had it that my next duty station would be Quonset, Rhode Island—good news, for that would probably allow visits on liberty in New York. But when the orders came they were for the Naval Air Station in San Diego.

Despite my initial disappointment, I was soon delighted with the city, the countryside, and the dry, gentle climate. My duties often entailed flights in aircraft up and down the coast, and I savored the unfamiliar coastline (my Gothamite insularity shedding off in tiny bits along the way). *You're going to love it here,* I wrote Aline, *You can have a picnic any time and not worry about rain!*

Aline was hardly thinking about picnics. She was having a miserable winter in New York. Susie was ill much of the time. Aline herself had to go to the hospital for surgery where a small area on her chest had been accidentally burned by an X-ray years before. She wrote me from the hospital that the operation went well (she made sketches of it); she was passing the time by making drawings of doctors and nurses; and Susie, staying with Mrs. Ray, talked about Daddy and "the spring." The letters were calm and factual. But there were messages subliminal or barely coded: "P.S. I dreamed about you last night. Yep!" And little line drawings—of Susie (angelic), herself (seductive), and me (flattering)—all in the nude.

The "spring" of our hopeful correspondence seemed to recede as time wore on. There were delays at both ends: at mine due to the scarcity of housing for families, at Aline's due to the follow-up operations and the assembling of another show. I spent most of my time off looking for quarters in San Diego or La Jolla, and I advertised in the papers, offering $50 to the finder of a place for us. The papers had many such ads.

Eventually my efforts paid off. I found an apartment, two rooms in a small house near a beach in La Jolla. Spring had arrived at last! By mid-June the New York apartment was sublet, and Aline and Sue were on a sleeper bound for the West Coast.

We were to have barely six weeks of family life together before moving on, but it was a welcome period of rest for Aline, who arrived looking sallow and weary, and for Susie, who came pale and fretful. They changed perceptibly from day to day as they relaxed in the sunny environment. They spent much of their time on the beach, where I usually found them when I returned from work in the evening. Together we would have supper, walk along the shore, and watch the red-gold sun melt into the sea.

So, physically at least, we were prepared for another move. We had known I would have to return to the East Coast, and on August 3, 1944, I received my invitation. It began, "When directed by your commanding officer . . ." and ended a few lines below, "Potomac River Naval Command, Washington, D.C."

Three weeks later we were on our way, marveling at the lush greenery of the Maryland countryside. Before evening we arrived at the National Naval Medical Center in Bethesda, where I checked in while Aline consulted with a social worker about housing. As expected, the prospects were poor, and we were glad to get lodging at a farmhouse a quarter of a mile up on what is now Rockville Pike: bed and breakfast until we found something more suitable. (We were almost a mile from the center of Bethesda, where there were a handful of restaurants and other conveniences.)

The "something more suitable" turned out to be a modest apartment, which we got by buying the furniture of an outgoing tenant.

Our neighbors were mostly young adults, civilians in the downtown bureaucracy, or military people brought here by the needs of war. Some had children, and Susie soon found playmates. Aline lost no time exploring the Washington museums and looking up old friends, especially Prentiss Taylor, whom she had known at the Art Students League, and Belle Boas, her first art teacher, now at the Baltimore Museum. As for myself, I found the duty at the Naval Medical Research Institute interesting and stimulating. Life, in short, began to seem normal.

I am sure at that time we had no intention that this toehold in Maryland should be any more than a step toward eventual return to New York. We could not know that the war had a year to go before Hiroshima and that, by the time our desires and daily realities came into balance, we might change our minds.

Finally the war did end; it was V-J Day, and we celebrated far into the night. Neighbors went jubilantly from apartment to apartment to savor the news and speculate on what was to come. Aline sat at a piano and played for hours, while I served drinks to all who came. (Never mind charred flesh and smoking ruins; we had learned to shut out news of suffering, especially that of enemies.)

After that first flush of jubilation nothing much changed in our lives for a while. Demobilization did not start abruptly. It was as if the earth had reversed its polarity, yet everything remained in place. It would take time to adjust. The naval research organizations had a great deal of cleanup work to do, unfinished business; and we heard of great plans for a peacetime medical research institute. Some officers who had academic tenure managed to get out quickly; others were encouraged to linger. I was allowed to edge away from the work in altitude physiology and devise projects in endocrinology.

1947 was the watershed year for us. We decided to stay in the Washington area. I got out of the Navy and accepted a civilian post at the Naval Medical Research Institute to set up an endocrinology unit. We bought a house across the street from a junior high school. These outward acts of implantation in Maryland soil were matched inwardly by that singular expression of hope and faith in the future: "we" were pregnant again.

We expected the new arrival early in the next year, and it was already summer. In the first months as homeowners, even before moving in, we cleaned the house from attic to cellar and freshly painted every inch of wall and ceiling— Aline seemed to enjoy the freedom of attacking such large surfaces. Then we moved in, blending the contents of our Chevy Chase and New York apartments. We even got acquainted that fall with the garden that came with the house. Our pent-up need for a permanent base was satisfied, and we settled in as if forever—which, for Aline and me, it essentially turned out to be.

Our second child, Deborah Ann, was born January 15, 1948, early in the baby boom. She was an imp with a challenging air who quickly staked out her own sphere of influence. She would be nurtured through childhood by a team that included not only parents but also Margaret Monroe, our esteemed part-time helper for decades to come, and Susan, who kept us informed of the views of Dr. Spock on how to raise children.

This was to be our Era of Domesticity, a long period of relative calm in which each year, whatever its joys and troubles, seemed to differ little from the one just past and the one to follow. Not that nothing at all happened; to be sure, there were memorable events such as school and college graduations (Sue and Debbie were growing up and suddenly were adults), Aline's shows, and changes of direction in my career. But what did happen seemed to fit normal, expected patterns. Indeed, one might say that our existence had that sameness-in-change over the years that Tolstoi saw as the banality of "happy" families (no grist in such lives for the storyteller's mill).

Aline's entry into the Washington scene was greatly facilitated by Prentiss Taylor, already recognized as a leading painter and lithographer. In looking through old papers recently I came across a short essay that he apparently wrote in connection with one of Aline's shows in 1950. Though written with humor it contains accurate observations about Aline and her way of going about her work:

HOW IT FEELS TO BE A VICTIM

Until the opening of an exhibit of caricatures by Aline Fruhauf one does not know how one looks as a victim but one does know how it feels. Naturally this makes for suspense.

This suspense has the artist herself on tenterhooks about what the reactions will be & it whets the victims' anticipation. As Miss Fruhauf says shrewdly it makes the opening more exciting. However there is an even shrewder reason for not allowing the subjects to see their portraits until the series is complete. Miss Fruhauf finds that if her subjects see themselves in her mirror they go out & lose pounds, or recoiffure or resort to plastic surgery & psychoanalysis. As she is a painstaking worker she can not risk such drastic changes & the falsifying of what her discerning eyes had truly perceived.

Those dark & electric eyes increase their voltage & x-ray intensity when one has been chosen as a subject. No matter how long one has known her, & I have known Aline for almost 25 years, one finds himself getting looked at in a thoroughly new way. As long as one is being worked on the old association is not the same. Conversations are no longer the bright & easy things they were whether with her or in some group in the same room with her. One finds in talking that his face is being attended but his words are not. At the opening or in conducting a meeting one finds himself suddenly being studied & sketched from a far corner. In the midst of a farewell there may be cries of Hold It! Then there are her visits to one's "background" & one's possessions undergo a scrutiny equalled only by moving day when all one's things are starkly revealed on a sunlit sidewalk.

This goes on for weeks or months for these pencil & water-color portraits are long & thoughtfully studied syntheses. For all their smallness of scope they are quintessential character studies. They are conceived & executed with a lapidary perfection. They are delicate & subtle without any lack of delight, wit & vitality. There is too much real affection for the shrewd eye, the just & penetrating eye, ever to be unkind. Rather these are discerning portraits with a wry twist.

I can vouch for the reformational effects of the caricatures on some subjects, at least to the extent of two instances of weight reduction and one of facial repair. As for anyone's being driven to psychoanalysis, I think the idea fanciful.

Quaintance Eaton, a friend who knew her from the early 1930s on, describes her as of those beginner's professional days:

> She was one little independent soul, every inch herself, a complete individualist. Her viewpoint was a little sardonic, sweetened by a genuine affection for people. I knew her in the early Musical America days, when she did a regular caricature for the mag, and we were close friends thereafter. . . . She was indeed a blithe spirit, in touch with the gods.

But Aline was something more than the "Blithe spirit" who set the tone and delimited the subject matter of her memoirs. She was an interesting, multifaceted woman, dear to those who knew her well, full of enthusiasm, and possessed of some unusual talents.

Aline's ready sense of humor tended to obscure the fact that in the ordinary business of living she was really a straight arrow who hated to be late, took commitments seriously, and insisted on a clean, orderly home. She had a social conscience and took civic action and politics seriously. On a personal level she was quick to rally to a friend sick or in trouble. And she bore her own troubles well; she was never a complainer. These qualities remained with her over the years and served her well, not only in her art but also in her life as wife, mother, friend, and neighbor.

But Aline had another quality, which I got to know only through long and intimate association, and find it easier to illustrate than describe. Shortly after her death I wrote this note:

> One evening I found her sitting in our dining room, so quiet I thought she was ill. She motioned me to silence. Her back was to the window. Over her shoulder a ray from the setting sun crossed the room to a cranberry vase on the desk. It splayed a pattern of pink whorls on the off-white wall. From moment to moment the pattern shifted, without apparent movement, into new forms. She sat entranced. Each day thereafter, she would be there watching, sometimes ahead of the sun, until the season changed and ended the gratuitous marvel.

That is the woman, able even in her sixties to retain the bright sense of wonder that most of us lose after childhood, whom I most want to remember.

ERWIN VOLLMER
May 1987

For caricature, not less than for every other art, beauty is a primal condition. . . . The most perfect caricature is that which, on a small surface, with the simplest of means, most accurately exaggerates, to the highest point, the peculiarities of a human being, at his most characteristic moment, in the most beautiful manner.

—Sir Max Beerbohm, "The Spirit of Caricature"

MAKING FACES

Policeman's Miracle

In the Phillips Collection at
Washington, D.C., there is a little portrait of
Niccolò Paganini by Eugène Delacroix. It is one of
the jewels of the collection. Painted on oil on a
piece of cardboard only 17-1/2 by 11-1/2 inches in
size, Delacroix's *Paganini* has a concentrated intensity that enchants the beholder. The shadowy little
figure of the violinist appears in a velvety
penumbra. Wearing patent leather shoes—still the
height of elegance to me—he stands on a platform
bathed in a golden light, brilliant where it falls on
the hands that hold a barely indicated fiddle. The
expression on the bony face is typical of all musicians playing a slow movement. With eyes at
half-mast and nostrils dilated, as if inhaling a
delicate fragrance, Paganini has the lento look. As
portrayed by Delacroix, this performer and composer of almost unplayable bravura variations
ceases to be a legend and momentarily comes to
life.

There is an element of caricature in this work
that is found in all great portraits, from the Greco-
Egyptian mummy portraits of the second century
to the works of the great Spanish painters, El
Greco, Velázquez, Goya, and, to the ultimate
degree, Picasso, the prime wit of them all.

It is my element. I have spent a lifetime "making faces," with occasional excursions into landscape painting and printmaking, only to return, refreshed, to the thing I do best. Whenever I see *Paganini*, the portrait of an artist at work and a musician to boot, I get the feeling that "this is where I came in."

I WAS BORN AND LIVED MY YOUNG YEARS IN an apartment house near Riverside Drive on the upper West Side of New York. My bedroom window was a proscenium for the musical-comedy setting three stories below, a tree-shaded beer garden, where waiters in scarlet coats made bright spots of color as they moved among tables covered with cloths of sparkling white, and where a tenor sang Neapolitan love songs, accompanied by the tinkling tremolo of guitar and mandolin supplied by a small band of musicians. In my mind the visual counterparts of this sound were dark and shimmering spangles, blue and purple and iridescent green. Ladies in enormous hats and sweeping gowns sat at tables with their escorts, eating and drinking, enjoying the evening air, and watching the broad and ever-changing ribbon that was the Hudson River.

One day, when I was old enough to climb and too young to be a good judge of distance, I saw from my window proscenium one of the great white boats of the Hudson River Day Line. As it slowly steamed by, I noticed something in the center that looked like a black coat hanger; it was going up and down, up and down. Slowly, in time to the motion, I began to move my forearm, elbow up, wrist down, wrist up, elbow down. I was positive I could hear the boat sigh and exhale in rhythm: it was talking to me, and I wanted to get close enough to touch it. When I tried to scale the black-iron stalks of the window guard, a neighbor saw me teetering dangerously, telephoned my mother in a hurry, and I was pulled back to safety.

My life of adventure continued, but on a more visual plane. Sunsets on the river were evening spectacles in which clouds of molten copper and gold changed to shreds of crimson and violet, like dahlia petals, and sometimes the sky turned a mysterious apple-green just before dusk. Then the sun went down like a red-hot penny, and after cobalt-blue twilight, the stars came out, diamonds in the sky, bedded jewels, like my mother's brooch in its blue velvet box.

With nightfall the spectacle took on a more subtle splendor. Lights went on in the amusement park across the river, strings of jeweled light. A Ferris wheel turning slowly was a magic circlet of fire-gilt beads against the dark curtain of the Palisades.

In the winters I was bundled up to the eyes—two sweaters under my heavy winter coat—and was taken for walks along Riverside Drive. Across the Hudson in New Jersey, the Palisades were whitened cliffs, and flat chunks of ice like great slabs of vanilla coconut fudge floated on the river. Down in the park, the slopes were covered with snow, and trees made of glass sparkled in the sunshine and crackled with the wind.

One afternoon in early summer, when the park slopes were green and weigela bushes bloomed with pink trumpet-shaped flowers that tasted of honey, I saw my first artist at work. He was a young policeman, standing by a low stone wall, sketching the river. Under his visored cap was a clear-cut, high-cheekboned profile. His eye was dark and alert, as it squinted in the sun from time to time. I fell instantly, headlong in love.

Although I had been scribbling since I could hold a pencil, I had never before seen anyone else draw. The process was rhythmic and fascinating. The policeman held a small notebook in one hand and a pencil in the other, and as his gaze shifted from the scene before him back to the paper, his pencil hand kept up a steady obbligato of quick short strokes. With the breathless feeling that still overtakes me on approaching a personage, I asked the policeman if I might see what he was making. He handed over his notebook. There, in rich black and white, and the silvery tones in between, I saw a miracle. He had conjured up all the magic of my river. I knew then that I wanted to draw.

I saw him again, perhaps twice. Each time he showed me his work in progress. Then he disappeared forever.

My lifelong love affair with drawing had begun. I scraped the surface of the gravel in the park with sharp stones or sticks, and penciled every unguarded surface in the apartment. Soon, the idle scratchings took form. One day I swung my pencil around a surface in one continuous line and discovered to my astonishment that I had made a circle. The triumph was followed by other enclosed shapes. I made squares and ovals and filled them with crosses and diagonals. Experiment continued, and it wasn't long before I put two dots for eyes in a circle, added a vertical for a nose, and finished it off with an upcurving horizontal, symbol for a mouth. All at once I saw that the thing I had made was looking out at me from the paper. It was a face.

And then they came, faces by the dozen, on desk blotters, walls, paper bags, and envelopes, used and pristine. Gradually they acquired hats of all shapes and sizes, then blobs for bodies, arms and legs that looked like sticks, and hands that looked like chicken feet. I was following the patterns of children's art, which is virtually the same the world over.

The next step in the development of this primitive art form is the child's discovery of the profile. I remember my first experience with it. One evening just before bedtime, I was lying on my bed, my nocturnal glass of water in its accustomed place on a little wicker washstand. The cool glass in my encircling fingers was pleasant to the touch, and the crystal light that played about its contents was hypnotically beautiful. I tipped a little of the water into the china basin, found some dust, and dabbled a finger in it to make a design. I poured on some more water, and the design disappeared. On the lookout for a less fugitive medium, I picked up a stub of pencil and a used envelope that had a worn and slippery surface. They had a natural affinity for each other, and soon the pencil was sliding along with the greatest of ease. What emerged was the profile of a fabulous-looking female, with long wavy hair and one enormous eye, heavily fringed, top and bottom. In the heat of creation, I had smudged the lady with the graphite-blackened side of my hand, and I found that, instead of spoiling the drawing, it had produced a rich bloom that added depth and lustre. I went to bed bliss-fully happy.

Aline Fruhauf

Inspirations

My vast output puzzled my parents. If they had drawn at all as children, they had forgotten about it. "I don't know whom she takes after," my mother would say. "There were no artists on my side of the family." And my father claimed to have known an artist once, an old fellow in Cincinnati, who was drunk most of the time. "He'd sober up long enough to paint pictures of naked women on beer mugs and vases and give them to me to sell for him; then he'd go out and spend all the money on liquor." The shocked tone my father used in telling this story demonstrated his poor opinion of artists, and he was never to be quite free of it.

Although Harry Fruhauf, manufacturer of men's clothing, would be the first to deny it, he had more than his share of the creative temperament. Dark, heavyset, and solemn looking, he had a dedication to fine workmanship and beautiful fabrics that bordered on the religious. With pencils sharpened to a needle point, he wrote a fine copperplate hand, and when he dipped a new pen into dark green ink, the writing was penmanship in every sense of the word; his capitals were elegantly flourished, and he made shaded downstrokes by pushing down on the nib to broaden its opening to allow a greater flow of ink. He played the piano by ear, and I listened gravely to his version of "Don't you remember sweet Alice, Ben Bolt?" a rich-toned, ominous sostenuto. Once he told me he would rather have been a lawyer or a violinist than a businessman, climaxing the statement by producing a fiddle I had never seen before—or since. He let me pluck the strings and finger the bow and rub it on a cube of rosin, which, I was disappointed to find, didn't taste at all like butterscotch. Then he tuned the violin. But I never heard him play it.

From my earliest recollections of my father, I was aware of his mountainous business worries. The theatre relaxed him. He enjoyed musicals featuring such comedians as Weber and Fields, Sam Bernard, and Raymond Hitchcock. He loved the sound of spoken French and couldn't wait until I would be old enough to take lessons.

My mother, Selma, was a small-boned, sharp-featured, rather pretty woman, hazel-eyed and copper-haired, with a natural intelligence and a keen-edged wit. Although, throughout her life, she ignored drawing and painting, she understood my involvement and campaigned long and fiercely for my art lessons. She loved the theatre, but unlike my father she preferred serious plays. She was fond of golf, and she swam well, crocheted and embroidered with mechanical perfection, and played the piano, by sight, in much the same way.

Her housekeeping duties were limited to marketing. All the others were taken over by Kati (pronounced *Kah'di*), a stalwart young Slovakian, who had left her own baby in her native village to be brought up as her mother's son. Kati took me over bodily and wrapped me in swaddling clothes, middle-European style; and I basked in the warmth of delicious cooking smells, plenty of cuddling, and the sound of Slavic folk songs. Everybody seemed tall to me in those days, but Kati towered; her magnificent carriage gave the illusion of great height. She had a long symmetrical face. Her eyebrows met in a straight line, and her black eyes

7

could dance with merriment or blaze with maniacal fury. I learned very early to stay out of her way when she had headaches, probably migraine, for then she wrapped a wet towel around her head and, radiating storm clouds, took to her room until the agony abated.

Before her apprenticeship to a pastry cook in one of the "great houses of Vienna," Kati had worked in the fields barefoot. Her peasant feet were out-size, and the only comfortable footwear she could find were men's shoes. Her work clothes were spotless: cotton housedresses and long white aprons. When she went out, her basic costume was a high-necked white shirtwaist and a long, black gored skirt. Her handbag was a black leather, satchel-like affair, fragrant with hard white rolls, which were very convenient for afternoon snacks in the park and came in handy when we encountered a gaggle of geese or swans on our travels abroad. She was adept at prestidigitation, and although I watched her very closely in breakfast dining rooms in hotels at home or abroad, I could never see her actually secrete a roll into the cavernous recesses of her satchel.

Kati and I adored each other. She was the third parent, standing between my real ones. I came flying to her and buried my face in her long apron whenever things got rough between me and Harry and Selma. We were, all three of us, a temperamental and intense-looking lot, and there were explosions, short-lived but vehement while they lasted.

In the evenings, after the supper dishes were cleared away, I was allowed in the kitchen where Kati entertained her friends, friendly servant girls who, like Kati, had crossed the Atlantic in the crowded steerages of North German Lloyd steamers. Their hair was dragged back from their pale shiny faces, and tiny earrings of gold or turquoise glinted in their lobes. Most of the girls were homesick, and they sang sad folk songs. Soon I was singing along with the company. They taught me to say "good-day" in Czech: *Dobra Rana*. It had

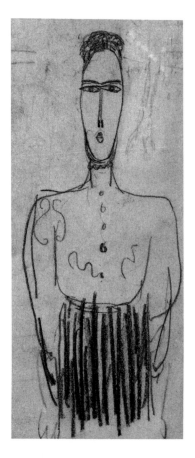

Kati, unpublished drawing, ca. 1977.

a fine sound; the *r*'s, it seemed to me, were hard and sharp and as green as blades of grass. (I was still, more or less unconsciously, collating sounds with objects.) I was taught to count to ten, to ask for a kiss, to ask for bread and milk, and to say "good-by." My accent was flawless, but I remained forever lacking in vocabulary. Kati and the girls laughed at my parrotings, and we drank coffee and ate *buchtli,* Kati's delicious saffron-yellow buns, crusty and brown on the outside, each with a dollop of ruby-red jelly in its fragrant center.

Then there were the horrors: terrifying shadows that lurked in the window-glass late at night, and the crack in the ceiling that managed to form itself into one hideous, grimacing face. And the cold fear that gripped me when Kati took me for walks in the park on windy fall days and leaves that smelled like strong tea swirled in circles; Kati told me they were witches dancing, and I believed her. It must have been Kati who was with me when I met the artist-policeman in Riverside Park, although neither of us mentioned the encounter.

My nostalgia for Kati's workshop is the basis for my abiding love of what are known in the trade as "kitchen antiques." There was a black iron gas stove ringed with circles of blue flame; the warm raw sienna of natural wood cupboards and long-handled spoons, butter paddles, and the potato masher; an enormous mustard-colored mixing bowl ringed with white. My attraction to blue-and-white china began with the glossy, white barrel-shaped canisters, decorated with cobalt flowers and rich, black Gothic letters reading "Coffee," "Sugar," and "Salt." Best of all was the coffee pot of that marvelous blue that is somewhere between bristol and turquoise. I am writing this now in a little room of that color, which makes a delectable background for the objects that have collected me over the years: a fleet of antique duck decoys; a miniature black iron coal stove; two Indonesian marionettes with carved headdresses of scarlet and gold; and a delicate celadon Chinese plate enameled with birds, butterflies, and flowers.

The overstuffed furniture in my family's parlor was a bright green plush with the hard, smooth surface of a shorthaired dog. No one ever sat on the slipper chair twice because one leg gave way. The fireplace was tiled in yellow and marbled with white, like scrambled eggs. The gas log, when first lit, emitted tiny spurts of vivid blue fire. I was fascinated by the color and liked it better than the feathers of gold flame that came immediately after. There was a fire screen my great-grandmother Freedman had painted—purple velvet on one side and ornamented with a brace of birds of paradise; royal blue on the other, a background for large brown and gold poppies. Both sides were liberally sprinkled with glitter. I had just discovered that fingernails made excellent tools and tried them out by picking the glitter off the screen. No criticism was intended; I just liked the feel. But when the last particle of the shiny stuff was off, I was sorry. I had rather liked it the way it was. What surprised me was that no one noticed the vandalism, or at least no one ever mentioned it.

A *vernis-martin* curio cabinet with bowed glass doors was my museum. Its glass shelves held a number of silver-gilt spoons whose enameled bowls depicted tiny scenes of far-off places, all with the same cloudless blue sky. There was a little, carved ivory figure of a Chinese sage, a minute set of silver-filigree furniture that could be held in the palm of my hand, and two cloisonné vases, one the blue of lapis lazuli, the other a most marvelous luminous white with scarlet flowers and brilliant green leaves.

The cabinet was not without its little horror: a bronze Japanese demon, squatting, glaring, making a fearful face, and beating the top of his bald head with rage. One day, I took my courage in both hands, picked up the little devil, and turned him around, only to find that his hair was long in back and ended in a double row of curls. Since I was a curl victim myself, I felt a kinship with him and my fear vanished. There was also a miniature mandolin, covered with a thin veneer of tortoise shell, with tiny ivory keys and strings of hair-thin silver wire. When plucked, the strings emitted a wee sound, like a mosquito. And there was a turtle about an inch long, silver gilt and enamel. I still have it and the Japanese demon.

Another treasure I kept—the others disappeared or were given away—was a daguerreotype of my grandmother Anna Freedman Frank, the daughter of the fire-screen painter, as a little girl of four. She was an arresting-looking child, with piercing black eyes, short hair dragged back from her forehead, and a tiny sparrow-beak nose. She was wearing a grown-up dress with a tight-fitting basque, a crinolined skirt, and big butterfly bows at her shoulders.

Green plush portieres divided the parlor from the dining room, which, in the approved rathskeller style of the period, was paneled in a dark stained wood. Up near the ceiling, a shelf going round the room displayed a collection of putty-colored beer steins and some plates painted, after Henner,* with red-haired ladies whose deep décolletages had no end. The furniture was heavy golden oak. The chairs were upholstered in nail-studded black leather, and carved lion heads with sharp teeth peered wickedly over their backs. I put my fingers in their jaws, pretended the lions were biting me, and felt very brave indeed.

I learned to recognize the seasons and holidays by the papier-mâché favors sold in ice cream and stationery stores. Washington's Birthday brought forth hatchets imbedded in logs decorated with sprays of glossy red cherries, which, on dissection, proved to be stuffed with cotton. Thanksgiving was heralded by bronzed turkeys of all sizes with fanlike tails. Their bottoms lifted out so they could be filled with candy: small gumdrops like frosted

*A French portrait and figure painter who did many pictures of nymphs in woods.

jewels and nonpareils, chocolate disks studded
with white sugar icing. There were masks at Hallo-
ween, false faces painted vivid pink and orange,
and orange paper pumpkins with unlikely blue
eyes and toothy grins. At Easter, the store windows displayed hard-surfaced brown bunnies
with carrots in their mouths; the tops of the carrots
were bright green feathers. And there were wonderful white eggs, fashioned from sugar crystals,
hard as ground glass and sticky to the touch, each
girdled with a sash of hard pink frosting. The eggs
had round glass windows through which you
could see little scenes done in shiny, bright-colored
oleograph.

Country-bred, Kati had a light touch with real
vegetable colors. She could dye eggs by boiling
them with onions or beets, and they emerged
polished in rich, melting earth colors: deep Venetian reds and glowing siennas. The deep-toned
eggs were beautiful to hold and, later on, to eat.

I went to Europe twice with my family before the
outbreak of the First World War. The trips are
difficult for me to pin down chronologically, but
they must have been made when I was five and six
years old. They were related to my father's business, and a postcard, saved by my mother, has a
picture of an old woman carding wool in Shetland
and is dated London, August 10, 1913.

Paris was a city of gold, from the coaches of
Versailles to a shop window on the rue de Rivoli
filled with gold kid footwear of all kinds, including
the tiniest baby shoes, strapped slippers for a little
girl, a lady's high-buttoned boots, and a gentleman's dancing pumps.

I remember that we visited an art gallery in
London, where I saw an artist at work, a lady
copying a landscape. Her medium was oil paint,
rich and unctuous. I watched her dip her brush in a
worm of white paint on her palette. With little, caressing strokes, she made an exact replica of the
cloud in the picture she was copying. She talked as

she worked, a running commentary in a lilting, very British voice, and I thought that someday I wanted to be able to paint clouds like that.

Aline Fruhauf

When we came home, I discovered another artist at work I could watch, but only from a distance. She was Miss Emily Goldberg, in the apartment across the street from ours. She wore a purple smock, and her hair was as red as the ladies' on the Henner plates in our dining room. I watched her dabbing at her palette, then at the invisible picture on her easel, and wondered what on earth she was painting.

Soon I was given a box of watercolors in tubes, and I painted imaginary ladies in flaring tunics and skirts edged with fur. When my father's shirts came back from the laundry, I commandeered the shirtboards. They made a new and interesting drawing surface and held the promise of exciting experiments to come.

Little Girl in White

My friend Bitsy,
Elizabeth Enright, a writer of children's books and
short stories, remembered me from our first day
together in kindergarten. Apparently we were
both actively clothes conscious. She wrote,

> *You were wearing a high-necked, lacy white dress
> and a marvelous wilderness of dark curls with a
> huge hair-ribbon afloat at the side like a little
> boat. I think the shoes were white.*

The shoes were indeed white, and they had
mother-of-pearl buttons with tiny silvery centers.
The only way to fasten them was with a but-
tonhook, an essential item in those days in every
toilet set.

Bitsy told me she thought I had great elegance,
but I thought her clothes were by far more chic and
avant-garde than mine. She wore a brown satin
smock, with decorative stitching that started
directly under the Peter Pan collar and with long,
loose sleeves that were gathered at the wrists and
ended in ruffles. Although her shoes were also
high-buttoned and her stockings were long—we
were allowed to wear socks only during the summer months—they were both black, surely a mark
of sophistication.

My clothes had been carefully planned for the great day by my mother, grandmother, and Kati. The buckskin shoes had a fine, mat finish of Blanco, a chalky white substance that came in a round, tin box. Two coats applied with a barely dampened sponge assured a streakless surface, and I was a real pill about this.

I had been starched, ruched, petticoated, edged with lace, and urged to keep it all clean. I agreed, not knowing how rugged a first day at kindergarten could be. After Kati brushed my hair until my scalp tingled, she made curls by wrapping a strand of my hair around her forefinger, giving it a swipe with the brush that had been dipped in water, and then releasing the curl. There were, I think, about six such curls. My mother dressed up in her new brown suit trimmed with gunmetal buttons. Her blouse had a high collar of cream-colored net held up by little wiggly wires called collarbones. Her hat was brown, trimmed with a becoming ostrich plume that swept nearly to her shoulder. Bitsy said she looked very pretty.

At school, most of the boys wore knickerbockers and long stockings; some, more flashily dressed, wore blouses with Eton collars and shorter, less baggy pants with three or four useless buttons running up their outer sides. And there was a good supply of wash-suits with big white buttons that secured the pants to the shirts. For some reason these were called Oliver Twists, but, unacquainted as I was with Dickens's character or his wardrobe, I failed to find the parts of the garment that had a twist of some kind. One of the boys, an infant prodigy called Edward Hardy, was brought to class in his mother's arms wearing pale blue rompers. I could never forget him. Years later, when he was nine, he amused himself by deciphering the hieroglyphics on packages of Egyptian cigarettes.

The girls wore long-waisted dresses like mine or smocks like Bitsy's. No one but me wore white.

Our teacher introduced herself: Miss Garrison. She had pink cheeks and a taffy-colored pompadour. Her manner was brisk, her voice high and ringing. Bitsy supplied the following notes on her costume:

> *A white blouse, voluminous skirt, high-buttoned shoes, and a green, accordion-pleated, taffeta petticoat. Very beautiful.*

The classroom was enormous. The little chairs were safely tucked under the long, butterscotch-colored tables, and the floorboards were a pinkish gray, the color of used chewing gum. While Miss Burke played a march on the piano—Bitsy said it was from *Aida*, but I was just as sure it was from *Faust*—Miss Garrison marched us round and round the room and, when the piano ceased, bade us to form a circle, sit on the floor, and listen to a story. The other children sat down with a massive thumping, like elephants. I stood perfectly still.

"Won't you join us, little girl," trilled Miss Garrison, smiling winsomely. I dissolved into tears but didn't move. The elephants hooted loudly, and, remembering the warnings to keep my white clothes clean, I was very miserable.

I stayed on at the Horace Mann School until the fourth grade. And I made a lifelong friend of the art teacher, Belle Boas. She was tall and erect with an ivory-colored face. Her nose was straight and delicate, and her thin-lipped mouth was mobile and sensitive. Unlike the other teachers, who wore their hair in forward-sweeping pompadours, Miss Boas wore hers parted and drawn in soft, dark loops over her ears and pinned in the back into a graceful knot. She wore unusual colors: burnt orange, gold, or olive green. I remember her voice, a low musical monotone, and the pleasant way her eyes crinkled up whenever, over the years, I brought her new examples of my work. She was my friend and mentor until her death in 1954.

In introducing us to the use of watercolors, she taught us to keep our paint, water, and brushes clean, and to float a wash of color onto paper. She was skilled in magic; once she recreated a daffodil before our eyes, all in brush work, with no pencil lines to guide her.

At home, it was decreed that I learn French, and Mme. Renaud, a tall, stern lady, was introduced to the household on afternoons from half past two to half past five. She took me for long walks on Riverside Drive for "conversation." We sat on dark green park benches overlooking the Hudson, and she taught me to read and write in French. The double-decked buses that passed by had signs, "Fare Ten Cents," which I read as *fah're-tahn sahn*. Soon I was rattling off the names of the *grandes couturières* of Paris; my primers were my mother's copies of *Vogue*.

When we returned from those sometimes icy promenades, Madame and I discussed clothes over cups of hot chocolate. "A lady," said Madame, "was always *comme il faut* and *bien tenue* in black; if it was well brushed, it did not show soil. *Pratique!*" She wore large hats, dotted-net face veils, and tight-fitting kid gloves, and she seemed to me the most stylish person I had ever seen. One afternoon we eschewed the Drive since Madame had some shopping to do; she was going to make herself a ball gown, surprisingly of pale pink tulle, and we walked miles up Broadway to a department store called Koch's in search of artificial forget-me-nots, understated accents for the gown to be.

Madame dispensed unusual bits of information and advice. The Empress Eugénie, I learned, was very beautiful, but her teeth were not; one could still die, horribly, from the black death; and the best French accent came, not from Paris as was supposed, but from Lyons. I was never, under any circumstance, to talk with anyone from Bordeaux for fear of polluting my accent, which, up to then, she pronounced *pas mal du tout*, a great compliment from her. Madame, of course, was from Lyons.

I yearned for black patent leather slippers but wasn't allowed to wear them because of weak

ankles; consequently, I was a slave to the but-
tonhook. Each time I went to Mr. Livingstone's
shoestore with my mother, I gazed longingly at the
Mary Janes on display. How lovely they were,
with dear ankle straps and only one button apiece,
like little licorice candies. Their flat bows of dull
grosgrain ribbon made a nice contrast to the slippers that were shiny enough to reflect your face.

   Mr. Livingstone understood my longing. "Tell
you what I'll do," he said in a confidential tone.
"The next time you have your picture taken I'll
lend you a pair of patent leathers." Soon afterward,
on a trip to the photographer's with my mother, I
tenderly carried the borrowed slippers, nested in
pale blue tissue paper in a shoebox. When the
photographer stuck his head under the black cloth
that covered the camera and told me to look at the
birdie, I first stole a quick glance at my feet, beautiful with shoes, and instead of the usual glower, I
gazed back at the camera with a look of seraphic
happiness.

   Still bedeviled by fears of catching the black
death and of witches disguised as swirling leaves
dancing in the park, I was also terrified by the
moving pictures, so much so that I was usually
carried screaming from the theatre. And when my
parents took me to what they thought might be a
relatively harmless production of *H.M.S. Pinafore*, I
took one look at Dick Dead-Eye, as played by
DeWolf Hopper, and hid under the seat. He had
two sets of eyes: his own, heavily made up, and
another realistically painted on his eyelids.

   "Keep quiet," my mother whispered soothingly,
"here comes Little Buttercup." I calmed down
enough to get back in my seat and listened to a
middle-aged soubrette tunefully insist that she was
Sweet Little Buttercup, but I hid my face when the
four-eyed monster reappeared. Later, it didn't
help me to know that the bogeyman incarnate,
who was to inhabit my nightmares for weeks, was
called a "wolf-hopper."

Aline Fruhauf

Girl in White, ca. 1913.

Somehow I lived through a performance of *Snow White and the Seven Dwarfs*, but after seeing the lifelike pig's heart that the huntsman showed the cruel stepmother-queen, I was ready to abandon the theatre forever. It was only after I saw a Christmas pantomime, featuring young people dressed as Reddy Fox and Peter Rabbit, that I decided to give it another chance. Three years later, I was to see Sarah Bernhardt.

Divinity on the Boardwalk

Duringthe summer of 1916, my parents rented a cottage at Long Beach, Long Island, and my Grandmother and Grandfather Frank stayed with us. There I was taken to Castles-by-the-Sea, a restaurant in a white building on the boardwalk, to dine and to watch the famous dance team, Irene and Vernon Castle (for whom the restaurant was named) as they danced the fox-trot, the maxixe, and the tango. Irene was slim. "Not pretty," my mother said, "sweet looking, but stylish." I thought she was pretty. She had very level eyes and brown bobbed hair, the first bob I had seen.

My father liked to dance, and my mother wore a beautiful dance dress: Chantilly lace, black over white, with a silk sash of a reddish color called tango orange. Together, as I watched, they whirled decorously around the dance floor.

Many celebrities, including theatre people, came to Long Beach to dine and dance at Castles or at the Hotel Nassau. They walked on the boardwalk or allowed themselves to be pushed in big, comfortable, canopied roller-chairs. One day my father pointed out Diamond Jim Brady, the millionaire who collected jewels. He was a heavy man with the complexion of boiled ham. Like the boys in the song "Green Grow the Rushes-Oh," Diamond Jim was clothed all in green, and he was studded with emeralds to match. They gleamed on his hands, in his cuffs, on his tie. We saw him again, dressed in blue and ablaze with sapphires. I have always regretted not seeing him decked out in rubies and wondered if he had a red suit to match.

The great French actress Sarah Bernhardt was staying at the Nassau. She was seventy-two. Since she had had a leg amputated the year before and never wore an artificial one, both she and Grandpa Frank, whose legs were paralyzed, were taken for airings on the boardwalk in their wheelchairs. They never met *en passant*, or we surely would have heard of it. Grandpa was a gregarious soul despite his disability, and he talked to anyone who struck his fancy. He was just as proud of his Hanoverian German as Mme. Renaud was of her Lyonnaisian French. But I doubt that he would have tried it out on Sarah Bernhardt. There was a war going on.

Grandpa was a handsome old man, very pink and white, with flashing blue eyes and a neat moustache and goatee, snow white and silky. In the summer, he wore a student's visored cap of blue serge, a sealskin hat in the winter. He loved children and had many young friends in New York's Central Park. He could always beat me at checkers, but then anyone could.

One afternoon Grandma and I were sitting on the porch sharing our mutual passion: chocolate peppermints left over from a carefully guarded prewar box. We ate them slowly to make them last as long as possible. Anna's black hair had scarcely any gray in it, and she wore it in a sort of roll on the top of her head. The black eyes that had burned in her daguerreotype as a little girl now sparkled behind thick-lensed, rimless glasses attached to a black string.

"I used to have beautiful eyes," she said. "When Grandpa was courting me, he said 'Your eyes are

21

like black cherries.' I ruined them making a crazy quilt."

She admonished me to take good care of my eyes: "They're your most precious possession."

"My Mutzi," she added fondly and patted my hand.

She was looking very nice in a summer dress of black-and-white figured silk. She wore her pearls and a rope of intricately strung jet beads, the size of poppy seeds, and her tiny bunioned feet were strapped uncomfortably in black kid slippers. We munched a while in silent happiness; then she broke out with "You ought to talk to Sarah Bernhardt."

"Why, Grandma?"

"She's the greatest actress in the whole world. It's an honor to have her in this country. Besides, what's the use of all those lessons if you're never going to use your French. Anyway, I'm sure she'd be pleased if you went up to her."

"What would I say to her?"

"Just say 'howdy do' in French."

The next afternoon I was out on the boardwalk with my friends. We saw the Bernhardt entourage leaving the hotel. An attendant was pushing a roller-chair with a heavily made-up old woman in it. Two mustachioed men and a woman walked alongside. Jacques, a handsome Belgian boy who knew everything, said, "That's her son, her doctor, and her maid."

Sarah Bernhardt's face, though ravaged, had a terrible beauty; I knew I was in the presence of a personage. Her rouged mouth was the shape of the masks of Comedy and Tragedy, somewhere in between. Her gray-green eyes were luminous and like a lion's, with thick tarry lashes; her nostrils were imperious and sharply defined. Her clothing was all silk and velvet in shades of dark red and purple. A pouf of red hair showed under her ruched hat. Cream-colored lace cascaded at her wrists and throat. Jewels gleamed on her fingers that had rouge on them. Even though it was a warm day her lap was covered with a fur robe. I advanced toward her, curtsied, extended my hand, and after I had caught my breath I said, "Bonjour Madame, comment allez-vous?" The leonine eyes widened. I was so close I could see the little red veins in them. Not a wrinkle in her face escaped me. Suddenly, the mask-mouth parted in the most beautiful smile; she took my hand and pressed it to her lips.

When I got my hand back, it was stamped with big red parentheses. I forgot my politesse, and holding my hand aloft like a banner I ran all the way home to show it to Grandma and anyone else I happened to meet on the way. I didn't wash the hand for a week; it wasn't easy keeping it out of the tub. Eventually the mark of the kiss wore off. I went swimming.

That winter Sarah Bernhardt appeared at the Keith vaudeville houses throughout the country, playing scenes from her most popular plays. Because of the amputation, she played *L'Aiglon* and the trial scene from *Jeanne d'Arc* sitting down. Mother took me to the Palace Theatre in Times Square to see them all. The one that impressed me most was the deathbed scene, the last act of *La Dame aux camélias*, which she played in a huge canopied bed, banked with drifts of white lace. Mme. Bernhardt as Marguerite Gauthier—Marguerite Gauthier! One of the young women who came to a bad end!—was nightgowned in billowing white. The haggard face under a red-gold wig still held its terrible beauty.

The house was hushed as she intoned, "Ar-r-mand! Ar-r-mand!" and cold chills gathered between my shoulder blades.

"*Je n'veux pas mour-ri-re—maintenant!*" the voice came clarion clear through clenched teeth that acted like a sounding board; every syllable could be heard in every part of the house.

Armand, played by a handsome young actor—Lou Tellegen, I think—was overcome with emotion. He tried to comfort Marguerite. They would go away together. She would get well in the country of the sun.

"Au pays—du—soleil—," she repeated after him in a haunting, thrilling singsong.

And with these words, Marguerite Gauthier exhaled and expired. The audience, silent for a moment, exploded into thunderous applause. I hear that voice every day of my life.

Present for a Vampire

The First World War had been over for nearly a year when we moved from 112th Street near the river to West End Avenue at 84th Street. I left Horace Mann and my beloved art teacher, Miss Boas, to attend a private girls' school. On Saturday mornings I was enrolled in the children's class at Frank Alvah Parsons's New York School of Fine and Applied Art. When the classes at Parsons were over in the late spring, I took home my Sho Card colors, wonderfully soft and gooey pigments in glass jars. Water on top of the thick paste of paint stayed suspended in jewel-like transparency until one stirred the contents of the jar with a stick. When the water evaporated from the light green, the paint developed a gentle fuzz of mildew, like mouse fur, with a heavenly smell that no one but me seemed to appreciate.

At home I discovered practical uses for the colors. The first was to touch up the daisies on the ends of the black ciré-ribbon streamers of my wide-brimmed black straw hat. Then I learned that in all the processes of art one thing invariably leads to another. I spied some empty pillboxes on my father's chiffonier and, with brushes still full of paint, I put daisies on them. Since regular school was also closed for the season and the days were long, I cadged more pillboxes from a friendly druggist and gave him a hand-painted present. I bought some coat hangers from Woolworth's, purloined some lead pencils from the household supply, and decorated them all. I made matching sets and gave them to friends. Blondes would get turquoise blue with rosebuds or pink with forget-me-nots; redheads got Nile green with daisies—I could use the heavenly smelling light green—and brunettes ended up with anything from cherry red to orange with blossoms in appropriate colors. These applied-art projects triggered my contact with the outside world and were a welcome change from my one artistic household chore, the gilding of radiators.

I made friends with the children in the new apartment house, and one of the first things they told me was that the actress Theda Bara lived on the sixth floor. She was the original movie "vamp," who foreshadowed such later temptresses of the screen as Pola Negri and Nita Naldi. According to the movie magazines I was beginning to devour, Theda Bara was born on the Sahara Desert in the shadow of the Great Sphinx. Her first name was an anagram of *death*, and her last, *Arab* spelled backwards. Arrayed in tight, high-necked black velvet dresses, even on hot days, she gave dramatic interviews to the press, and the reporters were forced to peer at her through a blue smog of incense. Her face was made up in chalk white, her mouth in vivid scarlet, her eyes were underlined for emphasis with black, and every lash stood out under thick applications of mascara. The titles of her films were as startling as her appearance: *The Vampire, Cleopatra, The Eternal Sin, The Rose of Blood, Her Double Life, Forbidden Path,* and *Tiger Woman.*

She was born Theodosia Goodman in Cincinnati; Bara was taken from the name of her Swiss maternal grandfather, Francis Bara de Coppet. Theodosia's parents, according to the report, had a little money and helped to further her career on the stage. When William Fox engaged her for the film

adaptation of the stage play *A Fool There Was*, she
submitted to a complete change of personality, and
her pale makeup, dark eyeshadow, and lashes
thick with mascara influenced the look of the era.
Little girls dressed up in their mother's long
dresses, festooned themselves with strings of
beads, walked with a measured and hip-swinging
slink, and pretended they were Theda Bara.

"Kiss-s me-e, my fool!" they hissed in playrooms
across the country, "I-y-ee am-m Clee-oh-patrah!"

I know, I was one of them.

Evil though she might be, she appeared to live
quietly with her husband, her sister Lori, her
parents, and her dog, Petey, a combination bulldog
and fox terrier. At least one iconoclastic report
described her apartment as "not luxurious," and
the background music supplied by her Victrola
was a recording of the Irish tenor John McCormack
singing "I Hear You Calling Me." It went on to
describe her dress as "plain and serviceable," the
kind that "social workers recommend to working
girls." She always came home from the studio
about five in the afternoon, and the neighborhood
kids lined up to watch Theda Bara step out of her
car. She looked younger than she did on the
screen, and her figure was "girlish."

It was at this time of day that I aired my canary,
Dickey. There was only one convenient way to
take him out for a walk on the busy street, and that
was to include the cage. And the hour for my first
glimpse of the vampire had come. Gripping the
birdcage, I joined the four or five children who had
gathered as the brown and beige Rolls Royce with
brass fittings rolled up to the curb. There was a
hood over the passenger section, but the chauffeur
and footman sat open to the weather. The chauffeur, in brown and beige livery, was the only man
on the box. Mike, our doorman, sprang out to
open the car door, and the first member of the Bara
family to alight was a brindled brown dog with
touches of white. He walked on his hind legs,
marcato, as if listening to a roll of drums. Then

came a tall slender lady, all in frothy beige, like a coffee soda. Her dark eyes looked straight ahead, at nothing in particular. Her face was very white, and her thin mouth was accented with medium-red lipstick. Black hair showed in deep scallops under a cloudlike hat. Theda Bara, much milder looking than the sultry pictures in *Photoplay*, was followed by her husband, the director Charles Brabin. He had a long pale face and a nose shaped like a metronome. He wore a ginger-colored topcoat of some soft expensive material and a brown beaver hat pulled jauntily over one eye. A meerschaum pipe was gripped firmly between his teeth; it, too, was brown. The color scheme changed when sister Lori, a blonde version of Theda, and the parents of the girls, a pleasant-looking middle-aged couple, emerged dressed in subdued gray, black, and navy blue.

I was impressed, and I wanted to give Theda Bara one of my hand-painted sets. I had given a set to Polly, one of the elevator girls, who was a good friend, and I told her I was thinking of making one for Theda Bara.

"That's a real nice thought," Polly said. "I think she'd like that very much. I'll deliver it for you when I bring up the mail, and I'll tell her it's from the little girl in 2C."

Beige would have been a nice color for the presents. It would have blended with her outfit, the car, her husband, and the dog. But I settled on sulphur yellow, liberally sprinkled with blood-red blossoms and poison-green leaves, as colors more suited to a vampire. I wrapped the gifts in tissue paper, enclosed a card, and gave the package to Polly.

"I know she'll be delighted," Polly said, "and the next time you see her you must go up and say hello, so she'll know it was you who made the presents."

My imagination, sparked by my reading the *Arabian Nights* and having seen a performance of *Chu Chin Chow*, a musical extravaganza based on

Ali Baba and the Forty Thieves, painted a vivid picture of what the Bara domain might look like. The walls were hung in black velvet. There were wild animal skins on the marble floors, and a python was curled on a scarlet cushion. Gongs crashed at intervals for no apparent reason. Silent servants wearing long robes and turbans glided in and out of the incense-filled rooms, obedient to every command.

In my reverie, Theda Bara opened the tissue-paper package and inspected its contents. Then she clapped her hands and a servant appeared noiselessly, agate eyes burning in his impassive face. With a flourish, she handed him the coat hanger; he took it and hung it in a closet filled with exotic, scented silken robes. A second servant, who looked just like the first, received the pencil and laid it on an escritoire of carved ivory. The third to be summoned was a Chinese maid in a beautifully embroidered mandarin coat and with long fingernails like talons, who took the pillbox and carefully placed it in a medicine chest that was carved from a solid block of imperial jade.

The day after the package was delivered, I took Dickey for his walk and waited expectantly for Theda Bara. On the dot of five the car drew up to the curb. But when Theda Bara followed Petey across the sidewalk, I moved toward her and froze. I couldn't tell Polly that I really believed all the lurid stories in the fan magazines and was literally scared stiff.

"She won't eat you, you know," said Polly.

"I know," I said ruefully, "maybe—tomorrow."

The next day I managed to walk up to Theda Bara, switched the birdcage to my left hand, and swallowed.

"How do you do," I croaked hoarsely. "I hope you liked the presents."

In a low pleasant voice, she thanked me "for the pretty-uh-things" and disappeared into the entrance to the building. Polly looked at me with real concern.

"What's the matter, honey?" she asked. "You all right? You went white as a sheet!"

The next day, I received a large brown envelope, courtesy of Polly. It was a photograph of Theda Bara, dressed in a light, full-skirted chiffon dress and a single row of graduated pearls around her neck, a clear attempt by the film industry to change her image. Her hair was looped over her forehead in two large scallops and hung in loose strands over her shoulders. It looked well brushed but could have stood a little judicious trimming at the ends. Her hat was wide brimmed and floppy, the kind one wore to a garden party or an afternoon wedding. Her expression was guileless and demure. I sighed, looked again, and decided that the dress and hat were probably pink, and if the picture were in color and someone had tied it with a satin bow, it would have done very well as the cover of a candy box. I showed it to my mother who thought it was very nice. Kati had no comment.

I went to my room, took the black straw hat out of its box, and put it on. I pulled scallops of my hair down over my forehead and looked deeply and steadfastly into the mirror. When I took the hat off, I noticed that the Sho Card color was chipping off the daisies. I brought the hat to my mother and said I thought I could fix them to stay with oil paints.

"All right," she said, "get me my handbag, and while you're at the store get some gold paint for the radiators."

The Face Makers

As my art work progressed, I found that I could make likenesses of my friends, which began to take the shape of paperdoll portraits, colored back and front. I also made my first self-portrait: a paper doll, dressed in a white slip, with replicas of articles from my own wardrobe—a hat, a coat, and my favorite dress, a cobalt blue and bright yellow affair of checked gingham—all cut out to fit over the slip. And in a nostalgic mood for the Theda Bara of the old movie fan magazines, I made a cardboard portrait of her as the queen of the Nile, which I kept as a bookmark. It disappeared, however, along with many other works; although Kati was a feminist at heart, anxious for me to pursue a career in the arts, she managed to throw out some of my better drawings.

My mother loved the theatre and, now that I was older, she took me with her to matinees. (On Saturday nights with my father, the three of us went to the musicals he liked.) Mother belonged to several clubs dedicated to the study and support of the theatre, one of which, called the Drama Comedy Club, was presided over by Edyth Totten, a flamboyant brunette and former actress. The club met on Friday afternoons in the ballroom of the Astor Hotel. I liked to sit on the little gold chairs

31

and watch actors and actresses do scenes from their current plays. Miss Totten arranged theatre parties at reduced rates, so the members of the club saw many of the plays they had sampled at their meetings. Some plays were probably kept alive by this device, and we were kept au courant with what was going on in the Broadway show shops.

There were also discussions at the club—I don't remember them—and we listened to an occasional speaker, sometimes a musician. The only performer I remember at all was Margaret Severn, a dancer, who had made a reputation by wearing masks designed by W.T. Benda in dances inspired by them. One of her masks was of Silly Doll, a vacuous creature with puffed-out cheeks, round staring eyes, and a tiny pouting mouth. Another was Golden Beauty, the archetype of all the fairy princesses I had ever read about. I desperately wanted to take a close look at the masks, to meet their creator, and to find out how he made them so I could make some too.

Benda, whose initials stood for Wladyslaw Theodor, was born in Poznan, Poland, in 1873. He grew up with a family of actors; all the artifices of the stage were his daily fare. He came to the United States in 1899 and established a reputation as an illustrator of books and magazines. By 1918, he had made twelve masks, which attracted the attention of Frank Crowninshield, the editor of *Vanity Fair*, and they were first used on the stage in 1920 in the *Greenwich Village Follies*. I found him listed in the telephone book and called him, and he said he'd be glad to see my mother and me and show us his work. His Gramercy Park studio had a vaulted ceiling, a wrought-iron balcony overhung with antique fabric, a large easel, and a drawing table with a black-and-white illustration of a lady that looked just like Golden Beauty.

He was a slender man of medium height, with black hair and moustache, and friendly eyes. He wore a green smock over a business suit. I went to the wall to see the bodiless people that hung there:

a monster, painted in green and blue; another that looked like the enlarged head of an insect with headgear that curled like flames; a geisha, with an elaborate coiffure lacquered in black; an unpainted version of the face of Abraham Lincoln; and Golden Beauty, in all the glory of the most magnificent headdress I had ever seen, shaped like the tail of a peacock, covered with gold and decorated with feather designs that simulated rubies and emeralds. I stared at it in open-mouthed admiration, and Benda handed it to me.

"It's all right," he said, "you can hold it."

Wonder of wonders! It was as light as an enormous peanut shell. I turned it around and saw that the inside was lined with innumerable strips of paper fitted together in fan-shaped patterns. I asked him how he made the masks.

"Cardboard," he replied with a shrug, "little pieces of paper, plaster, oil paint."

He handed us the other faces, and we inspected them with care. Then, fearing we were taking too much of the artist's time, we thanked him for his courtesy and left.

My one effort to make a Benda mask was hardly a success. I tried to build a face by pasting ribbons of bond paper on a shirtboard, but the thing looked dreadful, like a flattened human face in bandages. Then, remembering that Benda had mentioned the use of plaster, I bought a bag of plaster of Paris, poured some on another shirtboard, made a valley, poured in some water, and began to knead, a procedure I had watched Kati follow with flour and water and eggs in making noodles. I covered the bandaged face with the plaster-dough as quickly as I could and molded it into the recognizable features of a face. When I thought the plaster had hardened enough to paint, I took out my oil colors and rubbed some flesh tones into the face. The thing began to have a life of its own, quite different from anything resembling Golden Beauty. I put in blue eyes, black eyebrows, and thick eyelashes like Sarah Bernhardt's.

"For heaven's sake!" my mother exclaimed when she saw it. "What are you going to do with it?"

"I was thinking of giving it to Margaret Severn," I said. "I don't think Mr. Benda would want it."

My mother agreed that Mr. Benda would not want it. But she took me to tea at Margaret Severn's, where the mask, courteously accepted by our hostess, was left on the hall table, still moist with paper soaked in library paste and damp plaster mixed with oil paint.

Levy Brothers stationery store on Broadway at Eighty-third Street was my uptown rialto. It supplied me with drawing materials, excellent raspberry lollipops an inch thick, and movie magazines. And I pored over the spinach-green rotogravure photos in the movie magazines, alternately working on a lollipop and making drawings of the movie stars. I noticed that an artist named Ralph Barton, who drew for the magazines, was able to get likenesses with a very simple and beautiful line and a very subtle exaggeration of features. I admired his style without knowing that the drawings were caricatures, or that my own efforts would, in time, fall into the same category.

A few years later, in 1922 I think, I was to see Ralph Barton's work on a much larger scale, an entr'acte curtain for the *Chauve-Souris*, Nikita Balieff's revue imported from Paris. On a chalk-white background, Barton had drawn, in his usual smart and sensitive line, a typical Broadway first-night audience, row upon row of the faces of every imaginable celebrity of New York and Hollywood. One I remember particularly was of the diminutive Anita Loos, the author whose *Gentlemen Prefer Blondes*, published in 1925, was illustrated by Barton. Miss Loos's linear image was seated like a doll on the lap of her husband, the actor John Emerson. When the asbestos curtain was raised and the line-drawn audience stared implacably at the live one, the effect was electrifying and the applause was great.

I began to copy photographs of actors on shirtboards, painting them in oil. They were fair as likenesses but dreadful as drawings. Nevertheless, they bore fruit. I sent them off to their subjects, and in return I received autographed photos of the stars—Lillian Gish, Norma and Constance Talmadge, and Richard Barthelmess—which I treasured for a long time. One day, I saw an actual filming on West End Avenue. The actors' faces were covered with sulphur-yellow powder, which photographed as white, and their lips were stained a vivid purple. They looked masklike and grotesque, and I loved them dearly.

I was suddenly fourteen, then fifteen and sixteen. And although I wore paper clips on the edge of my felt hat, unclasped and flapping galoshes, short skirts, and long-waisted dresses, I didn't consider myself a flapper. I wore the outward accoutrements with a kind of loathing, an unwilling concession to the times, and longed for the day when I could wear more picturesque clothing. I had a Latin teacher who said I had a Rossetti neck. I immediately looked up Rossetti and the Pre-Raphaelite painters and felt a little less hopeless about my appearance. And I let my hair grow—I had had it bobbed—but Kati never forgave my loss of curls.

I still attended the Saturday morning classes at Parsons and was enrolled in a class called Costume Illustration, under the direction of Grace Fuller and Marion Barnes, pleasant ladies who wore identical chokers, balls of clear crystal that caught the light in a most agreeable way. Once I heard them discussing my work in tones just loud enough for me to hear. I thought they were most considerate, since they spared me the embarrassment of appearing to eavesdrop.

"She's got something," said Miss Fuller.

"Yes," said Mrs. Barnes, "isn't it too bad she can't draw?"

To remedy the situation, I joined the Saturday afternoon life class conducted by Harry Baker, a jolly gentleman with a handsome ovoid bald head, great shadowed blue eyes, and a little, waxed white moustache turned up at the ends. According to Baker, "once you learn to draw the figure, you can draw anything." He illustrated stories for Western magazines and amused us by drawing cowboys on horseback, galloping across the plains. He wore a cream-colored ten-gallon hat, and I made a pretty good caricature of him, which he autographed.

Saturday nights were gala. I went to the theatre with my parents, and my Monday morning class-room doodles turned into caricatures of the actors and actresses I had seen two nights before. They were done on newsprint, a beige paper, which, though of miserable quality, was the basis of a good flesh tone, so all these drawings of stage folk were in color. I sent them off, as usual accompanied by fan letters. Correspondence became more exciting when I enclosed art works; one star, Eleanor Painter, and her husband, the tenor Louis Graveure, were so enchanted with my offering that they sent me one in return: a corsage of sweet peas. This was high tribute, but since I couldn't figure out how to press an entire bunch of flowers, I saved the ribbon and one or two dried blossoms.

As I became aware of the work of contemporary caricaturists, Ralph Barton's drawing still seemed the most interesting. I had followed it from *Photoplay*, around 1920, to *Judge* and *Vanity Fair*. A book of his light verse, *Science in Rhyme Without Reason*, which was, of course, illustrated by him, had just been published, and I studied the drawings with devout fixity and memorized all the verses.

In April 1924, a month or so before I was to graduate from high school, I wrote to Barton, asking if he knew of any school where I could study the art of caricature, adding that I liked his book very much and would be pleased if he would autograph my copy. In a few days the reply came; it was a nice letter. He wrote that as far as he knew there was no such school; the important thing was to have the urge to draw. If I had that, nothing could stop me. He went on to say that he would be glad to autograph my copy of his book and suggested that I telephone for an appropriate time. I did call him and was asked to tea to meet Mrs. Barton.

At the time, I was trying to look like Katharine Cornell, the young actress who had made an instantaneous hit in Clemence Dane's play *A Bill of Divorcement*. I parted my hair in the middle, wet it down to make it lie flat and straight across my forehead, secured it with "invisible" hairpins (which showed), drew it down over my ears, and pinned it into a little sausage in back. I dressed carefully, put my book under my arm, and set out for Forty-seventh Street, west of Fifth Avenue. As I rang the bell to the walk-up apartment, I took a hurried look at my reflection in the polished brass of the row of letterboxes, decided that my cheeks were much too fat for me to look like Katharine Cornell, and when the answering click came I walked upstairs with a breathless feeling, not unmixed with stage fright.

The Bartons were waiting for me on the landing. Ralph was a slender man in his early thirties, with brown hair parted in the middle and slicked back, and sideburns. He had dark blue eyes and deeply furrowed cheeks, and his mouth curled about his uneven teeth in a slightly apologetic manner. He was scrupulously neat, unaffected, and charming. Carlotta Monterey Barton was stunning, a black-and-white drawing by Ralph Barton. Her profile looked as if it had been cut out of rice paper. She wore her smooth black hair cut short like a Pierrot's cap, and she had small perfect ears and wore sideburns like brushstrokes of india ink. Her generous eyebrows were shaped like circumflex accents, and her long, dark eyes sparkled under half-closed lids. Although her mouth was rather thin in profile, from the front it was shaped like the ace of diamonds. I was happy to see that, in direct defiance of the modes of the day, she wore a long, full-skirted dress of heavy black silk with snow-white organdy at the bosom. Her shoes were smartly styled oxfords, round-toed and tied with wide laces, and she wore very sheer black silk stockings. My admiration showed, and Mrs. Barton, quite accustomed to being admired, responded with a devastating smile.

We went into the living room. Pictorially, the couple could not have been placed to better advantage. The wall behind them was covered with what seemed to be sheets of beaten gold. I touched it in wonder and asked what it was.

"It's tea paper," Barton said, "the kind they once used to line tea chests in China. You can get it at the Japan Paper Company."

I savored the rest of the room. There were several Oriental rugs on the black painted floor, and there were chairs made of some woven reed. Bookshelves, four feet high, stood against one wall; the top shelf served as a mantel holding an early American clock, a parade of ivory elephants in graduated sizes, some Chinese puppets, a kachina doll, an old pewter gill measure, and various other small and curious objects of carved wood, brass, and ivory. Mounted down the length of one door were Chinese idiographs cut from black velvet. My mouth opened for the question, but Barton was ready for it.

"It's Chinese," he said with a smile, "for 'jade and gold all over your house.'"

I sat down on a chair slipcovered in gray-green and violet striped silk, only to get up again to look at the artist's caricatures grouped on the wall above the bookshelves. There was my favorite wash drawing of Eleanora Duse as she appeared in New York in 1923 in Ibsen's *The Lady from the Sea*, even more delicate than its reproduction in magazines. And there were the *Vanity Fair* series of painters, hypothetically appearing in their own pictures. The one I remember best was of Degas being kicked in the teeth by one of his ballerinas. Matisse and Picasso also found themselves

inextricably trapped in their own paintings.

Barton called my attention to two of his favorite caricatures; one of Paderewski, the world-famous pianist who was also the premier of Poland, his bushy hair topped with a tiny derby; the other of General von Hindenburg, in full uniform with all his medals. At the far end of the wall was a watercolor portrait of Barton's little daughter by a former marriage, Natalie, aged ten, wearing a blue dress, crossbarred in red. All had been framed in narrow moldings of park-bench green. Barton even supplied their source: "Mr. Denks of Hanfstaengl's on Fifty-seventh Street."

We talked of the theatre and of Paris, the Barton's favorite city, "the most civilized place in the world," and of drawing paper. Barton used

Ralph and Carlotta Barton at home, 1925. Inscribed, "To Aline with our love. Carlotta Monterey Barton, Oct. 1925."

39

Whatman's five-ply watercolor paper; he preferred it to the bristol board we used at Parsons.

I asked if it was a good idea to copy the works of other artists.

"Only the Old Masters," he said.

"Any one in particular?"

"Rubens," he said, a touch weary, but still polite. Then I asked if there was anything else I should know in case my work was good enough to be published.

"Yes, indeed," he replied, "always leave plenty of white paper around your drawings. The engravers like that."

Then he showed me one of his latest works. It was a tour de force, a monumental map of Paris, complete with every building, cathedral, park, the Eiffel Tower, and peopled with tiny figures, on bicycles, crossing streets, fishing on the banks of the Seine. It measured nearly two feet across, and in the lower right-hand corner was his signature, "Ralph Barton, for CM." I murmured inarticulate admiration.

A maid brought in a red lacquer tray of thin white porcelain cups. Something was floating around in the pale amber liquid. I looked more closely.

"It has flowers in it!"

"It's jasmine tea," Mrs. Barton explained.

I drank some, flowers and all. It was delicious. I looked around the treasure-filled room, at the two shining ones smiling at me, and I felt that somehow I had stepped into the Arabian Nights. Jade and gold all over your house, and jasmine tea. I swept the room with my eyes—all the objects related to form a harmonious atmosphere—and I walked around it again, talking incessantly, pointing to pictures and artifacts, behind in general like an uninhibited tourist.

"How lovely it is," I said, very close to tears.

I had been there a little over an hour, and the smiles on the Bartons' faces were becoming a little fixed. Fearing of wearing out this of all welcomes, I rose suddenly, dropping my handbag. Everything in it fell out—coins, mirror; my Dorine compact opened and the puff rolled out like a little wheel spilling Rachel powder on the shiny black floor; the top came off my Tangee lipstick disclosing an inch and a half of aniline orange.

"Now you know all my secrets," I said lamely, as scalding embarrassment covered me from head to toe.

Their smiles were now kindly.

"Goodbye," I said, "thank you for the tea," and started for the door.

"Wait a minute," Mrs. Barton called to me, "you forgot your book."

I came back. The artist found a pen, hesitated a moment, then inscribed the flyleaf:

For Aline Fruhauf, who is in danger of coming down with a serious attack of caricature.

Backstage

After the memorable tea with the Bartons, I bombarded them with their caricatures, drawn from memory and executed in Higgins-ink, black and green, and in *pourpre*, an eye-shattering cherry-purple, manufactured by Pelikan in Germany. I mounted these offerings on concentric squares of cherry-colored and electric-blue construction paper. I also modeled a tiny clay head of Mrs. Barton, painted and shellacked it, and mounted it on a minute cube of black wood. And, as a house present, I covered a dime-store bud vase with melted black and vermilion sealing wax, which, I thought, was very Chinese and would look well against the gold wallpaper. The Bartons asked me to tea frequently and encouraged me to bring my latest work.

Conversation with them was interesting. They quizzed me on the Younger Generation. Was it as lurid as Scott Fitzgerald had made it out to be in his writings? I couldn't be very helpful on that score. I had never known people like Fitzgerald's characters although I certainly enjoyed reading about them.

Carlotta Barton called me "our child," and I was happy to have a set of glamorous foster parents who "understood" me.

Both the Bartons had been married before.

Theirs was, in fact, the third marriage for each. Carlotta had a daughter, Cynthia, in California, and the little girl in the portrait, Natalie, who attended a convent school in Kansas City, was Ralph's daughter. "She's charming," Carlotta said. "She looks like a Greuze."

Carlotta, who appeared on the stage from time to time and who posed for the more elegant fashion magazines, had a flair for dramatizing her white-skinned, brunette beauty with correspondingly striking black-and-white costumes. One day I met her walking along Fifth Avenue, looking especially handsome. It was fall, and she wore a fitted *tailleur* of black-and-white sharkskin and a small hat with the same blend of black and white. The hat was covered entirely with guinea-hen feathers.

Both the Bartons encouraged me to read. Carlotta led me to Walt Whitman and Montaigne; Ralph, to Balzac, Rabelais, and Flaubert.

"*Salammbô*," Ralph said, "was one book worth saving."

I read it dutifully, didn't like it, and much preferred *Madame Bovary*. Ralph's favorite painter was still Rubens, and he thought I should investigate him for myself. He also introduced me to the works of Max Beerbohm, both the essays and the caricatures, and he stressed the importance of familiarizing myself with the satiric artists of the past: Gillray and Rowlandson, Cruikshank, Daumier, and Lautrec. Under his influence, I began to haunt the art galleries and museums. History had been my worst subject in school; now, at least, my sense of history was reactivated, the blanks filled in, as it were, by the paintings, drawings, and sculpture of the past. More important to me as an emerging artist was the realization that caricature was not only a respectable form of art but also a valuable way of documenting human beings.

After graduating from high school, instead of college, I chose to enter the class in stage design at Parsons and to continue the Saturday morning classes in costume illustration. The school emphasized the importance of research, so we made field trips to museums to make watercolor sketches of objects, clothing, and furniture that ranged from Eskimo garments and beadwork at the Museum of Natural History to the long-buried, ancient Roman glass in the Cesnola collection at the Metropolitan Museum of Art. I discovered that as soon as I had made a color sketch of any object it was fixed in my memory.

The stage-design class had occasional lectures by scenic and costume designers. One was given by James Reynolds, who, at the time, was deeply immersed in the Empire period. He had just finished work on a production of Rostand's *L'Aiglon*, and he wore his pale yellow hair combed foreward in a Napoleonic forelock. He brought some of his designs for the sets and costumes with him; their predominant colors were shrimp pink, lime green, and dried blood.

The Parsonage, as the school was sometimes called, was under the influence of Dynamic Symmetry, a mathematical system of drawing formulated by the American artist and author Jay Hambidge, and in the life class on Saturday mornings, we constructed the figure according to this method. Claude Bragdon, the architect and author, a proponent of Dynamic Symmetry and also a stage designer, was one of our visiting lecturers. He had based his whole philosophy of design on the method and equated it with the fourth dimension, which he called an "expanded thought frame." I asked him what he meant by an expanded thought frame.

"If you're going on a trip," he replied, "and think you're all packed but find you have some clothes left over, you put the extra ones in another bag; that bag is your expanded thought frame, your fourth dimension."

All that this cryptic information gave me was a name for my hatbox. It was not, however, the first time I had heard of that elusive element. In the same year, 1925, S.J. Kaufman, a columnist on the *New York Evening Globe*, referred to it in connection with caricature, which he deemed the fourth dimension of portraiture. And the dean of American caricaturists, according to another of Kaufman's columns, was Alfred Frueh, whose name was enough like mine to cause some minor confusion later on.

At school I waged an unsuccessful battle with mechanical drawing and got so behind in my work that I got up early in the morning and the school janitor let me in at seven-thirty so I could make up work on my drawings of ground plans and elevations of stage sets. But the more I drew mechanically, the more I wanted to make faces. Between bouts with T-square, triangle, compass, and ruling pen, I experimented with caricatures, using Dynamic Symmetry as a means of construction. I managed to direct the features of Glenn Hunter, the matinee idol currently appearing in *Merton of the Movies*, into the figure known as Root 2; the effect was like a poster.

Frank Alvah Parsons, the director of the school, was a man of exquisite taste and charm. He was elderly, white-haired; his nose had a corrugated bridge and his face was the color of a deep-pink carnation. His eyes were small and sharp and bright blue. He had quite definite ideas about women's dress. Among his prejudices were large cameo brooches and red apparel. The latter sent him into blistering rages, one of which was directed at me. One morning he was lecturing on one of his favorite subjects, the mistresses of the French kings and how they influenced the furniture and architecture of their times. I was writing at the back of the room, but he saw me. My buff-colored smock was open at the collar and showed about two inches of scarlet sweater. Parsons took swift leave of Diane de Poitiers and Madame Pompadour, his carnation face grew alarmingly pinker, his eyes narrowed to pinpoints of blue fire, and his voice shook with fury as he bit off his words:

"There-is-something-very-disturbing-in-this-room."

All eyes turned to me, alias Hester Prynne. Hastily, I buttoned my smock, pulling it almost to my ears.

"That's much better," he said. But the thread of his discourse had been broken, and the class was dismissed. It was years before I wore red again, except as an accent.

Up to this time, my tastes in art were rather florid. Zuloaga's portrait of the Marchesa di Casati, a spectacular blonde whose black eyes the artist had shadowed with iodine brown, was my idea of a stunning piece of portraiture. And the air-brushed slickness of Maxfield Parrish's youths and maidens, with omnipresent five-foot earthenware jugs with purple shadows, were equally satisfying. Then, somewhere, I saw van Gogh's *Arlésienne* (Madame Ginoux), the version that was formerly in the Adolph Lewisohn collection and is now in the Metropolitan Museum of Art, with its brilliant yellow background and its central dark figure of a woman reading. But, like Gully Jimson in *The Horse's Mouth* on seeing the work of Manet for the first time, my eyes were skinned, and all other paintings seemed inconsequential.

The Bartons, who had been spending time in Paris, returned to New York and to a larger apartment. I missed the gold walls, but there were other wonderful things in the new abode: a pair of Chinese pewter ducks and two heads, caricatures in the round of Ralph and Carlotta. They had been cut from a cotton fabric, stuffed with sawdust, and lacquered by a Russian artist, Marie Vassilieff, who lived in Montparnasse. And Carlotta had brought back an evening coat she had had made of quilted white cotton sprinkled with tiny flowers. It was made from a peasant's petticoat, a traditional part of the trousseaux of Provençal brides. She gave me the address of the antique shop on the boulevard Raspail in case I went to Paris and wanted to buy one for myself.

"They also come in a wonderful bright yellow,"   *Aline Fruhauf*
she said.

My stage-design class was on its way to a new
adventure. In exchange for lectures on lighting and
for firsthand information on the operations of a
theatre, the class was to work on scenery, costumes, and props at the Neighborhood Playhouse,
a nonprofit organization built and supported by
two wealthy spinsters, the Misses Alice and Irene
Lewisohn. The playhouse had an impressive
history of successful experiments in drama and the
dance. Ellen Terry had given a reading of Shakespeare in 1915, and in 1919, Yvette Guilbert had
directed and appeared in *Guibor*, a French mystery
play of the fourteenth century. Ballets being currently produced were *Ma Mère l'oye*, a children's
production by Maurice Ravel, and *La Boutique
fantasque*, a pantomime with music adapted by
Frederick Jacobi from Rossini and Respighi.

I associated pleasant smells with the playhouse.
They began with the burnt sweet odor of roasting
coffee that permeated the subway cars as the train
approached the Chambers Street station; then
there was the fragrance of the theatre itself, a
tantalizing bouquet of freshly sawed lumber, of
glue sizing and dry pigments for painting flats,
and of the mildewy scent of the brick wall at the
back of the stage.

Aline Bernstein, the stage and costume designer,
took us on a tour of the theatre. She was a small
woman with a natural, warm, russet complexion,
delicate features, and soft brown hair with just a
hint of gray. She wore a beige smock over a brown
silk dress, a short necklace of antique gold, and
beautifully made shoes of brown leather. Her eyes
were tired, and her soft straight mouth drooped a
little at the corners. She looked like the very pretty
little girl she must have been.

The play we would be working on was *The Little
Clay Cart*, a centuries-old Hindu classic, translated
by Arthur William Ryder in 1905 from a French
version by Gérard de Nerval and Joseph Mery, and

the playhouse production was to be its first performance in English. Aline Bernstein explained that
she had used Indian miniatures as her source for
the costumes and setting. And in a small, light
voice she told us how costumes for the theatre
differed from street wear. "They have to be more
emphatic in line and color in order to project across
the footlights."

"Come up to the workshop," she added, "and
I'll show you how we make them."

We followed her up two flights, past Helen
Arthur's office. Miss Arthur, small, pert, shorthaired, and snub-nosed, was the brisk manager of
the playhouse, who attended to all the business
and sent out all the press releases. Agnes Morgan,
the director, stole a glance at us; she was a quiet,
blonde woman with a twinkle behind her glasses.

The top-floor workroom was well lighted. It
opened onto the roof, which, when the weather
was good and the workroom crowded, was used
as additional work space. The first things I noticed
as we entered the workroom were some detailed
pencil sketches on the wall, working drawings of
the costumes for *The Little Clay Cart*. Full skirts and
short jackets were sketched with one arm out-
stretched to show how the sleeves were set into the
shoulders. Alice Beer, a red-haired woman with
red-brown eyes, was bent over a stove stirring
something in a vat with a glass rod. I looked in;
yards of silk were steaming in purple dye. And
there were other vats of dyes: saffron yellow,
crimson, and peacock green. Every now and then,
Miss Beer lifted the cloth with the rod to see how
the color was progressing, and when it had reached
the proper hue she plunged it into a washtub of
cold water.

We went down to the floor below. Stanley
McCandless, the lighting expert, showed us a
small model of a stage, complete with footlights
and miniature spotlights equipped with different
colored sheets of thin gelatin.

Russel Wright, the tall, blond technical director,

was waiting for us backstage to show us the new cyclorama, a smooth plaster wall that took lighting beautifully and didn't show wrinkles like the old-fashioned cloth backdrops.

The class was over for the day. Mrs. Bernstein gave us our homework: "Go down to the public library and read *The Little Clay Cart*; everyone connected with the production of a play should read the play itself."

An integral part of Mrs. Bernstein's designs for the play-to-be was a graceful openwork fence of interlocking arabesques. For some reason I called them squircles and, just as unaccountably, the name stuck. The next time we came to the playhouse, Russel showed us a wooden frame about four feet square enclosing a clay model of a section of the squircle fence. He poured wet plaster over the clay lattice until it was completely covered. After the plaster had hardened, he turned over the heavy cast and proceeded to dig out the wet clay; we all helped. After the cast was clean and dry, he applied a coat of varnish to the inside. He tore triangular strips of heavy building paper and put them to soak in a pail of warm water. He felt the cast to see if the varnish was dry, then rubbed the surface lightly with Vaseline.

"That's so the first layer won't stick to the cast," he said.

Then he wrung out the triangles of wet paper and pressed them into the mold, allowing some paper to overlap several inches outside the mold.

"Now," he explained, "on the second layer, and three or four layers after that, we'll apply Fox paste."

We all joined in, tearing, soaking, wringing, and pasting. In a day or so the section of fence would be dry enough to be pried up and easily lifted from the mold, and the whole process repeated until there were enough sections which, fastened together, would stretch the width of the stage. The result was a light, sturdy, and durable shell, hollow inside, but, outside, the exact shape of the original

Aline Bernstein "as she was in 1925." Unpublished drawing, ca. 1977.

clay model. So this was papier-mâché! Comprehension dawned slowly; I had learned the secret of Mr. Benda's masks.

The class was invited to the dress rehearsal. Mrs. Bernstein, flushed and apprehensive, hurried backstage for a last-minute tour of inspection. She then stood in the back of the house to see the performance.

Seeing me, she said, "I feel as if I'd swallowed the eggbeater."

I had brought along a sketch pad. The curtain went up on the first scene. To the left and right, respectively, were the two little houses of Vasantasena, the courtesan, and Charudatta, the bankrupt prince. Between the houses stretched the exquisite, bronzy green fence, silhouetted against a sky that seemed to be made of blue enamel, like the spoons in our old curio cabinet. The audience gasped. Our squircle fence had become a thing of beauty. The actors appeared; dressed in luminous silks, they looked like Mughal paintings come to life. Albert Carroll, the actor who played the shampooer-turned-Buddhist-monk, had transformed his face into a living mask. It was a wonderful thing to draw.

In a group caricature I drew of the stage-design class, my own face showed no distinction at all. Surely, I thought, I must look more definite. I began working toward a self-caricature, believing that somehow, if I could reduce my own features to lowest terms, it might help me establish my own identity. I doodled, starting with my beetling eyebrows and then latching on to my nose as a keystone. The nose was my worst feature; it stuck out too far and was bulbous at the end. The eyes were all right. They would counteract, somewhat, the overprojecting nose. I added the eyes, two ovals ending in dark pupils. They slanted parallel to the eyebrows, which were so close together they almost met, giving me a look of permanent intimidation. The mouth was good, so for some reason I made it smaller. Then came the chin, small and receding even after all those years of orthodontics, and the cheeks, round and puffed out like Benda's Silly Doll mask. And, to support it all, my best feature: my Rossetti neck became a long stalk encircled with the birthday present I had asked for and prized above all my earthly possessions—a choker of crystal balls. I put in the hair, still long and pinned up in back but cut short in little wisps at the sides, an ambivalent hairdo. I inked in the drawing, added a little watercolor, and showed it to the Bartons on my next visit. They said I certainly hadn't flattered myself, but they found it amusing.

Long after the other members of the class had ceased to work at the playhouse, I stayed on as a part-time volunteer. I was a complete disaster as a seamstress, but I shone in papier-mâché. I was put

Aline Fruhauf

51

to work on props and helped to make the parts of the costumes that didn't require sewing, all for a production called *Sooner and Later*, a ballet conceived and directed by Irene Lewisohn. It was laid in the future, and, like most concepts of this period, it emphasized the super-skyscraper motif, sharp angles and metallic surfaces. Donald Oenslager, a rosy-cheeked young man with a high forehead and an anxious look, had designed the costumes and sets. He took me out on the roof and showed me how to transform powdered metallic radiator paint into a semblance of molten gold or silver by mixing it with Valspar. The paint flowed onto the buckram sections of the costumes like syrup and dried like burnished metal. After years of touching up radiators with dingy gilt powder mixed with banana oil, I was glad to know about "Oenslager gold."

At other times I painted flats after sizing them with a hot glue and whiting solution. One day I was put in charge of the glue. I had been warned to keep enough water in the *bain-marie* under the glue pot and to be sure to turn off the gas before I left, but I forgot and went home. Fish glue on the boil has a characteristic fetor. When it is burned, it gives off an unequaled mephitic stench. That night, they burned incense at the Neighborhood Playhouse.

The members of the cast were used to seeing me working around the theatre and showed no surprise when I began to sketch them. I made many drawings of the cast in their final production of the year, the *Grand Street Follies*, a lighthearted review satirizing the uptown show shops of Broadway. Albert Carroll, of *The Little Clay Cart*, was the star performer. He was a pallid, thin-lipped young man with gelid eyes and a languid manner. But when he made up his face to look like John Barrymore in *Hamlet*, his nose, aided by dark liner, took on the knife-edged contour of the famous Barrymore profile, and the pale eyes were transformed into caverns of madness. He was equally

successful with impersonations of actresses. Affect-
ing a red wig and flowing draperies, he reduced
the voices and mannerisms of such worthy ladies.
of the stage as Minnie Maddern Fiske and Emily
Stevens to the lowest possible terms. His was
in-the-flesh caricature, especially enchanting to
me. I was glad, however, that I never saw him do
Bernhardt. I wanted to keep that image intact.

Meanwhile, back at the Parsonage, there was a
new life class teacher, Howard Giles, an earnest
devotee of Dynamic Symmetry. In the front row of
his semicircle of students, a slim girl with a ruddy
complexion and straight, brown, bobbed hair
turned out one marvelous drawing after another,
beginning by setting down a network of guidelines,
the verticals, horizontals, diagonals to the left and
to the right, and their diagonals that made up the
six directions of Dynamic Symmetry. Our results
were more or less wooden in comparison with
hers. During rest period I heard Giles call her Miss
Hokinson, and I wondered if she could be the
author of the clever cartoons that were beginning
to appear under that name in the *New Yorker*.
When I asked her, she told me she was and seemed
pleased to have been recognized.

We got to be good friends. She came to lunch,
and my mother, who liked her immediately, asked
if she wouldn't like to come to one of the Drama
Comedy Friday afternoons at the Astor to draw the
clubwomen in action. Hokie, as I called her, said
she'd like that and met us at the Astor, where she
settled down as much as was possible in her little
gold chair, took out a hard-covered, handbag-sized
notebook, set down her penciled filaments, and
began to draw "the girls" she would grow to love.
The innocent-looking, culture-driven, large-
bosomed ladies with tiny feet in high-heeled
pumps, even in her most casual sketches, were
depicted in a style that combined rock-solid drawing with playful grace, a style I tried unsuccessfully
to imitate. Hokie, on the other hand, admired the
way I made faces. "We ought to collaborate," I

Aline Fruhauf

53

said, half jokingly, and in a way we did. I submitted cartoons to the *New Yorker* that were turned down. But when I showed them to Hokie, she made rough drawings, submitted them, and they were accepted, and she sent me a check proportionate to the size of the reproduced cartoon. In this way, for a short time, I was a gag writer.

Hokie had a passion for pictures and so did I. We hoped someday to be painters. Some years later, Howard Giles developed a color theory also based in some mysterious way on Dynamic Symmetry, and Hokie, still cherishing that hope, joined his class.

Interlude

Early in the summer of
1925, my parents gave me a delayed graduation
present, a trip abroad with four girls. Our chaperon
was a robust, sharp-witted woman in her sixties
who had recently retired from teaching English at a
private school. The Bartons said I would adore
Paris but loathe London. Our chaperon, whose
tastes were different, thought it might well be
otherwise but didn't insist.

England came first on our tour, and I made my
first outdoor sketch in Worcester Gardens at Oxford. It was a botanically accurate account of an
ivy-covered wall and a profusion of flowers in the
order of their appearance—delphiniums to the
rear, pink phlox in the center, and orange and
yellow marigolds in the front. When I showed the
sketch to Barton on my return, he shuddered and
said I had committed every sin known to the
amateur watercolorist. My sketches of people were
more successful. Emulating Hokie, I bought a
small, hard-covered notebook that would fit in my
purse and made pencil notes of flower sellers,
London bobbies, children, and taxi drivers. In the
evenings, while resting from sightseeing, I redrew
the sketches in a Whatman watercolor sketchbook
and colored them. And by the end of the tour, I

had added similar pages on Amsterdam and The Hague, Volendam, Brussels and Bruges, and, of course, Paris.

Despite the Bartons' prediction, I loved London, especially the theatre. The five of us went to Hammersmith to see *The Beggar's Opera*, which had been running for years, and *Iris* by Sir Arthur Wing Pinero, which starred Gladys Cooper, a typically English beauty. *The Man with a Load of Mischief*, by Ashley Dukes, was an attractive comedy set in the Regency period, and I enjoyed Fay Compton, whose profile was like a Greek coin, and Leon Quartermaine, who had such beautiful hollow cheeks.

We visited a shop that sold Indian and Persian miniatures, and I bought two Mughal miniatures, both portraits of ladies. The better of the two showed the central figure wearing a diaphanous green bodice and a rose-colored skirt dotted with gold; her feet were painted with henna. To her left stood a pair of trees shaped like elongated artichokes and painted a dark bronzy green just barely brushed with gold, the exact color of the squircle fence. The miniature was to influence my later caricatures, in which I flattened the perspective.

Paris retained some of the glamour fired by my earlier memories of the window full of golden shoes and the Cinderella-like coaches at Versailles. The faces that appeared in my sketchbook were finely drawn and agitated, the women carefully made up. I had mixed reactions to the Louvre because there was too much to digest. The Venus de Milo was impressive, but I envisioned too many plaster casts in her wake to fully enjoy the original. Only the Winged Victory, poised at the top of a flight of stairs against a burnt-orange background, lived up to my expectations. Like most tourists, I found the Mona Lisa to be smaller than I expected, but I thought she might be a good face to caricature.

More and more, I realized my ignorance of painting. Portraits by Van Dyck in English country houses had reactivated my sense of history. But quite suddenly my taste regressed and I was enveloped in a passion for the Pre-Raphaelites. I don't remember seeing any van Goghs, but Madame Ginoux's influence came back to haunt me when I visited the antique shop on the boulevard Raspail where Carlotta Barton had bought her Provençal petticoat. Just as Carlotta had reported, they had some bright yellow ones, and the quilted cotton was patterned all over with tiny flowers that echoed the colors of van Gogh's portrait. I like to think that Madame G. herself had such a petticoat, and I bought two for what would someday be made into bedspreads and valances for my yellow room.

I came back to New York, to the bosom of my family and to my aging canary, and found that the Bartons had moved again, this time to a studio apartment at the Hotel des Artistes at 1 West Sixty-seventh Street. I had brought them some gifts, a calf-bound volume of Restoration plays I had found in an old bookshop in Torquay and a woodcut by a Dutch artist. "I wanted to get you a Masereel," I said, "but I couldn't find any but reproductions."

"You have some new things," I uttered at the sight of two masks—one painted in yellow clay with three gashes on each cheek and in the middle of the forehead, and a carved headdress that looked like a bishop's miter; the other, a black wooden face. Ralph said the big one was from Dahomey, from West Africa, one of the few places where masks are painted; and the smaller, a Congolese fetish. "We got them from the Algerian consul last time we were in Paris." And there were some new pictures on the wall, original caricatures by Miguel Covarrubias from his recently published book, *The Prince of Wales and Other Famous Americans*. One was of Charlie Chaplin, and the other, which appeared in black and white in the book, was a brilliantly colored version of Barton with flaming orange hair and a flamboyant suit, quite

Aline Fruhauf

Ralph Barton (undated).

57

Making Faces different from the artist's customary subdued elegance. Barton, however, liked his new image.

Between magazine assignments, Barton managed to work on several books, including *But They Marry Brunettes,* Anita Loo's sequel to *Gentlemen Prefer Blondes,* and his most ambitious work to date, a two-volume edition of Balzac's *Droll Stories,* which would be completed three years hence.

Mourners' Bench

Paula Trueman, a member of the permanent company of the Neighborhood Playhouse, was a vivid and charming little person, a fine dancer and a talented actress, whose pixie face was remarkably suited to my type of expression. During a rehearsal of *A Burmese Pwe*, I made some sketches of her, then borrowed a photograph of her wearing a Burmese headdress and took it home to combine headgear and face in a pen-and-ink caricature. I brought the drawing to the business office to show to Miss Arthur, who, in turn, showed it to Thornton Delehanty, a sandy-haired young man who was the new press agent. Delehanty took it down to the *New York World*, and the drama critic, Alexander Woollcott, said he would use it on the theatre page the following Sunday.

That Sunday in March of 1926 was a day of glory. I was a little delirious with joy, my mother and grandmother were jubilant, and my father was very proud. I called Barton, who congratulated me and said that I should get a scrapbook and recommended Styles and Cash as a reliable firm from which to buy it. The next time I saw Hokie, I showed it to her; she thought it looked very professional.

Making Faces

PART OF "THE BURMESE PWE"

Paula Truemaan, One of the Neighborhood Playhouse Troupe Which Presented a New Triple Bill Last Week

ALINE FRUHAUF.

Paula Trueman in the *New York World*, 1926.

The die was cast, and at the playhouse my dive into the *World* changed my image from amateur propmaker to newspaper artist. I was encouraged to make more drawings and to come to as many rehearsals as I liked. I never lacked sitters.

I did a little research and found that press agents of Broadway shows arranged for qualified artists to sketch actors backstage at rehearsals and at out-of-town tryouts. They paid the artists $12.50 a column for drawings that appeared in approved newspapers. Miss Arthur, dear soul, had paid my amateur standing a final tribute. Her check was $10, short of the prevailing rate.

The logical place for me to start peddling my work was the *New York World*. Tuesday afternoons at the old building on Park Row would find an assortment of artists waiting for Woollcott in the dingy waiting room outside his office. They sat on or stood around an ugly yellow-oak settle called the Mourners' Bench.

On my first visit, Irving Hoffman sauntered in. He was the youngest of the mourners, then about seventeen, a tall, black-haired youth with a triangular face and huge goggles. He was good-humored and full of stories, and his rapidly executed caricatures were sharp and incisive. Many theatre people commissioned them for their personal Christmas cards. Irving knew everyone and everything that was going on in the world of the theatre and the movies. If Shubert Alley ever needed a mayor, he would have qualified. He kept abreast of show business by subscribing to the *Zolotow*, a newsletter edited by Sam Zolotow of the *New York Times*, which listed all current and incoming plays, together with their respective producers and press agents. And he was Walter Winchell's "leg man": for years he gathered items of gossip for the well-known columnist, spending most of his time at Sardi's restaurant, Lindy's, or other haunts of show folk and the press.

Irving was usually accompanied by Alex Gard, a sardonic Russian, a little over five feet tall, dressed in a long, belted camel coat and a snap-brim fedora of the same color. Alex was a prolific on-the-spot caricaturist, and in exchange for meals, his framed works were beginning to cover the walls at Sardi's. And there were many others who made the rounds to sell their work.

Malcolm Eaton, a rotund, affable man, specialized in caricaturing movie people. His drawings had great style and humor, and his woodcut of two monkeys, a snake, and lioness, which was featured in a jungle picture, led to his syndicated comic strip featuring animals. Abe Birnbaum, whose story headings and magazine covers with a painterly quality enlivened the *New Yorker*, had a richness and sparkle that bore no hint of the commercial. Al Hirschfield, "The Beard," was more often seen at the *Times* or *Tribune* than at the *World* with his portfolio, heavy with full-page spreads. They were, and still are, action-packed, well-designed, and excellent caricatures, lovingly executed in an expert pen line. William Auerbach-Levy, a great favorite of Woollcott's, who gave him special assignments, was a little round-faced man, an excellent draughtsman, whose caricatures were close to portraits. He taught at the National Academy of Design and was also a well-known painter and etcher. Alfred Frueh, whom S.J. Kaufman called the dean of American caricaturists, was a tall, rangy man with a pleasant grin and a sandy forelock that gave him a deceptively hayseed look. He was probably the most brilliant draughtsman of them all. When I met him at a party, he confessed to being fonder of growing trees on his country place upstate than of "making funny pictures." We joked about the slight similarity of our names, which had a tendency to confuse people. I once had a lecture canceled when it was found out that I was not the Frueh whose work appeared in the New York dailies and the *New Yorker*.

Sometime before 1931, when the *World* merged with the *Telegram*, a very pretty blonde from Chicago, Irma Selz, joined us at the Mourners'

Bench. Her caricatures were lively and well designed. They always hit their mark. She was also a proficient watercolorist, a sculptor, and a writer and illustrator of children's books. We took long walks together on Riverside Drive when we thought our drawings were getting stale, and we attended exhibitions, preferring the artists who concentrated on the human face. Giacometti was one artist we were particularly drawn to.

My first Tuesday at the Mourners' Bench was my introduction to Alexander Woollcott, the drama critic, who was also the "Town Crier" in a weekly radio broadcast devoted to the literary scene and the model for *The Man Who Came to Dinner*, a play by George S. Kaufman and Moss Hart. A little after two o'clock, a short, fat man in a wide-brimmed hat and a cape swung into the waiting room. He had a milk-white face and very blue eyes, magnified to almost double their size by thick horn-rimmed glasses. His owlish look was intensified by a sharp little beak of a nose, which overhung a neatly trimmed chestnut moustache.

"Who's first," he called out. I moved forward, and he motioned me over to an ancient and scarred oak table. I spread out my wares. Looking them over with a detached look, not unmixed with derision, his only comment was "Who's next."

After that meeting, I did a caricature of Woollcott. Barton thought it was "marvelous" and suggested that I "drop it off at his apartment, he lives in this building." Then, noting my hesitation, he added, "I'm sure he'd love to have it."

I wasn't quite so sure, but when I got in the elevator I asked the operator to let me off at Mr. Woollcott's floor. In response to my ring, a butler in a white coat came to the door. "Come in, come in," he said, obviously taking me for a guest, "let me have your coat." I heard many voices and the clinking of glass and ice; there was a party going on. They were all there; they must be, I thought, the Algonquin crowd, that special elite of critics, writers, humorists, and illustrators — among

Aline Fruhauf

Alexander Woollcott in 1934.

them, Dorothy Parker, Neysa McMein, Alice Duer Miller, Robert Benchley, and Deems Taylor —that made up the luncheon group that met at a special Round Table set up for them by Frank Case, the hotel's manager. The names were as familiar to me as the days of the week. It would be fun to join them. But, no, shyness overtook me, and with a whispered "This is for Mr. Woollcott," I pressed the drawing into the butler's hand and fled.

When I went down to the *World* the following Tuesday, the climate for showing pictures was no more propitious than it had been the week before. After Woollcott had dispensed with my portfolio in the usual way, I said, all winsomeness and girlish enthusiasm, "Mr. Woollcott, I was the one who left

63

that caricature of you at your house last week." He looked at me coldly. "I threw it," he said, "out the window."

A few years later, however, in 1931, he sat to me backstage when he was appearing in S.N. Behrman's *Brief Moment*.

"Where do we go from here?" I asked Irving Hoffman, who was among the mourners that morning. "To the *Post*," he said, "75 West Street, John Anderson." Anderson, who was a tall, lanky, and courteous man, had an easy, affable way with artists. If he suspected that his desk was a catchall for hordes of Woollcott's rejects, he never mentioned it. He took my drawing of an unknown actor, Mitchell Padraic Marcus, who played a leading role in the Lenox Hill Players' semiamateur production of *The Cenci*, and soon I had another clipping to keep Paula Trueman company in my brand-new scrapbook.

In 1927, the *Morning Telegraph*, which some unkind souls called "a ten-cent paper for ten-cent readers," featured news of horse racing but gave second place to show business. Its editorial offices were housed in a rattletrap of a building at Fiftieth Street and Eighth Avenue, and at the time of my first visit the city fathers were blasting through solid rock building the Eighth Avenue subway. As I went up the broad, rickety, wooden stairs with my portfolio under my arm, I felt the building tremble with each detonation and wondered if the next boom might be the last. Like the Neighborhood Playhouse, the "Telly" had its own unique bouquet, not as attractive but just as unforgettable, a combination of printers' ink, acetic acid, and bad drains.

At his desk in his shirtsleeves, oblivious to noise and odors and pecking away at his typewriter in the approved two-finger fashion of the newspaperman, was the tall, bald, Texas-born Burton Davis, the drama editor. A cigarette was stuck inside his lower lip. I introduced myself and said that Irving Hoffman had sent me and that I had some caricatures. I watched him, fascinated; the cigarette stayed stuck even while he was talking.

"I can use this," he said, taking the caricature of Albert Carroll and Betty Linley as they appeared in a revival of *The Little Clay Cart*, "and I can use some individual heads for one-column cuts." I said I would bring some in, and after studying the *Zolotow* I had borrowed from Irving, I made my rounds of the various press departments, collected photographs, and got permission from the press agents to sketch actual performances at rehearsals and sometimes sketch backstage. If there were tickets available I was given a pair, and I took my mother to many matinees.

I took the drawings that were turned down by the New York dailies across the river, by subway, to the *Brooklyn Daily Eagle*. Across the street from the *Eagle* was the absolute last gasp for unpublished work, the *Brooklyn Standard Union*. For some reason, its tiny office had an indefinable air of unreality. Yet it must have existed, I told myself, because my scrapbook contained examples of my work it published. Its spectral editor looked like a boy making believe he was an old man by dipping his face in a flour barrel, and to add to the illusion he wore steel-rimmed spectacles far down on the bridge of his nose. The city editor was a lady, obviously not as young as she was painted, with flaming hair worn Gibson-girl fashion and a frilly white blouse of the same period. She sang out for the copy boy in a vibrating coloratura soprano, the type of voice I always associate with the operettas of Victor Herbert. One day, loaded with *Eagle* rejects, I made my way across the street, went up in the elevator, and found that the *Brooklyn Standard Union* had disappeared without leaving a trace. When I made inquiries about its whereabouts, no one knew what I was talking about.

On my way home one afternoon after peddling my work, I stopped at the Hotel des Artistes and found Barton at home. He seemed upset but asked me in. "She's gone," he said, and it sounded final.

Aline Fruhauf

Albert Carroll and Betty Linley in the *Morning Telegraph*, 1926.

I watched him dumbly, my world crumbling. Then he said something about New York State divorce laws and Carlotta having just cause for filing suit.

"Why don't you go to see her?" he said at last. "I know she would like to see you; she's very fond of you, you know."

At the time, it didn't occur to me that he might be using me as a messenger. "Are you sure she's in now," I asked doubtfully. He was sure. He had just talked with her and she was in her room. I went across town to her hotel, and Carlotta, in obvious distress, received me. As always, she was astonishingly beautiful. Her hair was now long, but again, as at our first meeting, she was a startling study in black and white. Her dark hair swept almost to the waist of a flowing Japanese kimono, which was all black except for a single white dot in the middle of the back, and her face, devoid of makeup, was paper white. Frustration and deep disappointment were mixed as she told me that the marriage was finished for her. There was apparently nothing I could say or do. For the second time that afternoon, I stood by in helpless inanition.

"I just hope to God he's happy!" she said, pacing the floor and weeping.

I called Barton when I got home to tell him that I had seen Carlotta and how badly I felt about the whole thing. He asked me not to be upset and to stop by when I was in the neighborhood, that he had something for me. It was a print of his *Map of Paris*, which I framed in park-bench green.

A deeply unhappy man, Barton never got over his break with Carlotta. During the summer, I saw him in Paris, and this time he was definite about wanting me to be his messenger. "When you are back in New York," he said, "call her at Elisabeth Marbury's and ask her if she'll take me back." I did call her but to no avail. I never saw or heard from her again. Three years later, she married playwright Eugene O'Neill.

That was the summer, 1926, I went abroad with

my maternal grandmother, Anna Frank, and her
youngest sister, my favorite aunt, Lena Goodman.
They had invited me to spend part of the time
traveling with them, then to go back to Paris to
spend a whole month at a pension, chaperoned by
the tour guide's wife. Barton was in Paris, and his
fifteen-year-old daughter, Natalie, was visiting
him. "She wants to become a nun," he said. "I'd
like her to see something of Paris first."

As soon as I was settled in the pension, I called
on the Bartons, *père et fille*. Natalie was a very
charming but serious girl, with dark blonde hair,
blue eyes, her father's uneven teeth, and a fair,
dimpled face. She did, as Carlotta had said, look
very much like a Greuze.

The apartment, a sublet from the writer Louis
Bromfield, who had sublet it from someone else,
was filled with Empire furniture and lamps made
of fat glass jugs filled with colored water and
topped with shades of pleated book linen, a current
vogue. Besides producing masses of work, Barton
was living the life of a well-to-do Parisian. He
shunned the Left Bank cafés, frequented by expa-
triate Americans, and went only to the best restaurants. His clothes, too, were of the best—shoes by
Hellstern, haberdashery by Charvet—and in lieu
of a scarf pin, a scarab seal ring encircled his cravat.

One weekend, when Barton was off to Dieppe,
he gave Natalie and me the use of his chauffered
limousine and told us to have fun, to do some
sightseeing, and he gave Natalie the money to take
me to dinner. "I assume you'll want a fish dinner"
(it was Friday), "so why don't you go to Prunier's."
We visited the Musée Carnavalet and the Musée
Cluny and ended up in the place Saint-Sulpice,
where Natalie bought rosaries for the nuns back
home. Prunier's was wonderful; I had fish with a
sauce verte.

As soon as the divorce became final, Barton was
married again, this time to Germaine Tailleferre,
the only female member of the group of composers
known as The Six, of which Auric, Durey,

Honegger, Milhaud, and Poulenc were the other members. I met her in New York; she was a very quiet, very pretty natural blonde.

When the illustrations for Balzac's *Droll Stories* were finally finished and privately published by Liveright in a special edition, I wrote to Barton to tell him that I liked the books and to ask him if there was any truth to the rumor that he and Madame were expecting an heir.

"There isn't any baby," he replied, "and Nat has become a nun! She is now Sister Marie-Madeleine." The illustrations in *Droll Stories*, he said, "were about as bad as they could be as reproductions. . . . I feel a little guilty, just the same, that the engraver didn't have his name with mine on the title page as he did almost as much work on the drawings as I did."

I had enclosed a sketch of Maurice Ravel in my letter and was delighted with Barton's acknowledgment of it:

> L[uc]-A[lbert] Moreau, the very excellent painter, told me he had seen a fine caricature of Ravel in a musical paper in America by a young girl. I got your letter the next day and, by putting two and two together, decided he could have meant no other caricature but yours. This is a Grade A compliment and should make you feel very stuck up. The caricature of Ravel in your letter is indeed first class.

The caricature was published in *Musical Courier*, January 19, 1928, so Barton's letter, not dated, must have been written shortly thereafter. Later that year, during the summer, when I was in Paris again, I called on him and saw the house on the rue Nicolo that he and Germaine had bought. It was a smart-looking, modern town house with a dining room that opened on a garden. The top of the dining table was a long rectangle of black glass with an indirect lighting fixture in the center. Twelve little fruitwood chairs embroidered in bright petit point stood around the table.

"They're the signs of the zodiac," Barton said. "I made the designs, Germaine did the needlework."

A flight of stairs, carpeted in Higgins-ink green, led up to the bedrooms. Germaine's was all white except for one note of subdued color, her portrait in red conté crayon by Alexandre Iacovleff. Ralph's room was all black "because I like to sleep in the daytime. How do you like the house?"

"Beautiful," I said, "looks like *House and Garden*."

"Oh, they've been here."

I stood in the foyer, taking a last look at the Higgins-ink green carpet; then I spied a black and crystal star-shaped lantern hanging from the ceiling.

"Black Starr and Frost," I quipped.

"Oh, Aline!" he said, made a face, and countered with "Reed and Barton." We had a good laugh and said good-bye.

Back in New York, I resumed my art studies and continued to free lance for the newspapers. Ralph's marriage to Germaine also ended in divorce. He had dedicated his last book to her, *God's Country*, a brilliant satire on American history. Although the book had value, I didn't like it, and in a fit of candor, I told him so in a note. He replied from "Bastide du Bois Sacré," La Seyne sur-Mer, Varennes:

> *I have, alas, sold my house, but I am building another one, whose name is inscribed above. Just now I call it the sacré bois, but it will soon be finished and I will like it again. . . . Didn't you like my book? I am cast down and wretched. Do read it again.*

The house was built and sold, and Ralph came back to New York, taking a penthouse apartment. I met him by chance on Fifty-ninth Street, when he called to me by name. I hardly knew him. He looked much older and somehow extinguished. He asked me if I had a beau, and when I answered, "Yes, a very serious young man," he countered, "Well, you are a very serious young girl," and he let it go at that. His apartment was nearby, and as I

Aline Fruhauf

Maurice Ravel in the *Musical Courier*, 1928.

was always interested in his various dwellings, I asked to see it. It was disappointing. I remember only a number of chairs made of chromium tubing and upholstered in a plastic material that was neither park-bench nor Higgins-ink, but a dull lustreless shade of green somewhere in between. I never saw him again. On May 21, 1931, he typed a letter headed "Obit" and shot himself through the head.

"My remorse is bitter," he wrote, "over my failure to appreciate my beautiful lost angel, Carlotta, the only woman I ever loved and whom I respect and admire above all the rest of the human race."

The Seat of All Learning

Hokie was also in Paris during the summer of 1926. She stayed at a little hotel on the Left Bank and occasionally went to a sketch class at the Académie Julian. I, too, wanted to study, but the one artist I wanted to work with, André Lhote, was out of the country, so, instead, I went sketching with Hokie. We sat on the banks of the Seine and did watercolors of the trees and the fishermen, and I made a back view of Hokie in her brown jacket and skirt. As a drawing, it showed more evidence of our mutual exposure to Dynamic Symmetry than any of Hokie's. Although she set down her formidable-looking network of filaments, her finished studies were full of vitality and of movement.

We walked together along the rue du Bac and the rue des Saints-Pères, looking longingly in the windows of the antique shops at the tiny boxes of Battersea enamel that were, we decided, too expensive. For consolation, before I left Paris, I bought a little Meissen box painted with moss roses. I also acquired a lithograph by Marie Laurencin of some young ladies in pink and yellow, and, at the Algerian consulate, I was lucky enough to find a Congolese fetish, very inexpensive and very much like the one Barton had.

When we didn't go sketching, we went to the

71

Louvre, where I kept returning to the Mona Lisa, who looked as if she had been washed in a pale green syrup. I bought a postcard reproduction of her, and back in my room at the pension, I made a linear breakdown of the face on a leaf of my Whatman sketchbook. For the nose, I drew a vertical line and ended it with a symbol for the slightly overhanging tip. For the almost imperceptible brows above her long, ovoid, horizontal eyes with some puffiness under the lower lids, I made slightly upcurving horizontal lines parallel to the eyes and added pupils, flat, dark, and noncommittal. The famous smile became a horizontal line curving upwards ever so subtly at the corners. I drew in the neck, shoulders, arms, and hands, and with the simplest possible linear rendering indicated the pleated material over the bosom and, as in the original, just the barest suggestion of cleavage. Then, I reduced the landscape to the lowest terms and strengthened all the lines with diluted brown ink, Gunther Wagner's "Pelikan."

The work was going to be a labor of love, I could see that, so I decided to take my time over it. The leisurely pace, as it turned out, became a necessity, with one interruption after another. First, I caught a cold, then sprained my ankle, and a virulent attack of food poisoning followed (Prunier's *poisson* with *sauce verte*?). For a week I lived on yogurt and tea. Between bouts, I applied thin washes of color to my painting and blessed the British Isles for having produced Whatman paper and the best watercolors in the world, Winsor and Newton.

My Mona Lisa was almost finished. The doctor came by and said I could supplement the yogurt and tea with, perhaps, a little broth and some *pain grillé*, and Mona Lisa, too, was ready for some extra nourishment, a glaze that would simulate the patina of centuries. I tried a solution of glue and water, but it needed something stronger. I went to the paint store on the corner, bought a small bottle of shellac, and managed to make it back to the pension without falling down. I could hardly wait

The Fruhauf Mona Lisa, ca.
1925.

to apply the final touch, but all was not yet over. The finish was about to turn into a double shellacking. I discovered that the shellac of the French, like their champagne, is bubbly and requires a practiced hand, which, it was soon obvious, I didn't have. I pulled out the cork and a jet of fiery liquid spurted into my eyes. The spirit of Leonardo, I began to think, was tormenting me.

Somehow I made it to the elevator, an art nouveau cage, which for once descended without interruption, and I headed for the pharmacist, also conveniently located next to the paint store. I explained my predicament to the ministering angel in a white coat, who quickly applied a rosy, healing liquid. I found it hard to believe that anything so soothing to the eyes could be powerful enough to dissolve shellac.

In the fall, back in New York, I exhibited the caricature at the annual exhibition of the Society of Independent Artists at the old Waldorf Astoria Hotel. It amused so many of my friends that I used it as a Christmas card. I had a halftone engraving made and had well over two hundred cards printed in brown ink on beige stock. I colored every one of the prints by hand without accident, but when it came time to simulate the glazed patina, I took care to use a varnish that came in a screw-top can.

Since I still had an absorbing interest in masks and puppets, the built-up faces that are caricatures in three dimensions, I planned to look up Marie Vassilieff, who had made the portrait heads of the Bartons. She was a sculptor who had also been an actress, composer, librettist, puppeteer, poet, painter, and producer of mystical marionette plays. The portrait-dolls—made of cloth, stuffed with sawdust, and handsomely lacquered—were her invention. She lived on the rue Froidevaux, opposite the Montparnasse cemetery. I knew I would never forget the name of that street; I had only to think of the French word for calf's liver and add the *r*. I called her on the telephone, and she asked me to come over.

Mme. Vassilieff, a tiny woman with close-cropped gray hair, the face of a Russian peasant, and a deep bass voice, lived and worked in a studio full of her brilliant creations and reeking of lacquer fumes. She agreed to do a portrait head of me and got to work sketching me from all angles. It was pleasant being the subject for a change, and I basked in a glow of narcissism. I looked at the paintings on the wall, colorful murals, stylized, hard-edged, and heavily varnished, like Russian toys. There was also a charming portrait of her little son, Pierrot, who was away at school, and a doll-sized sewing machine on a table. The dolls, her versions of Parisian notables, were lounging around on two couches. They had extraordinary presence. She told me who they were: Count Boni de Castellane, Colette, Matisse, Picasso, and the couturier Paul Poiret. She had given Poiret a face the color of a steel-blue bottle fly and decorated his chin with whiskers of henna-colored yarn. Apart from the cluster of celebrities was a brooding little character, a young man, perfectly proportioned; she hadn't exaggerated any part of him. His neatly fashioned face and hands were of pale brown suede, and the hair, plastered down to the delicate skull, was soft black kidskin. She had dressed him in a beautiful hand-tailored suit of pure white wool.

"Who is that?" I asked, and Madame mumbled something about a young Pole she knew. I wondered if he was or had been a *chéri* of Madame's, but I didn't ask. Although I might have—all the time I was posing, she asked me the most intimate questions about my personal life.

When my sawdust portrait was finished, I went to the studio to claim it. I was glorious in gold lacquer, my hair was black raffia, and I had lustrous glass eyes, straight from a taxidermist's supply store. My eyebrows were black kid, and I had long, luxuriant eyelashes made of strips of monkey fur. My Rossetti neck was a long cylinder that made my head look poised, as someone had described it, like a crystal ball on a needle. It was a mask, a puppet head, a caricature, and to me a highly flattering portrait, all in one. It became the first item in my narcissus corner.

I thought a page of Madame's portrait-dolls might be an interesting item for *Vanity Fair*. She sent me some photographs and some biographical information, and the story and pictures appeared in the January 1930 issue of *Vanity Fair*.

Shortly after my return from Paris, I had tea with my old friend and teacher Belle Boas, who never seemed to age. Time had only mellowed and enriched her beautifully boned face. I brought along my Paris sketches and the caricature of the Mona Lisa.

"Well, what are you going to do next?" she asked over cups of tea and delicious little cakes she had baked, mounds of meringue that were kept from being too sweet by small bits of crystallized ginger.

"I need more drawing," I replied. "I think I should go to the League. Can you suggest anyone for me to study with?"

"Boardman Robinson," she suggested. "He's a fine draughtsman, has done some caricatures, also political cartoons for the *World*. He'll understand you perfectly."

At supper that evening, I discussed the matter with my parents. My father was dubious but resigned, even though he still associated art as a way of life with that old painter he knew in Cincinnati and hoped that I might carry on the family tradition in the clothing business, perhaps as a designer of women's wear. Mother thought the League was a good idea, especially because Miss Boas had recommended it.

The next day, at Parsons, I proposed my next step in art education to Miss Fuller and Mrs. Barnes.

"You're going to be a painter?" Miss Fuller asked.

I told her I didn't know, perhaps later, but that

right now I wanted to improve my drawing and try to be as good a caricaturist as I knew how.

Mrs. Barnes shook her head, "That's all you'll ever do, just one caricature after another."

"But look at Peggy Bacon!" Miss Fuller exclaimed. "She studied here with us, with Mr. Baker, and she does excellent work besides carica-tures—illustrations, etchings, wonderful draw-ings."

I said good-bye to the ladies, who looked at me fondly, wished me luck, and asked me to keep in touch. They were smiling when I left, and the sunlight glinted on their chokers of crystal balls.

Fifty-seventh Street was *grande luxe* in those days. The shop windows were showcases for the best in industrial design, fashion, and the fine arts: Isotta Fraschini's highly styled motorcar; Bendel's, Tappe's, and Stein and Blaine's dressmaking salons; Orrefors's tempting displays of Swedish glass; and, close to Fifth Avenue and east of it, the art galleries displaying paintings framed in gold like large, brilliant jewels. And west of Sixth Avenue was the seat of all learning, the Art Students League of New York.

After I signed up, paid my fee, and bought a newsprint pad at the supply store, I mounted the stairs of the old building with a portentous feeling. On the way up, on the walls, I noticed some of the works by artists who taught or had taught there, a still life of a plate of fish by William Merritt Chase, charcoal nudes by Kimon Nicolaides, and some drawings by the famous anatomist George Bridgman. The smell of turpentine that pervaded the building was intoxicating. Through half-open doors I saw students in bright smocks working behind forests of easels. Robinson's class was on the top floor.

I entered and found a high stool in the back. The model had just taken her pose. She was a large woman with a classic symmetrical face. Her blonde hair was brushed up and pinned in a topknot.

Occasional obscenities slid from the corner of her mouth, which the class politely pretended not to hear.

I adjusted my pad and penciled in a Root 5 construction, the standard Dynamic Symmetry formula for the standing figure. And, knowing from long experience that there were only six directions into which the human figure could fall, I put them all in as guidelines, as I had done for years. I could see it wasn't going to be easy, the model was all melting curves; there wasn't a straight line in her body.

Robinson came in, a great, jolly, bearded man in a rough tweed suit. He made a beeline to me and my pad. "What's this: the Brooklyn Bridge?"

"It's Dynamic Symmetry," I said in a small voice.

He laughed, he roared, and everybody looked around. "Nonsense," he said. "Learn to draw, you don't need a crutch."

Robinson went to the head of the class and began drawing the figure on the stand on a large sheet of paper tacked to the wall. He had a scratching technique, full of vitality, not unlike Forain's. Then, on another sheet, he illustrated the technique of contour drawing by outlining the entire figure without once glancing at the paper.

"Get the gesture, get the form, relate, relate," he said, and made another sketch, putting in the darks in the forms with more brier-patch scratchings. It was a powerful drawing.

I enjoyed the class and, like all of Robinson's students, I took on his manner of drawing. He was sympathetic to my caricatures, and when I took him some of my published work, he criticized it as if it were classroom material. I asked him what he thought of Max Beerbohm's caricatures, and his reply was laconic: "As drawings, bags of wind. Purely literary. He depends on his captions."

I pondered the comment and, although I could see his point, wasn't sure that I agreed entirely. I considered Max's caricatures to be in the great tradition with a distinct aesthetic quality. And, after all, isn't caricature in itself a literary art?   *Aline Fruhauf*

It is difficult to say what an art student gets from a teacher. Sometimes the results are not immediate but cumulative over the years. Belle Boas, who was my mentor and friend long after she had ceased being my teacher, continued to influence me and my work, prompting a never-ending quest for quality; an appreciation of the work of art, whether it was a painting, a piece of pottery, or a length of fabric; and the knowledge that one's personal pursuit of art, coupled with the constant viewing of the work of others, new or old, was in itself an enrichment of life.

As to acquiring technique, however, a student can absorb just so much of what a teacher has to offer and has to move on in his own direction. There are times when a little push is needed. Mine was on the way. It came when Robinson, peering at me from beneath his bushy brows, blurted out, "How long have you been in this class?"

"Two years," I said.

"That's long enough," he laughed. "Out! Out!"

I had been fired. The next step was painting in oil, that mysterious medium of masterpieces, of the Mona Lisa and of Madame Ginoux. I gravitated to Kenneth Hayes Miller, who led a kind of cult at the League. Many of his pupils, mostly women, adored him and stayed with him for years. I doubt that he ever told a student to leave for his own good.

The combined teachings of Robinson and Miller had produced some fine artists, among them Arnold and Lucile Blanch, Abe Birnbaum, Peggy Bacon, Yasuo Kuniyoshi, and Reginald Marsh. At the time I came into his class, Miller was under the influence of Giorgione and counseled his class to underpaint all their pictures with raw umber and white. The two colors, mixed, produced a putty color in various values, depending on how much white was used, and when it dried, it permeated the colors that were glazed over it. The result was deadly, and it was not difficult to spot the work of

Georgia O'Keeffe, unpublished drawing, 1960.

Miller's students. I knew one talented girl who found that raw umber had so infiltrated her color sense, even long after she had left Miller's class, that she quit painting altogether and became a sculptor.

I had a new box of oils and a piece of canvas board on my easel, and I was ready to work. Miller hadn't yet come in, and I was curious to know what he was like.

"Tell me about him," I whispered to the monitor.

"If he likes what you're doing," she replied, "he'll give you a criticism. If he doesn't, he'll walk off without saying anything at all."

My drawing had been stimulated and strengthened by working under Robinson, and I was ready to apply an equally vigorous approach to painting. The model on the stand was a young coffee-and-cream-colored girl. She was standing in front of a green burlap screen overhung with a triangle of scarlet cloth. "Ah, Gauguin," I thought, and set to work brushing in gold ochre, viridian green, cobalt blue, and rose madder. I had the whole canvas covered with paint straight out of the tube by the time Miller came in and got to me. He looked at the canvas in silence, smiled his famous smile—half fiend's, half archangel's—and walked on.

Some time later, I did a caricature of Miller. When I offered it to him, there was silence again, but he pocketed the drawing and then said, "Very amusing," before he moved on to the next student.

Hokie and I covered the art galleries regularly. She called me to tell me there were some new paintings by an artist named Georgia O'Keeffe at a gallery called An American Place. It was there I encountered another kind of silence. Miss O'Keeffe was a painter of unusual and vibrant talent. She was also the wife of Alfred Stieglitz, one of the foremost photographers of his time, who became the director of the gallery in which he became a passionate crusader for the new in American art. His reputation for buttonholing visitors and engag-

ing them in challenging argument was well known, and innocent art lovers complained that the noisy old man talked so much they couldn't see the pictures. But not so that day.

Alfred Stieglitz, unpublished wash drawing, 1960.

As we walked into the gallery we saw him, an intense, sharp-eyed man with unkempt gray hair, some of it issuing from his nose and ears. He wore a battered black hat and a black cape. He watched us and so did the dark handsome woman sitting next to him, hunched on a high stool. She looked glum. She, too, wore a cape, and her black felt hat was pulled up into a peak. I recognized O'Keeffe from having seen Stieglitz's photographs of her. The silence could almost be felt, and the gallery was so small it was almost impossible to walk around without bumping into the two black-robed figures who surveyed us like predatory birds. On

81

the walls were the paintings—enormous, glowing studies of flowers, giant purple clematis and other blooms with every detail of their organs, not only faithfully represented but magnified many times. They were framed in half-round moldings of silvered wood. The paint had been applied so smoothly there were no visible brushmarks, and the colors had an extraordinary freshness. I had never before seen pictures like these, yet I yielded to idiotic impulse, the giggling-in-church syndrome, and my inane whisper, "The frames are pretty," echoed from wall to wall.

The two pairs of dark electric eyes increased their voltage, and the quiet became a dead calm. Sensing thunder and lightning, Hokie grabbed me by the elbow and hustled me out of An American Place.

A few weeks later, I went back to the gallery. Fortunately, Stieglitz didn't remember me. There was a new show on the walls, watercolors, the rocky seascapes of the Maine coast by John Marin. Stieglitz stood by, ready for talk. I asked the price of the picture I was looking at.

"How much is it worth to you?" he rumbled.

I explained that I was spending my mornings at the Art Students League and at present was not buying, just looking.

"What do they teach you there?" he asked.

"We underpaint the composition first, like the Old Masters, Veronese, Giorgione. . . ."

Stieglitz said yes, he'd heard of them, "go on, go on."

"When the raw umber and white has dried we glaze on the colors, red, blue, yellow. . . ."

This time Stieglitz exploded, "Why-why-why-that's like kissing a beautiful woman through a veil."

His statement had a profound effect on me, and shortly after, I left the Miller class under my own steam.

Roses for Act I

A mutual friend suggested that I do a caricature of Remo Bufano, who was running a marionette and puppet theatre on Macdougal Street. I found him to be a small, compact man with a handsome projecting nose, curly light brown hair, a thin humorous mouth, and heavy lids that overhung half his eyes. He had the voice and temperament of an actor, and had he been a few inches taller he might have been a successful one. He managed, however, to combine his histrionic ability with expert craftsmanship. He was a diabolic mimic and a good sculptor, and the combination of these two qualities made him one of the outstanding puppeteers in the country.

I was a child when I saw one of his earliest performances. It was during the summer at a hotel in the Catskills. Remo and a companion, Philip Loeb, were touring the mountain resorts in an old Ford, giving performances of Alfred Kreymborg's *Lima Beans* and an unforgettable adaptation of the Italian classic *Orlando Furioso*, in which Orlando was the brave knight who rescued beautiful maidens in distress and drove the Saracens out of Sicily. I think he was Remo's favorite character.

Florence, Remo's wife, was doll-like and had the look of an Oriental although her maiden name was

Marionette Artist

Remo Bufano, as visioned by Aline Fruhauf, who is working with both actors and puppets in the Little Theatre enterprise which he is conducting at 28 MacDougal street, Manhattan.

Remo Bufano in the *Brooklyn Standard Union*, 1927.

Flynn. She was the business manager of the team. Sometimes she sewed on puppet paraphernalia, and she wore the black cotton smock and pants that are the uniform of the puppeteer. The Bufanos were accustomed to hear that they were charming little people who looked just like their marionettes and puppets.

Their studio apartment at 107 Waverly Place had two large rooms, a cooking area, a bath, and a large closetlike dressing room that was big enough to sleep in but was used as a storeroom. Two wooden cabinets were hung with marionettes of all sizes and descriptions.

The placed hummed with activity the day I came to sketch. In one corner, a seamstress stitched bright-colored little costumes at a whirring sewing machine, Florence divided her time between the telephone and the typewriter, and Remo carved small hands and feet out of soft wood. There were some ambitious examples of his sculpture placed around the working area: an enormous terra-cotta head of an old woman in a shawl, a portrait of his Sicilian mother; a smaller than life-size torso of Florence, looking like a little Buddha; and an unglazed clay version of Sparrow, the Bufano's cat. Other curious and lovely objects I noted were Japanese *No* masks hung on a door, a delicate pen-and-ink drawing of a child by Pamela Bianco, and a Modigliani-like portrait of Florence by Maurice Brevannes.

After I had made several sketches of Remo, he showed me the caricature Covarrubias had made of him as a marionette with a large head, small body, and strings attached to his hands, feet, and shoulders. It was a very good caricature and, incidentally, a hard act to follow.

On a worktable near the window were heaps of clay, sheets of paper, a bag of plaster of paris, and some empty cigar boxes. Remo said I could make a puppet head if I wanted to, so after I finished sketching, I dove into the clay and began to model a head the size of an orange. What emerged was a

84

composite portrait of Mr. Punch, Houdon's Voltaire, and a caricature of Remo.

"Cut it in half at the jaw line," Remo said, handing me a knife. After I sliced the head in two lengthwise, he told me to put each half in a cigar box; then he mixed some plaster and poured it over the clay halves. There was no time to wait for the plaster to harden and to go through the familiar routine of papier-mâché, but now I was fairly sure of at least part of Benda's secret of mask making. At home, I modeled a miniature Golden Beauty, headdress and all, cast it in plaster, and made a number of mashed-paper masks. I painted them with "Oenslager gold" and gave them as gifts to friends.

Burton Davis printed my first caricature of Remo in the *Telegraph* in March 1927, and another profile, facing in the opposite direction, appeared in the ghostly *Brooklyn Standard Union* before it folded its tents. In the latter, a slightly different treatment of the hair had appeared; I was learning to achieve halftone effects with closely juxtaposed pen lines, which I liked better than the use of benday screens with their evenly shaded areas of little dots.

The Bufanos and I became good friends. Over the years I worked with them when they were called upon to make masks and props of papier-mâché for various productions, one of which was *Golden Dawn*, an operetta with scenes laid in Africa. I continued to make drawings of Remo with his marionettes, and when they staged what was probably the most believable production of *A Midsummer Night's Dream*, I made a lithograph of it and gave them a print.

Every Christmas Eve, the Bufanos gave a big party in the studio. Remo loved folk singing and played the guitar and entertained the company with one Sicilian folk song after another. A frequent guest was Rufino Tamayo, a brilliant painter and a pure Zapotec Indian, who would pick up the nearest guitar, throw back his head, and rock the air with wild, ecstatic Mexican music, all glissan-

Aline Fruhauf

MARIONETTE PRODUCER

ALINE FRUHAUF

REMO BUFANO.
Who Creates Both the Body and the Characters of the Players in His Marionette Theatre on Macdougal Street.

Remo Bufano in the *Morning Telegraph*, 1927.

85

dos, quartertones, and shouts. His paintings at the time were primitive, and his palette was limited to a few earth colors. After Tamayo went to Paris, his paintings gained in brilliance. His palette became enriched with exotic blue-reds; his forms, more abstract and mysterious; and he experimented with textures. He turned up at a Bufano party on a visit to New York, and I didn't know him. He was smooth, polished, and urbane, and when someone asked him to play the guitar and sing, the performance was silky and bland.

I met Prentiss Taylor at the Bufanos. He was a gifted Washington artist; later, we became fellow students in the lithography class of Charles Locke at the Art Students League. Prentiss was cherubic, compact, and black-haired. He had a delightful sense of humor and a talent for friendship.

The Bufanos were involved in many interesting musical productions that required marionettes, including the League of Composers productions of Falla's *El Retablo de Maese Pedro* and Stravinsky's *Oedipus Rex*. The latter had giant marionettes twenty feet high. I made drawings of Remo with the marionettes for both productions. *El Retablo* appeared in *Musical America* March 17, 1928, and *Oedipus* in *Musical Digest*, April 1931.

The Bufanos signed up to do a few weeks of marionette and puppet shows at a new theatre on Cape Cod, the Cape Playhouse at Dennis, where Raymond Moore, a producer, was offering first-run plays with famous actors and actresses direct from Broadway and Hollywood. The theatre had once been an old church on the south side of Route 6 and was physically transported to its present site in 1926. I wanted to go with the Bufanos, but I first had to persuade them and then persuade my parents. While my parents found no fault with it, the Bufanos were not too sanguine about my proposal; during the previous summer, they had "looked after" a young friend of mine in Paris and definitely did not want to establish a pattern of chaperoning young females. I assured them that I

Marionette Rehearsal (*El Retablo de Maese Pedro*), 1930.

would be self-sufficient, and to prove my good will, I announced their connection with the Cape Playhouse by telling Burton Davis of the *Morning Telegraph* about it. It was a mild theatrical scoop for the *Telegraph*, and all the other papers copied it. The Bufanos finally gave in. I told Burton that I would mail him regular reports from the Cape, and he mentioned this in his column too. And that is how I became a volunteer press agent for a theatre I knew nothing about and whose manager had never heard of me.

Remo and Florence went to the Cape ahead of me and arranged for me to room at the home of a Dennis lady who took in boarders. Full of hope and the spirit of adventure, I packed my suitcase and the Fourth Dimension. After a night on the train, I took a bus to Dennis and walked to the white frame house where I expected to join my friends. A little, white-haired old lady met me at the door.

"I'm not expecting any more actors, that's for sure," was her greeting. "You can find your friends in the second house down the road."

She shut the door—rather more firmly than was necessary, I thought—and I trudged down the street weary and heavy-laden, but pleased that I had been mistaken for an actress.

Remo and Florence welcomed me gladly and introduced me to Mrs. Dixon, the landlady. She was a large, handsome woman with close-cropped, curly black hair and a penetrating church-choir contralto. Later Mrs. Dixon told me she didn't have much use for theatre people, either. They were, she was sure, in league with the devil, but all summer people were an odd lot and one couldn't be too choosy. She was fascinated by the caricatures and adored the Bufanos who, she rationalized, were not really actors. After a while, she became quite fond of me too, whatever I was, and used to wake me in the morning by singing, "Get up, small chee-ild!" in her powerful contralto.

The other guests she called The Boys. They were Wallace House and Peter Brocco, members of the puppet-theatre staff, and Paul Osborn, a former instructor of English at Ann Arbor, whose first play, *Side Show*, a satire on college life, was scheduled for production in the fall on Broadway.

When I asked Florence if she thought there was something I could do to help around the theatre, she introduced me to the tall, friendly looking director, Raymond Moore, who said he needed a head usher and put me to work that evening. Although my career was short-lived for want of a sense of direction, Ray Moore was very nice about it. "There must be something else you can do," he said kindly.

"How about working in the box office?" I queried. But the box office was already staffed with poets who wrote rhymed couplets for one another. Then I painted a vivid picture of myself as the backstage dynamo of the Neighborhood Playhouse, prop making, scene painting, et cetera, leaving out, of course, the part about letting the glue pot burn. I was put to work with the stage manager, Mogens Petri, and the technical director, Herbert Lutz, who worked at the Provincetown Playhouse in New York during the winter. I went to the hardware store to get a pair of overalls and was soon back painting flats.

The scenic designer, Mrs. Walter Knapp, an interior decorator from Great Neck, New York, was faced with a technical difficulty. A rose-covered trellis had to be ready for the stage by the next day, and the number of artificial flowers required more money than the budget would allow.

"I have an idea," I proposed. "Get me some pink crepe paper," and someone went to Hyannis for a couple of rolls.

It was as if I had never left kindergarten. I cut a circle of paper about two inches in diameter, folded it in half, then in quarters, pinched and twisted the base of the triangle, fluffed out the wide part with the palm of my hand, and displayed a rose. "Enough of these wired to the trellis ought to make a fine rose arbor," I said, and cut some more until I had enough for a bouquet. Mrs. Knapp got another pair of scissors, and soon we were sitting in the middle of the bare stage, snipping and folding as if our lives depended on it. Ray Moore, who hadn't been briefed on the happening, strolled by. "Paper dolls?" he ventured. Mrs. Knapp reached into the growing pile at our feet and pelted him with a handful of pink blooms.

"Roses for Act I," we told him. He thanked us

Aline Fruhauf

and said, "I don't suppose that in your adventure-some life in the theatre, Aline, you've ever been a property man?" And he explained that the property man took care of all movable objects in the production except furniture, and had to be familiar with the script. Then he underlined all references to said props, from umbrellas to cookies. Flushed with success as a rose maker, I agreed to take on the job.

The Cape Cod air stimulated my appetite to an alarming degree, and since Mrs. Dixon's New England cuisine leaned heavily to starch, I wavered between ravenous hunger and indigestion. Mrs. Dixon kept leftover squares of iced cake in a cupboard for The Boys to nosh on before bedtime. Nobody else was allowed to have any. One night, as I was watching The Boys having their bedtime snack, they thought I looked so mournfully under-nourished that they shared their bounty with me, and Mrs. Dixon caught us in the act.

"That cake's for The Boys," she sang out. I thought it better not to remind her that I was also a guest, American plan, but I finished the morsel of cake and waited it out until breakfast.

Opening night of the new comedy arrived. I tended to my props, one of which didn't appear until the last minute. It was a plate, always empty at rehearsals but now filled with enormous molasses cookies, freshly baked and still warm from the oven. Their smooth, pale brown surfaces were studded with plump raisins. When I smelled them, reason flickered and went out. In blind, mindless hunger, I devoured every one. When the actors, on cue, reached out for cookies and found emptiness, they held their fire until the scene was over, then quite justifiably exploded backstage. Petri and Lutz agreed that they could manage nicely, as they had before, without me.

That summer many of the actors wore white suits. Clarence Derwent, an actor-manager who played Napoleon in a revival of *The Man of Destiny*, wore snowy linen at rehearsals, and Michael

Strange (Mrs. John Barrymore), who played opposite Derwent, wore a white flannel jacket and skirt.
Helen Westley, the well-known character actress
of the Theatre Guild, who wasn't in the cast but
came to watch her daughter Ethel rehearse, wore
approximately the same tint and set it off with a big
picture hat and jade earrings. She was swarthy
with surprisingly light gray eyes. I sketched her,
and the drawing appeared in *Theatre Magazine* the
following year, August 1928.

I fulfilled my duties as volunteer press agent by
sending biweekly bulletins of the Cape Playhouse
to Burton: Irving Hoffman told me, when I got
back to town, that all the other papers were still
copying the information for their own show business columns. I also made drawings of the cast for
a small display in the lobby of the theatre. They
depicted the Misses Janet Beecher and Olive
Wyndham, who were sisters; Violet Kemble
Cooper, a pale blonde with a knife-edged profile;
and Mr. Derwent and Mrs. Barrymore in their
white suits. The drawings were completed while I
was literally burning the midnight oil; Mrs. Dixon
had not yet installed electricity, and I got to be very
fond of the smell of kerosene lamps. To add to the
primitive quality of my working conditions, my
fountain pen broke down so I was forced to use a
kitchen match dipped in ink for a stylus. Ray
Moore liked the caricatures and appreciated the
news releases. He rewarded my summer's labors
with a modest check: "All we can afford to give you
is twelve dollars. Is that all right?" I took a bus to
Hyannis and spent all the money on a set of bright
yellow Quimper dishes to go in what was to be my
yellow room.

The yellow room became an actuality when I got
back to New York. The Provençal petticoats were
transformed into bedspreads and valances. My
visiting friends, like Whistler's, felt they were
standing in the center of an egg. Still floating in my
aureate haze, or yellow fog, I wandered into
Frances Steloff's Gotham Book Mart on West

Aline Fruhauf

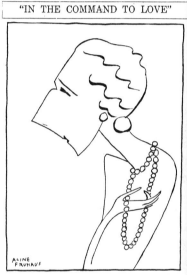

"IN THE COMMAND TO LOVE"

VIOLET KEMBLE COOPER.

Violet Kemble Cooper in the
Morning Telegraph, 1927.

91

Forty-fifth Street, where my bewitched eye led me straight to the shelf that held an appropriately bound copy of Aldous Huxley's novel, *Crome Yellow*. I wondered why the author had dropped the *h* in *chrome* and thought that, perhaps, it was an anglicism.

On a nearby shelf was a copy of a limited edition of Max Beerbohm's caricatures, *Things New and Old*. Leafing through it, I found a caricature of Huxley, done in 1923, which showed him to be a tall young man with the limp look of well-done asparagus. He had thick hair, ragged at the top; a generous moustache; and full lips that looked as if they were about to utter something devastating. The eyes, behind heavy horn-rimmed goggles, were pale. Somewhere on the long way down to his feet his legs had become mysteriously entwined; and one hand barely grasped a cigar with relaxed languor while the other hung loose, fingers parted like the petals of an upside-down lotus. I wanted the book but couldn't afford it. I did, however, buy *Crome Yellow* and another book by Huxley, *Those Barren Leaves*. Whatever the leaves were, they sounded as if they might be sere, hence yellow.

At home, I plunged into *Crome Yellow*, hoping to find some literary synthesis of the sulphurous tint that had taken me over, but I found nothing of the kind. *Crome*, it turned out, was the fictitious name of an English country house.

During my most recent phase of collecting holographs, I once again added drawings to my letters. One day, in bed with a feverish cold, I read *Those Barren Leaves*. On finishing it, I reached for paper and pencil and began the pleasant half-awake process of doodling. Presently little faces emerged, the characters in the novel. I cut them out in one-inch squares so that, when Huxley opened my letter, the drawings would flutter to the floor like so many barren leaves. I wrote him that I had enjoyed the novel and asked him if he

still looked like Max's caricature. He replied from
Lucca, Italy, on July 2, 1928:

Aline Fruhauf

> *Thank you for your letter & the very amusing*
> *caricatures of the people in Those Barren Leaves.*
> *Max Beerbohm's caricature of me is somewhat*
> *out of date, as I have shaved my moustache but I*
> *think the corkscrew legs are still correct.*

The English actor Basil Rathbone was a member of
the Cape Playhouse company during the summer.
Although I had seen him nine times in the revival
of *Outward Bound*, I had never met him. Florence
Bufano said he was a nice person and I ought to
draw him. He had just opened on Broadway in a
play he had written, *Judas*, in which he played the
title role. "The play isn't doing well," Florence
said. "I'm sure you can get a matinee ticket and
Basil would love to pose for you." She gave me his
telephone number. I saw the play and made an
appointment for the sitting.

"Oh, you're the caricaturist," was his greeting.
"I haven't much time. Will it take long? You know I
have a performance this afternoon."

He was a charming man, and his monologue
was so typical of what a celebrity has to say while
posing that I took it down along with my linear
notes:

> *You want my profile? Well, this is my best side.*
> Caricaturists *always seem to exaggerate my*
> *nose, but all the* artists *I've ever met tell me it's*
> *really very good. You know, I think your work*
> *must be fascinating. You must meet so many*
> *interesting people. I suppose that when you make*
> *a caricature, you bring out the dominant feature*
> *in a person's face, don't you? The last caricaturist*
> *made a terrible one of me. It was awful, really. It*
> *isn't as if I were, well, homely. My, you work*
> *quickly, don't you? You must know exactly what*
> *you want. I'm sure it's going to be lovely. Don't*
> *make me ugly, will you? Take your time. I've got*
> *plenty of time.*

Making Faces   After offering to show me photographs to help me out and suggesting that I leave out a certain blemish—"I know it's a salient point or something, but you know"—he asked to see my sketches. When I hesitated to show my rough notes, as I always do, he said, "But, my dear, I insist on seeing them. I always do. Give me that pad."

Taking the pad, he exclaimed, "Oh, my God! Do I look like that!"

Basil Rathbone in *Judas*, 1929.

Aline Fruhauf

Two Coins
From Two Musicians

I have always enjoyed drawing musicians, possibly because I started out as a very minor virtuoso, one of those precocious moppets who cause their teachers to alternate between pride and frustration. My teachers were happy when I composed, but not when I played by ear, or revised Chopin to suit myself, or transposed everything I could into the key of C to avoid sharps and flats.

At a birthday party given by a friend, the child-actress Lillian Roth, an occasion studded with celebrities from the Professional Children's School—Helen Chandler and Ben Grauer did the balcony scene from *Romeo and Juliet* just before the cake was cut—the inevitable photographers and reporters came in; Lillian's mother had seen to that. After the blinding bursts of the flashbulbs, a reporter asked me what show I was in and how old I was. I replied that I was twelve and that I wasn't an actress at all, but that sometimes I wrote music. The next day my mother found that I had been billed as a child-composer in one of the tabloids. And, for a while, I was just that. In celebration of *Peter Rabbit in Dreamland*, the Christmas pantomime that had liberated me from my terror of the theatre, I had written "The Peter Rabbit March," which

This Is Tom Bull

And This Is Billy Guard

Tom Bull and Billy Guard in
Musical America, 1927.

hinted strongly at the least-inspired works of John Philip Sousa. It was followed by two divertissements, "Reverie" and "Wood Nymphs," inspired by the works of Carrie Jacobs Bond and Delibes, respectively.

After that, I served the music world in a peripheral capacity, but even this was not until November 1927 when Mr. Viafora, the bassoonist of the New York Philharmonic, decided he no longer wanted to draw caricatures for *Musical America*, and I took on the job. I happened into the managing editor's office with my scrapbook at the strategic moment and thus began my seven years' association with *Musical America*.

"I want you to make a caricature of Rosa Ponselle, who is singing in Bellini's *Norma*, and one of Billy Guard, the press agent for the Metropolitan Opera," said Hollister Noble, a chunky young man, about thirty, with curly hair and black eyes. "And tell Billy I also want you to draw Tom Bull, the old gentleman who takes the tickets at the door. They've both been at the Met for more than thirty years. I'll call Billy now and let you talk to him." The editor telephoned the press agent, and we were introduced over the phone.

"I'd like to draw you now, if you're not busy," I said.

"My dear, I'm always busy, but I'd be delighted to see you," came the nasal voice at the other end of the line. "Come right over."

I went to the side entrance of the Met, which led to the press department, the retreat of William J. Guard. Don Quixote, as drawn by Daumier but dressed in pepper-and-salt tweeds, came out to greet me. His high cheekbones, cadaverous features, lank hair, moustache and goatee, and the Windsor tie were made to order for caricature. Once I knew I had set all this down in the proper order, I could settle back for a moment and enjoy this individual and his surroundings. An ancient, golden-oak rolltop desk almost filled the tiny office, whose walls were hung with photographs of opera stars of the past and some on-the-spot caricatures of Toscanini and Chaliapin that not only were very funny, but also had the air of un-mistakably authentic likenesses.

Billy noticed my interest. "Caruso," he said, "one of the greatest and a damn good caricaturist, too. He did one of me once." He then laid aside his thin black cigar and exchanged it for a flute; he played a few notes, sweet and wild, gave me an impish look, and said, "I'm blowing away my headache."

I gathered up my things, preparing to leave, and he told me to come back as soon after seven as I could make it. "I'll give you a pass," he added, "but mind you, be quiet when you draw. Don't disturb the singers or the audience." I promised to be as quiet as a mouse with gloves on. Billy bowed low over my hand. I dropped him a curtsy and headed for the subway and home.

Grandma was having dinner with us. She was an opera buff, who never missed the Met's radio broadcasts on Saturday afternoons. She was thrilled that I was going to the opening night of an opera. I got through dinner as quickly as I could, looked over my wardrobe, and decided on a two-piece velveteen dress, a color they called Dubonnet that year. It would blend with the red velvet orchestra seats and help toward making me invisible.

While waiting for my pass in the small room outside of Billy's office, I sketched a few of the "deadheads" waiting for their tickets and had another look at Billy, who had changed into white tie and tails. I caught a glimpse of the Met's massive impresario, Giulio Gatti-Casazza, and of Otto Kahn, the opera's banker-patron, a little man, impeccably dressed, with a gardenia in his but-tonhole. He had snow-white hair and moustache, soft black eyebrows, and the air of a sagacious pussycat. Billy gave me my pass, and I went to the front of the house to draw Tom Bull, the ticket taker.

Tom Bull was a very thin, gracious, old gentle-

Aline Fruhauf

Otto Kahn in *Top Notes*, 1929.

97

Rosa Ponselle—All Set for "Norma's" Immolation.

Rosa Ponselle in *Musical America*, 1927.

man in a top hat. My crystallization of him didn't take long. He had an angular face, a vertical nose, and a white moustache, and he wore eyeglasses. I had to spend more time drawing the top hat than making his face. Ticket taking was only one of his talents. He kept a little black book with the exact hour and minute of the beginning and ending of each opera, and those who wished to arrive late or leave early had only to consult him. He had a fund of information on the singers of the past and could tell you what drink Lilli Lehmann preferred, where Jean de Reszke had his moustaches trimmed, or the number of Victor Maurel's gestures.

From the moment the famous yellow curtains parted until they closed after the last act of *Norma*, I gazed upon Rosa Ponselle as the High Priestess of the Druids. I started in the standing-room area, then worked my way to the rear of the dress circle and tiptoed into an empty box, sketching the white-robed figure from whose mouth—a dark oval cavern in her pale face—came the sounds of a very capable operatic soprano.

I hated to disappoint Grandma, but when I gave her my report of my evening's work and entertainment, I had to admit that opera as an art form left me rather cold. The caricature of Ponselle appeared in *Musical America*, November 26, 1927, but I did a much better drawing of her at her birthday party a year later.

I hadn't ever caricatured a child, except unconsciously when, as a child myself, I made portrait paper dolls of my playmates. My next assignment, however, was to draw an infant prodigy, the boy violinist, eleven-year-old Yehudi Menuhin, and I was somewhat apprehensive of the sitting without knowing why. I needn't have been. He was a most cooperative sitter, and remembrance of the occasion still leaves me with a glow, for then, for one shining half hour, I was known as Mademoiselle Charmante.

The Menuhin family lived in an apartment on the upper West Side of New York during the time that Yehudi was playing solo with the New York Philharmonic. His father met me at the door. He was a small, darting man, terribly alert. I could hear sounds of laughter followed by an animated four- or five-way conversation in French. I followed Mr. Menuhin into the living room to meet his pretty blonde wife; their two little daughters, Hepzibah, age seven, and Yaltah, age five, who looked like Renoirs with their long flaxen hair and white dresses with blue sashes; Louis Persinger, Yehudi's teacher, a tall affable-looking man; a reporter whose name I have forgotten, a dark young woman; and finally, Yehudi himself, a plump boy with thick blond hair, round fat cheeks, and pursed lips that made him look a little like a drawing of the North Wind on an old map. His round luminous eyes looked black but were really blue. He was very self-possessed in spite of his clothes, which obviously had been selected to make him look younger: a long white cotton over-blouse and very short knickers that emphasized his rotund figure and chubby legs. Only his shoes suited him; they were mature in style as well as in size. Mr. Menuhin interrupted the French to introduce me. "*Charmante*," said Persinger, "I mean, *charmé*." Everybody laughed, and the ice was broken. It was an amiable way to start a sitting.

I gathered from the conversation, now in English, between Mr. Menuhin and the woman reporter that Yehudi, carefully tutored in French, spoke, read, and wrote excellent English and Russian, and that he had just finished reading Romain Rolland's life of Beethoven in the original French. The reporter was the gushing type. "Tell me, Yehudi," she cooed, "when you are alone in the country, surrounded by lovely flowers and singing birds, do you improvise on your violin? Do beautiful melodies come to you out of the clear atmosphere of nature at its best?" Yehudi looked the woman straight in the eye and said, "You know, my mother makes the most wonderful chicken pies."

Aline Fruhauf

Yehudi Menuhin, a Very Talented Young Man.

Yehudi Menuhin in *Musical America*, 1927.

At this time the boy was not allowed to play the works of modern composers. When I asked him if he liked George Gershwin's *Rhapsody in Blue*, he said he had never heard it. "But what a beautiful title," he said dreamily, *"Rhapsody in Blue, Rhapsody in Blue."* He savored the words.

When I left, the children all shouted, "Au'voir, Mam'selle Charmante!"

Although I continued to caricature theatre people, musicians got equal time, and I brought some of my leftover drawings to Burton, who printed them in the *Telegraph*. For a short time, the horse-racing fans saw the faces of Béla Bartók, Jascha Heifetz, and Maurice Ravel peering at them from between the news of daily doubles, pari-mutuels, and the latest reports from Hialeah.

I began to notice a marked difference between theatre and concert audiences. The music buffs had such sensitive ears that even the softest pencil moving over the smoothest paper provoked a

Béla Bartók in *Musical America*, 1927.

An Impression of Bela Bartok, the Mild-mannered Revolutionist Who Plays in New York This Week.

chorus of shushes sometimes loud enough to drown out the music itself. Drawing at press conferences suited me better. Not only was I one of the many taking down the news, but the atmosphere of exploding flashbulbs and the rapid fire of the interview were more conducive to sketching. I could linger over my drawings and scratch in the "form," Robinson style.

At one scratching session, I not only made enough sketches to fill a whole page of *Top Notes*, a subsidiary publication of the *Musical Digest*, but I had my own caricature drawn, as well. The occasion was Aleksandr Glazunov's birthday. Walter Damrosch gave him a concert and party, broadcast over NBC radio. I went along with one of the editors of *Musical America*, Quaintance Eaton, a tall, attractive girl with a piquant profile. She pointed out the celebrities, and I made quick line drawings. The first was of the birthday boy, who was heavy and dull-eyed, with a skin the color of a raw potato. Pianist Josef Hofmann was easy to draw; he had a little nose and an uncomplicated expression. I tried to get Damrosch, but he was too much in motion, and when he took the podium, all I could see was his back. Nevertheless, I decided to work in some form and scratched in a brier patch of penciled shadows.

When I got to Damrosch's ribs, I felt a light tap on my shoulder. I turned to face a very big, very rosy young man with curly hair. He wore a tuxedo, brown shoes, and what looked like a cockroach made of brass wire on his starched shirtfront. From his expression I gathered he had been watching me until he could stand it no longer. Monkeylike, he scratched his own ribs, pointed to my drawing, and shook his head in vigorous dissent. No doubt, he was an artist, I thought, and I knew from past experience that no matter what approach or technique I adapted, there would always be an artist looking over my shoulder and shaking his head. Continuing his pantomime, he requested my notebook and pencil, and as I faced him, he

Aline Fruhauf by Alexander Calder, unpublished drawing, 1928.

began to draw me in rich, baroque scallops, sweeping parabolas, inventive arabesques, and inspired curlicues. The result was a caricature that revealed not only my own shortcomings, but those of the poorly endowed relatives on both sides of my family. I asked him to sign it and he did.

In *The World of James McNeill Whistler*, Horace Gregory, quoting John Singer Sargent quoting Whistler, says, "It takes a long time for a man to look like his portrait." The axiom was proved by Alexander Calder's caricature of me made that evening. It has become my portrait.

Top Notes, Musical America, and its rival, the *Musical Courier,* kept me busy, and I heard a lot of good music in the process. Most of my sitters lived on the upper West Side, so I didn't have far to go. The sittings were usually held in the mornings, and most of the men posed in their dressing gowns. They were, with almost no exception, good, solid, happily married men. Often there was a baby carriage in the hall and a pretty wife who came in to be introduced and who invariably took discreet peeks at my sketchbook.

George Copeland, the concert pianist who specialized in playing the music of Ravel, Debussy, and Satie, although attired in dressing gown, disliked being photographed or otherwise depicted without a hat. After making me promise to draw him in a more conventional costume, he put on a wide-brimmed black fedora. He was a portly man, pink and white and bald. He had a button nose, round blue eyes, and the merest thread of eyebrows. Like Basil Rathbone, he was a talking subject, and I took down some of his comments. After lighting a thin cigar, he began his monologue.

"Modern music is getting tiresome," he said. "No one can achieve by striving only for new, stunning effects. The Spanish composers are the only promising people now; the rest are surprisingly unproductive. I hate musicians of all kinds. They're always talking about opus this and opus that."

The sitting took place in his hotel room, and a waiter came in with a breakfast tray. Copeland contemplated his cup of black coffee, and the monologue digressed.

"I like my breakfast things to be very white and very clean and very shiny," he went on. "The most enchanting breakfast I ever had was in Paris two years ago with Geraldine Farrar and her mother. We motored out to Armenonville, and the waiter

Aline Fruhauf

George Copeland in *Musical America,* 1928.

103

brought in a huge white platter of iced fruits, all cut up and shiny. Then he poured champagne all over the beautiful fruit, and we ate it with long silver forks. It was rather exquisite."

Changing direction again, he continued his monologue. "I don't want to convey any message. I play what I like the way I like, and the audience seems to like it too. And I don't give a whoop about leaving the world a better place when I die. Too much Beethoven never did anybody any good!"

Other sitters played for me. It was a privilege I enjoyed as one of the benefits of drawing for *Musical America*. Lotte Lehmann came into the living room wearing a long robe of sky-blue velvet that matched her eyes. "Sit down, *Kindchen*," she said. And, with a nod to her accompanist, she opened a little wordbook of sky-blue watered silk. In her unforgettably beautiful voice, she sang me a Liebeslied.

When Rachmaninoff opened the door for me at his apartment, he was so tall his head barely cleared the doorway. Very solemnly, he ushered me into a dark living room with heavy draperies, dark furniture, and innumerable framed photographs. He sat at the piano, fixed his somber gaze on a photograph of a little girl, and lifted his hands before playing; then came a thunderous cataract of sound. Something by Rachmaninoff, I pinched myself. He didn't say much. It was a short sitting.

The great Russian basso Fyodor Chaliapin was staying at the St. Moritz Hotel. He was a legend who had sung with Caruso. A magnificent-looking man, he posed like a veteran. I had never heard him sing except on recordings, and he didn't oblige me. Instead, he borrowed my notebook and pencil. Although he was somewhat unsteady from drink, the hand that dashed off a sketch and signed it was very sure. He handed the sketch to me and said, "This is how Caruso made a caricature of me."

A pianist friend of mine came one afternoon to try our new Steinway. After she had attacked and

Sergei Rachmaninoff in *Musical America*, 1934.

conquered the *Revolutionary Etude*, she played a
work unknown to me. It was as if she had dipped
her fingers into a shower of notes, glacial and
iridescent. It was the *Jeux d'eau* by Ravel. My yellow
period, triggered by van Gogh, had broadened
into an appreciation of the impressionist painters,
and this piece seemed like a musical translation of
the light that filled the canvases of Monet and
Pissarro.

Quaintance Eaton told me that Ravel was coming
to town; after I called his managers, Lucy Bogue
and Bernard Laberge, I went to the St. Moritz to
take my place among the photographers and
reporters. Ravel was a little man with an angular,
ruddy face, black brows, small alert eyes, and a
casque of beautifully waved white hair. His cheekbones were high, his nose was good-sized and
bony, his mouth was small and noncommittal, and
he had large, well-shaped ears without lobes. He
wore a bright navy suit, a blue shirt, and an elegant
brocade tie—blue, black, and silver like a blue jay's
wing. He was good-humored about posing and
had no apparent personal vanity. The reporters
fired their undistinguished questions while he
paced the floor and smoked a cigarette. He told the
press he was scared to death of American cooking,
especially of the fruit salads served at banquets,
but thought our red bananas were first-rate.

After the reporters left, I asked him if I might
make a sketch of him at the piano. I hoped he'd
play the *Jeux d'eau*, but he obliged with *Sonatine*,
which was lovely. His face assumed a languorous
expression, eyebrows up, eyelids down, nostrils
slightly dilated as if he were inhaling a light fragrance, the lento look. I made quantities of
sketches and inked them over at home. They had
spontaneity but were not realized caricatures.

After they were published, I sent him some of
the originals and wrote that I had enjoyed his latest
popular success, *Bolero*. At Christmas, I sent him
one of my cards, a self-portrait as a twelfth-century
saint, printed on gold tea-paper, and was surprised

Aline Fruhauf

Maurice Ravel in *Musical
America*, 1934.

Ravel's greeting card, 1930.
Freely translated: "With all
my thanks for the caricatures,
fond memories, and my best
wishes for Christmas, 1930.
Maurice Ravel."

Aline Fruhauf's 1929 Christmas card.

106

to receive a handmade greeting from him. On a three-by-five filing card, he had incised an arrangement of daisies. They had plumelike foliage colored with green crayon, and the centers of the flowers were yellow, shaded with red. One of the daisies, afloat, trailed a plume of foliage like the tail of a little comet, and in its center he had drawn, in ink, a copy of my Christmas card self-portrait. He inscribed the card,

Avec tous mes remerciments pour les caricatures, mes bon souvenirs et mes meilleurs souhaits du Christmas (1930)

And, under his signature, he added the first two bars of *Bolero*.

Ravel was the most congenial celebrity I have ever drawn. The last time I saw him was at a concert in the ballroom of the Plaza Hotel, when Madeleine Grey sang his *Chansons madécasses*. He accompanied her, and after the concert, he stood in the middle of the ballroom floor, completely alone, small, tired, elegant, very red in the face. I told him I enjoyed the concert, and he was pleased.

My Grandmother Anna was very proud of my development as an artist although she couldn't understand why anyone would want caricatures for any purpose, much less pay for them.

"Don't people mind what you do to them?" she asked. I told her that Caruso had been an enormous help in paving the way for all caricaturists of musicians.

"Only one of them complained," I said. "Andrés Segovia. I drew him bending over his guitar, and he told one of the editors I made him look as if he were biting it, and he threatened to sue me."

Anna was a great fan of the tenor Giovanni Martinelli, so I gave her the autographed photo he had given me at the conclusion of our sitting in 1934. She was very pleased, had it framed, stood it on her parlor window seat, and banked it with philodendron and grapefruit plants.

When I drew Jascha Heifetz during the winter of

Andrés Segovia in *Musical America*, 1928.

107

1927, she wanted a detailed report. He had been easy to do, I told her. He had well-defined features and hair like a cap of clipped, light brown wool.

"What did he wear?" she asked.

"Gray pants," I said, "black shoes with pointed toes, pearl-gray spats, a blue linen Russian blouse with red cross-stitching around the high neck and down the front."

Anna was interested to hear about the cross-stitching. She had taught me how to do it that summer at Long Beach.

Heifetz had smoked a cigarette in a long black holder, and like so many of the pipes and cigars I had drawn, it served as a punctuation mark for the caricature. He was seated in a low chair near a small eighteenth-century Florentine table that was painted yellow and glazed, like buttered toast.

During the summer of 1928, when Anna took me to Europe, I kept thinking of the table and, when we weren't sightseeing in Italy, I searched in vain for one like it. During the trip, I caught several glimpses of the table's owner. Once I saw him disappearing behind a marble column in a hotel lobby; another time, leaving the beach at the Lido. Anna was nearsighted and Heifetz was fast moving. He was always gone before she could see him. She accused me of hallucinating even after I told her I had seen his signature in the register at the hotel in Como.

Anna and I left Venice on the hottest day of the year. My dress, a silk print with a light background, had to last the journey, so I concentrated desperately on keeping cool. It wasn't easy. Our compartment on the train was like an oven. The highly seasoned soup we had had for lunch left us burning with thirst. A woman fainted in the corridor and revived only after repeated sluicings of bottled mineral water. I bought a pint and brought it back to the compartment, but there was no bottle opener to be found. We just looked at the bottle and grew thirstier. Anna was tired. Her glasses dropped and dangled from their black string, and

An Impression of Heifetz, Returned from the Orient and More Blasé Than Ever.

Jascha Heifetz in the *Morning Telegraph*, 1928.

her eyes, unsheathed from the heavy crystal lenses, were suddenly small and defenseless, like a baby sparrow's. She was suddenly old.

I went out into the corridor in search of a bottle opener and caught sight of the familiar-looking profile. He looked out of the window with blue-gray eyes at half-mast and puffed at his cigarette in a leisurely manner. Even in all the heat, he looked crisp and immaculate in white flannels and a flowing white silk shirt, open at the throat, like Lord Byron's. He saw me and smiled in recognition.

"How cool you look," he said. Outwardly, at least, concentration had worked. I told him that my grandmother was in the next compartment and that we were looking for a bottle opener. He said he thought he could help us out. I opened the door to the compartment and said, "Anna, I'd like you to meet Mr. Heifetz." Anna beamed. She extended her hand and said she was honored. He said he was, too.

A waiter came by and brought more water and some glasses. Heifetz reached into his pocket and brought out a shiny gold coin and deftly began to pry off the bottle cap. Anna clasped her hands and moaned softly, "Oh, Mr. Heifetz! Your precious fingers! Please be careful!" The operation succeeded without mishap. We drank deep draughts of lukewarm Pelligrino and chatted. Anna discovered that, yes indeed, he had been to the Lido, and to the Villa d'Este, and to Como, and he was now enjoying a two-month holiday before a concert engagement in Edinburgh.

Anna forgot the heat. She leaned back and looked fondly at me. At that moment, in the most recent of the procession of images of her granddaughter, I was the *Wunderkind* who had materialized, from thin air, "the greatest living violinist of the century. And just think," she added, "what he risked for us. If anything had happened to his hands, God forbid, I could never forgive myself."

A coin also figured in another experience with a

109

musician. Deems Taylor, former music critic of the *New York World* and composer of several operas, had just prepared elaborate program notes for the premiere, December 13, 1928, with the New York Philharmonic, of Gershwin's tone poem *An American in Paris* and assigned me to caricature the composer.

I went to the Gershwin residence early one afternoon. Gershwin had just begun to collect pictures. One of his first acquisitions, a print of George Bellows's lithograph of the Dempsey-Firpo fight, was hanging on a wall near the grand piano. George came in. He was slender, athletic-looking, with a dark rosy complexion and a very easy, unas-

George Gershwin, unpublished drawing, 1929.

suming manner. For some reason I couldn't fathom, he didn't look anything like his photographs. I soon realized, however, that his hair, instead of being smooth, stuck straight up, inches high, into the air. I told him he looked different from what I expected. "I know," he said, "it's my hair; I just washed it."

I made a lot of drawings, but the pompadour continued to confuse me; it upset the proportions of his face. "Stay as long as you want," he said. "I'll be practicing, anyhow." He adjusted his cigar at a diagonal and methodically attacked the piano. The live melodies of *An American in Paris* were so captivating I almost forgot to draw.

I was still struggling to get a satisfactory likeness on the night of the concert and caught Gershwin, dressed in white tie and tails, hair slicked down to normal, as he raced across the stage at Carnegie Hall to take his bow. The caricature appeared in *Musical America*, March 1929.

Four years later, after moving with my parents down West End Avenue from Eighty-fourth to Seventy-third Street, Gershwin and I shared almost the same view of the Hudson River and of the modified French chateau of Charles M. Schwab, the steel magnate. Sitting at my drawing table, puzzling out caricatures and wool gathering, I could look out at the familiar scene of the river, with its boats and its palisades along the New Jersey shore, and I could shift my gaze to the turrets and green lawns of the Schwab mansion or look straight across to the adjoining penthouses at Seventy-fifth Street and Riverside Drive, which Gershwin shared with his brother and sister-in-law, Ira and Lenore Gershwin.

I wondered how George's picture collection was progressing. At about this time, I was drawing caricatures of artists and art dealers for the handsome, glossy, and bankrupt magazine *Creative Art*. I had the privilege of picking my own subjects, provided that my choices met the approval of Walter Gutman, who ran a gossip column on the art world

Aline Fruhauf

George Gershwin in *Musical America*, 1929.

MR. GERSHWIN SETS THE PACE

111

for the magazine. One of my subjects was the artist Bernard Sanders, who told me that he was assisting Gershwin in selecting paintings for his collection. "I'd be glad to take you to see the pictures," he offered, and I accepted. "Bring a copy of *Creative Art* with my caricature in it," he added. "I think George would like to see it."

Bernard picked me up at seven-thirty, and we walked the short distance from my place on West End Avenue to the Gershwin penthouse on Riverside Drive. George came to the door. His hair was thinner, and he wore a well-fitted dark suit. At his side was a richly tinted young lady, elaborately furred and deliciously perfumed. George introduced her, and I took a quick look around the apartment. There were Navajo rugs on the floor, and the furniture was modern, with a custom-made look. The art collection had progressed considerably since the acquisition of the Bellows lithograph; the walls bloomed with paintings. I spied a Dahomey mask, took a wild guess, and said, "That was Ralph Barton's."

George looked surprised and said, "How did you know?" I wanted to say, "I never forget a face," but, instead, told him that I had seen it many times at the Bartons' and I wondered how it had come into his possession.

George appeared to be in a hurry to leave. Nevertheless, Bernard opened the copy of *Creative Art* to the page with his caricature. "Say, that's very good," said George. "Can I have it? I mean, I want to pay for the magazine." He flipped over the cover to see the price, reached in his pocket, and handed me a coin. "You can pick up another copy, can't you?" Before I could remonstrate, he said, "Stay as long as you want. You'll excuse us, won't you. We're already late." And he and the young lady were gone, out the door, into the elevator, and out into the soft New York night.

Bernard and I stayed to look at the pictures. There was a Rouault, a Chagall, a bust of George by Isamu Noguchi, and a screen by George's cousin Henry Botkin. Then we walked to the newsstand at the Seventy-second Street subway station, where, as directed, I bought a copy of *Creative Art* with Gershwin's fifty-cent coin. It was a futile gesture, too late to do the magazine any good. *Creative Art*, as such, expired with that issue, May 1933, when it merged with the *American Magazine of Art*.

Aline Fruhauf

Pablo Casals in *Musical America*, 1928.

Pablo Casals, One of the Week's Recitalists.

Just to the Poitrine

On a May morning in 1928, the telephone rang in the yellow room. It was Irving Hoffman.

"Do you know you made *Vanity Fair* this month?"

"Who, me? I never did any drawings for *Vanity Fair*. You must have me mixed up with Al Frueh. Lots of people make that mistake. It's very flattering, but!"

"Quit clowning," he said, "and listen. You are in *Vanity Fair*. George Jean Nathan mentions you. Something about the American credo."

Then I remembered. During a spell of letter writing, my means of collecting holographs, I had seen an article by George Jean Nathan, the well-known editor and drama critic, that was filled with sayings expressing American beliefs. I began to amuse myself by thinking up some of my own. I sent them off to Nathan, but they were never acknowledged. "I think I know what you mean," I told Irving. "I'll go out and get a copy."

Nathan's piece was entitled "La Philosophie Americaine, Being the Further Beliefs and Convictions of the People of a Great Democracy," and was introduced by the following paragraph:

Already in these pages and in several tomes,
under the general heading of The American
Credo, the writer has presented almost two thou-
sand cardinal articles in the doctrinal faith of the
American masses. But the end is not yet in sight.
With the valuable assistance of scholars both in
this country and in Europe, he is gradually
completing and perfecting this contribution
toward an understanding of the democratic mind.
For certain of the subjoined addenda to the Credo,
he wishes to acknowledge his thanks to the follow-
ing distinguished professors, Dr. John Larkin,
Dr. Joseph Wood Krutch, Dr. John B. Powell,
Dr. Sinclair Lewis and Mlle. Aline Fruhauf.

Nine of the credos had been selected from those I
had sent to Nathan. They included the following:

That the modern French painters are just
kidding the public, that they don't believe in the
crazy technique they practice, and that they are
all academicians at heart.

That all stage doormen are retired actors who
played with Ada Rehan or Booth and Barrett.

That all toe-dancers must have certain bones
in their feet broken before they can become pro-
ficient in their art.

That men who wear blue shirts have artistic
leanings.

Now that I had been acknowledged as a distinguished professor who had unwittingly joined
Nathan's staff of researchers, it seemed fitting that
my colleague pose for a caricature for *Vanity Fair.*
Frank Crowninshield, the editor of the magazine,
was out of town, but Donald Freeman, who had
taken over for him, said he would be happy to
have me submit a drawing of Nathan. "If you can
supply Nathan with more material assuring
another article for us," he said, "the drawing
assignment will be yours."

It was an odd arrangement. I had never before
worked that way. Nevertheless, I wrote to Nathan,

Helen Morgan, unpublished
watercolor, 1929.

informing him of the state of affairs, and he agreed
to help me in my career. Months went by. I received five notes from the credo collector, all
written on the green stationery of the *American
Mercury*, the magazine he and H.L. Mencken
launched in 1924, thanking me for my additional
contributions and assuring me that he really would
get going on another article.

Meanwhile, I was eager to get some of my caricatures in *Vanity Fair*; it seemed the sine qua non of
success. Frank Crowninshield was back in town,
and I was told that even if he didn't take any of my
work, meeting him would be an experience worth
remembering.

Crownie, as he was affectionately known to his
friends and coworkers, was reputed to be so fastidi-
ous that he proofread his morning mail. On the
afternoon of my appointment with him, his secretary, Jeanne Ballot, a pretty French girl with red-
brown bobbed hair and bangs, ushered me into his
office. I saw a dapper gentleman with a pink and
white complexion, crisp white hair and moustache,
bright blue eyes, and a little bump on his nose. He
was smartly dressed in a gray tweed suit with a
double-breasted vest. His bow tie was red paisley,
and his beautifully polished English shoes glowed
like dark honey.

My portfolio, as usual, was crammed with
drawings, and when I opened it they fell out and
scattered on the floor. "What a mess," he said,
clucking in disgust. "Remember, Miss Frühauf,"
hardly anyone ever used the umlaut, "this is your
sample case. Now if you were selling candy, you
wouldn't put it all helter-skelter, in one worn-out
paper bag, would you? No-o, of course you
wouldn't. You'd wrap each piece separately and
put each kind in a separate box. Hereafter, don't
show me anything that hasn't been properly
matted. But, come back!"

When I did go back, the drawings were not only
carefully matted, but invitingly wrapped in cel-
lophane. One of them was of Helen Morgan, the

popular night club singer, sitting on a black piano and wearing a bright red sheath. For contrast, I had silhouetted her against an equally bright blue background. Crownie held it up. "My," he remarked dryly, "I'll bet you thought you'd be knocking 'em dead with that one." The interview ended without sale or commission.

Later, however, I received a call from Donald Freeman. George Jean Nathan had come through with his end of our bargain, a new set of credos. I was to go ahead with my caricature of him. After firing off one more set of credos for good will, I wrote and asked Nathan for an appointment.

Nathan came out of his office into the waiting room of the Alfred Knopf Publishing Company at 730 Fifth Avenue, greeted me politely, and sat down to pose. He was shorter than I expected and better looking, with well-articulated features, smooth dark skin, velvety brown eyes, and an Italian bootblack hair comb. He was dressed in banker's gray worsted; my father's eagle eye would have approved the tailoring. The demon drama critic, whose crime, in the event of displeasure, was to leave the theatre before the play ended, looked as bland as a dish of junket and every bit as defenseless. The temptation was there to draw him equipped with horns and a tail, but I thought then, as I often do now, of Max Beerbohm's good words from his essay "The Spirit of Caricature," which Knopf had recently published in his *A Variety of Things*:

> *The perfect caricature is in itself a beautiful thing. For caricature, not less than for every other art, beauty is a primal condition. . . . The most perfect caricature is that which, on a small surface, with the simplest of means, most accurately exaggerates, to the highest point, the peculiarities of a human being, at his most characteristic moment, in the most beautiful manner.*

Aline Fruhauf

George Jean Nathan in *Vanity Fair*, 1929.

117

The drawing of Nathan, along with the new install-
ment of credos, appeared in *Vanity Fair*, November
1929, almost a year and a half after it was proposed.

In the spring of 1929, Peyton Maxwell, the editor
of *Theatre Magazine*, assigned me to make caricatures of six playwrights: Maxwell Anderson, S.N.
Behrman, Rachel Crothers, Floyd Dell, Philip
Barry, and Elmer Rice. The deadline was a short
one. All the playwrights were easy to approach
and had plenty of time for posing, except Behrman,
who faced a deadline of his own, working on the
Theatre Guild production of his play *Meteor* star-
ring Alfred Lunt and Lynn Fontanne. When I
spoke to the guild's press agent about a sitting with
Behrman, he said, "It's not going to be easy. He's
rewriting his second act. I can give you his phone
number, but it won't do you any good; he keeps
the phone in his closet." I told him that was too
bad; one more drawing would complete the page.

"Don't give up yet," he replied. "I'll see what I
can do." In some mysterious way, he was able to
reach Behrman and called me back to say, "If you
call him on the dot of two, he'll open the closet
door and answer the telephone." The plan worked.
Behrman answered the phone and asked me to
come right away.

S.N. Behrman in *Theatre Magazine*, 1929.

For one who led so cloistered a life, the playwright's appearance was far from austere. He had
an engaging grin, and his eyes were so turned up
with laughter they were almost invisible. He had
spent most of the day writing scintillating dialogue,
and the mood was catching. The quips were soon
flying, and I thought then, and also in the be-
clouded retrospect of years, that I had never been
so clever.

Unfortunately, the only notes I took were drawings, and all the memory of the verbal badminton
vanished by the time I got to the street. Exhilarated,
I walked four blocks in the wrong direction.

When in 1960 the *New Yorker* published his
delightful "Conversations with Max," an intimate
memoir of Sir Max Beerbohm, I wrote Behrman a

fan letter. His reply was cordial. "I am amused to discover," he wrote, "that I used to keep my telephone in the closet. I must have been more gregarious then because now I won't allow it in the room."

Earlier that year, 1929, I visited some friends, Leila Fisher and Minna Adams, in Washington. My pleasant stay with them marked my first encounter with a house in Georgetown. It had great charm, highlighted by the gleam of well-polished mahogany, open fires, and strategically placed bits of Waterford glass. And, with its Victorian furniture upholstered in velvet the color of dark geraniums, it was both warm and welcoming. My hostesses gave a party for me, and it was there I learned that the editor of a new magazine, the *Washingtonian*, a forerunner of the present-day *Washingtonian*, needed some caricatures of senators. Rixey Smith, secretary to Senator Carter Glass of Virginia, introduced me to the senator's sister, Marion Bannister, the editor of the magazine.

Rixey offered to take me around the Capitol. The next day we sat in the Senate gallery, and he pointed out Senators William E. Borah, Reed Smoot, Thaddeus Caraway, and others, while I made rapid sketches from a distance, amazed at the nonchalance of the gentlemen, who walked around, read papers, yawned, and paid no atten-

Aline Fruhauf

Senators Borah, Copeland, Caraway, and Jones in the *Washingtonian*, March 1929.

Copeland   Borah   Jones   Caraway

119

Vice-President Dawes and
Speaker Longworth in the
Washingtonian, March 1929.

The latest pen portrait of the departing
Vice President, with his famous underslung
pipe and best "Helen Maria" expression

The Honorable Speaker of the House of
Representatives, Mr. Longworth, looking, and
perhaps feeling, as if he had just swallowed
the canary

tion to whomever was speaking. Rixey told me
later that most of the work of the nation was done
in committee rooms.

We left the gallery, and Rixey and I took the little
subway to the offices of the vice president, where I
had a sitting with Charles "Hell and Maria" Dawes,
who smoked his famous underslung pipe. Then I
drew a quick sketch of the Speaker of the House,
Nicholas Longworth, who had a handsome bald
head and friendly gray eyes. His wife, the former
Alice Roosevelt, had just given birth to a daughter,
Paulina.

The caricatures of Dawes, Longworth, and
Caraway, together with those of Senators Wesley
Jones and Royal S. Copeland, were published in
the *Washingtonian* in March, just before the Hoover
administration took office; those of Smoot and
Senator Clarence Dill, in June; and one of Senator
George Norris, in May 1930. They represented one

Aline Fruhauf

Senators Dill and Smoot in the *Washingtonian*, March 1929.

of my few excursions from the world of arts and letters.

Back in New York, refreshed by the change of pace of my Washington visit, I went to a soiree at Quaintance Eaton's, where a group of "Musical Americans" were whooping it up, aiming limericks at one another. One of the editorial staff of *Musical America*, Winthrop Sargeant, directed his effort to me, and his aim had a far-reaching effect on my work. I don't think his verse got past the first two lines, but they were unforgettable:

> *There once was a girl named Aline*
> *Who drew, just to the poitrine.*

It was, alas, all too true. For years I had taken the easy way out, drawing heads and shoulders decorated with lapels or with beads, which in those days designated the sex of the victim. My full-length of Ravel was about the only exception. I resolved to do better, to draw the full figure with hands and feet whenever space would allow.

At the next performance I attended, a dance recital by Martha Graham, I made quantities of action sketches. But when I surveyed the results at home, I found my figure drawing rusty beyond belief. I put on a long jersey nightgown, similar in

121

cut to the gown worn by the dancer, and posed in front of a full-length mirror, contorting my body until I achieved a characteristic Graham stance. The ensuing caricature, showing both hands and feet, was published in *Theatre Arts Monthly*, May 1930. And it was followed the next month by one of Lillian Gish as she appeared in Chekhov's *Uncle Vanya*, wearing a long, ruffled, eyelet-embroidered gown. It, too, had hands, but I left out the feet, which were barely visible under her long skirt. I had begun to pay off my debt to Winthrop Sargeant.

My yellow bed-sitting room also became an influence on my work. I did two sets of my more successful caricatures, one in pen-and-ink or wash for reproduction, and one in color for my room. Many of the latter blossomed out in jonquil-yellow backgrounds, a color that heightened the delicate pallor of the dancer Anna Duncan and dramatized the actor Basil Rathbone as he appeared in *Judas*, with brown makeup and wearing a purple robe with a geranium-lake sash. Emerald green became the background of the to-the-poitrine portrait of the young actress Sylvia Sidney, dressed in black velvet. Sometimes I coated the pictures with copal varnish to give them a feeling of antiquity, adding a little "Oenslager gold" for accent. I became more and more interested in backgrounds and hoped some day to do a series of artists surrounded by their work and by the things they loved.

The first of these "at-home" studies was a Beerbohm-inspired wash drawing of the scenic artist Robert Edmond Jones, who had recently designed the sets and the twenty-foot marionettes for the League of Composers production of Stravinsky's *Oedipus Rex*. Remo Bufano executed the huge heads of the marionettes in papier-mâché, and his wife, Florence, suggested that I do a caricature of Jones and arranged the sitting.

Jones had just done the costumes and sets for Eugene O'Neill's *Mourning Becomes Electra*, in which both the interior and the exterior of the

Martha Graham in *Theatre Arts Monthly*, 1930.

Mannon's Greek Revival house reflected the stark tragedy of the play. The actresses Alla Nazimova and Alice Brady were regal and dramatic as they strode through the play in dresses of heavy black silk. Their dead white makeup was relieved only by the color of their hair, the rich dark auburn that reflects purple highlights.

Jones was a tall man with graceful arms and legs that seemed jointless, and his long white face had a heavy jaw. His living room, in which the sitting took place, was done in stark black and white. The carved wooden frames of the Victorian furniture were painted white, and the upholstery was black patent leather. The only notes of color were the predominantly tobacco-brown of an old Chinese painting that hung on the wall, the plum-colored dressing gown that Jones wore, and the dark auburn of his thick hair and moustache. All reminded me of his setting for the O'Neill tragedy.

After months of drawing for newspapers and magazines—over a hundred caricatures had appeared in nine different publications during 1929, and the tempo was increasing—I wanted to paint again. I was told that Woodstock, New York, was the place to go. Rooms for students were reasonable, and at the Art Students League, which had a summer school there, advertisements for the rooms were posted on the bulletin board.

As soon as I was settled in the home of one of Kenneth Hayes Miller's students, I took my box of colors and a small canvas board and sat under a tree. A good part of Ulster County was spread out before me, barns and trees nestled at the foot of Overlook Mountain. Despite the words of Alfred Stieglitz, I started a landscape in the Miller style, only to be interrupted by two young artists, Peg and Bill, who came rocketing by in a Model-T Ford. Although they were students at the tradition-ridden National Academy of Design, they were ardent disciples of Cézanne's. They descended from the Model-T and looked over my shoulder. From past experience, I knew what to expect.

Aline Fruhauf

Lillian Gish in *Theatre Arts Monthly*, 1930.

123

ALINE
FRUHAUF

Anna Duncan in *Musical America*, 1929.

124

"No, oh no, that's not the way to paint a land-scape!" said Peg. I muttered something about Courbet and Rousseau, but they pretended not to hear.

"For one thing, your brushes are too small," said Bill, "and your canvas! What are you trying to do, postcards?"

Again I muttered something about not being able to please everybody and waited for them to leave. But unexpectedly, they looked at each other with the beatific expression that proclaims the dawn of inspiration. "Know something? We need a model. If you will pose for us in the morning, we'll teach you to paint in the afternoon," they proposed. "We'll pick you up, give you lunch, and then later we'll take you home." I agreed. "You're to work on beaverboard, no canvas, and no brushes," Bill said firmly. "Putty knife only, and lots of inexpensive colors so you can sling paint around without worrying about how much it costs per tube."

My teachers set up a still life on a table spread with a white cloth. There was a green bottle and some books. After posing for them in a garnet-colored dirndl of mousseline de soie that I had made in Paris, I changed for lunch and my after-noon painting session. Applying paint on a large surface with a putty knife was like jumping into cold water, painful at first, but invigorating as I went on.

"Break up your color," they shouted, almost in unison. "Don't be afraid! That bottle's got blue and violet shadows; put one color alongside another. Make it shimmer!"

"But I don't see the colors you do," I protested miserably.

"Well, look for them. They're there."

By the end of the afternoon, my young instruc-tors thought I had done just fine, but the result seemed posterish to me. Under their dichotomous tutelage, my work showed that the Academy had won hands down over Cézanne. I continued to

pose for them for a week or so, long enough for
them to get a good start on my portrait, and then
excused myself.

Woodstock never lacked material for exciting
new projects, and when I heard that Don Oscar
Becq, a dancer who taught children at the King-
Coit School in New York, was looking for an artist
to illustrate his textbook on the dance, I visited his
rustic studio in Byrdcliffe, a hilly section of
Woodstock, completely surrounded by trees. The
children under Becq's direction were unaffected
and delightful to draw. One nine-year-old boy,
Robert, was particularly charming. He sat in a
canvas chair and posed for me. He had a long
head; apricot skin; small, round, slightly slanted
black eyes; and bangs like polished copper. My
pencil drawing of him had a richness I had never
achieved before, and when someone suggested
that I make a lithograph of it, I took it to the workshop of the artist-printer Grant Arnold.

"Do you think I could make a print of this?" I
asked.

"I don't see why not," Arnold said. "You'll have
to trace it on stone, then go over your line with
lithographic crayon—Number 5 ought to be about
right. I'll grain a stone with F carborundum; it
gives the smoothest surface."

I was learning a new vocabulary, and one word
printmaker held a special excitement.

The next morning, a stone was ready. I rubbed a
sheet of paper with red conté crayon, put my
drawing over it, and traced the drawing with a
hard pencil. Then I went over the red delineation
on the stone with a sharp Number 5 crayon. Because of the copal varnish content of Number 5,
the hardest crayon, it had to be used by itself. I did
not yet know how to reproduce on stone the rich
rubbed halftones of my drawing, so I indicated
them with timid strokings of crayon. When I had
finished, Arnold brushed the drawing with a
solution of gum arabic and left it to fix the image
overnight.

The next morning, he rubbed a brown substance called asphaltum over the stone and then wiped it off with a rag soaked in turpentine. I gasped as the drawing seemed to disappear.

"Don't worry," Arnold laughed, "it'll come back." He rolled a huge canvas-covered rolling pin on a slab covered with lithographic ink and rolled it over the stone. Robert reappeared as if by magic. There was a breathless moment when Arnold placed a sheet of dampened paper on the stone and turned the crank of the press. I hadn't counted on the drawing being reversed in the printing process, and the richness of the original drawing was lacking. The print had the powdery appearance of a lithograph by Marie Laurencin—nice, but not what I expected.

"Not bad for a start," Arnold said cheerfully.

For the next print, I did a preliminary drawing of the dancing class as a group. And when I transferred the drawing to stone, I asked Arnold if I could put in some rubbed tones. He told me it would be tricky, and they usually printed darker than they appeared on the stone. But if I were willing to risk it, I could take a piece of chamois, rub it on the softest crayon, Number 1, and rub the chamois on the stone. The print, though slightly smudged, had a richer quality than the first one, and since the likenesses of the children were all good, their mothers all wanted copies. The edition paid for itself.

The landscape with Overlook Mountain later came to life as a lithograph. My brief session of painting under the Cézanne-Academy dichotomy had loosened my attack on the landscape.

A Fudge Party

That winter of 1930, still in
love with the feeling of drawing on stone, I joined
a lithography class at the Art Students League. The
class met in the morning, and I was able to continue
to free-lance for magazines and newspapers in the
afternoon and evening. I haunted the galleries
where graphic art could be seen. There were the
masterly Daumiers and the atmospheric landscapes, like Chinese paintings, by the Minnesota-
born Adolf Dehn at the Weyhe Gallery and at the
Downtown Gallery; marvelously drawn caricatures, etchings, and lithographs by Peggy Bacon;
and lithographs by Yasuo Kuniyoshi, in which rich
swampy blacks contrasted with the merest whis-
pers of silver gray, wonders of technique and
imagination. Kuniyoshi's tones looked rubbed in,
but Arnold told me they were achieved with just
one grade of Korn crayon, Number 5, sharpened to
a needle point. The strokes, closely juxtaposed,
were applied with consummate artistry, and I
hoped someday to have the patience and skill to
work like that.

At the League, Charles Locke, our instructor,
came in twice a week to criticize our work from a
technical standpoint, leaving our aesthetic concepts pretty much alone. Something of a purist, he

127

frowned upon rubbed tints as being unreliable, printing too dark or not at all. Drawing with tusche, the lithographic ink that came in a bottle, was all but forbidden. And although mistakes could be erased by scraping the stone with a razor blade, the stone would be temporarily damaged and white scratches would show through the corrections, so erasures on the stone had to be made by a counterfix process, and the corrections refixed before the final printing.

One of the most talented students in the class was the Washington artist Prentiss Taylor, a mutual friend of the Bufanos. Although he was a proficient watercolorist and painter, his love affair with lithography has continued through the almost five decades I have known him. He became a force in the world of graphic art and served for many years as president of the Society of Washington Printmakers. While in the Locke class, he worked on four lithographs illustrating the poems of Langston Hughes that were published under the title *Scottsboro Limited* by the Golden Stair Press in 1932 when the Scottsboro case had become a cause célèbre.

My subjects at the time were those nearest at hand, a nostalgic view of the Hudson River from our dining room window and a dramatic view of a tugboat on the river in the early twilight of winter when the lights came on along the Palisades. Then, Brooks Atkinson, drama critic of the *New York Times*, who had posed for one drawing in the series of critics I did for *Theatre Magazine*, agreed to let me do another for a lithograph and posed at his desk reading galleys.

A new dancer, or as she called herself, a dancer-mime, Angna Enters, was a favorite subject for artists. The effect of her face was startling. In my mental filing system, I placed it somewhere between Alice Brady's and Lynn Fontanne's. It was rather long with a nose that came out in an upward sweep. Her mouth was the kind usually described as generous, and her small black eyes were made

Brooks Atkinson, 1931.

128

Aline Fruhauf

Angna Enters in *Aphrodisiac-Green Hour*, 1930.

to appear larger by short parallel lines drawn with a black liner at their outer corners. Angna Enters had studied art with John Sloan, and she knew history and painting intimately. She could recreate a whole period with gesture, costume, and music. Her vignettes were a keyhole through which the audience could view the past with the uncanny certainty that each highly charged theatrical piece was indisputably authentic. Her *Odalisque* recalled

129

the Delacroix-inspired painting of the same title by Renoir, and her *Pavana* was straight out of Velázquez.

Three of my drawings of her were published: one as she appeared in *Delsarte: With a Not Too Classical Nod to the Greeks* in *Theatre Guild Magazine*, another as she appeared in *Field Day* in the *Dance Observer*, and a head in *Musical America*. For a lithograph, I did her portrayal, in *Aphrodisiac-Green Hour*, of a weary *fille de joie*, resting her tired feet as she sat at a café table with a glass of absinthe. Her dress and hat, as well as the curtain behind her, were dead black. I used tusche right out of the bottle and scratched in my highlights with a razor blade, breaking in rapid succession two of the cardinal rules of my lithography teacher.

I had been drawing Katharine Cornell for years before I decided to do a lithograph of her. I saw her first in Michael Arlen's *The Green Hat* and still remember her first entrance, the long body at a slant in ochre crepe and the emerald-green felt hat pulled so far down over her face that only the tip-tilted nose, the chin, and the forward thrust of her lips were visible. In Arlen's novel, Iris March was a blonde, but that didn't matter to me. This was a completely different characterization, wonderful to draw. I also did a number of drawings of Cornell costumed for Edith Wharton's *The Age of Innocence*. They suggested her somewhat, and, as usual, I sent them off to her, receiving a nice letter in reply. In 1931, her press agent, Ray Henderson, arranged a backstage sitting for a large drawing to be used in the lobby of the theatre. Cornell was appearing as Elizabeth Barrett at the time Robert Browning was courting her in Rudolph Besier's *The Barretts of Wimpole Street*. Wearing a claret-colored silk gown collared with ecru lace and pinned with a cabochon garnet brooch, she was cooperative and unhurried, and as her fawn-colored spaniel, Flush—also a member of the cast—sat at her feet, she stroked his satin head and talked to him in low, caressing tones.

Aline Fruhauf

Katharine Cornell as Elizabeth
Barrett, lithograph, 1931.

But I was much too close to her. Each of her
strong features, the wide-apart eyes with heavy
lids, the full mouth with its cleft lower lip, the
tip-tilted nose with wide-winged nostrils, and the
calligraphic eyebrows like those on Indonesian
marionettes, all heavily accented with makeup,
clamored for immediate attention. Although the
sketch hung in the lobby for the duration of the
play, I wasn't satisfied with it and made another
from the back of the house. The stage lighting

131

accented the chiaroscuro of her broad, sculptural face with its high cheekbones and eyes in deep shadow, and it emphasized the soft sheen of her full-sleeved satin gown.

During the summer, at Woodstock again, I transferred the drawing to stone. One of the prints was purchased by Cornell's business manager for the company's collection, and Cornell said she liked it almost as much as Eugene Speicher's well-known, full-length portrait of her as Candida (Albright-Knox Art Gallery, Buffalo). Another print was offered for sale by the Weyhe Gallery, and one was reproduced in the *Morning Telegraph*.

Arnold was still printing lithographs for Woodstock artists that summer of 1931. One afternoon, two artists who did their own printing, Emil Ganso and Konrad Cramer, came into the shop to see how Arnold was getting on. Cramer said he was planning to make a batch of his own crayons from the recipes in Bolton Brown's recent book *Lithography for Artists* (Chicago, 1930). Brown had done printing for George Bellows, and I was a great admirer of the technical brilliance of Bellows's lithographs, so I told Cramer that I would like to see how the crayons were made.

"Fine," he said, "how about tomorrow afternoon?"

I looked forward to the experiment, hoping it would provide a crayon somewhat smoother than the widely used Korn crayon, which, unless skillfully used, is waxy enough to pick up foreign matter that leaves white specks in the printing. I would have liked something similar to conté crayon that would preserve, as in the lithographs of Toulouse-Lautrec, the feathery lightness of an original drawing. My idea of paradise would be to walk into a shop and draw freely on prepared stones, the way I was told that Lautrec worked. The constraint of tracing on stone, I was beginning to find, affected the quality of the drawing.

The session at Cramer's studio was a little like a fudge party, delicious odors and all. With Brown's manual as our cookbook, we made three types of crayon, ranging from very soft to very hard. Our utensils were a blowtorch and a small iron skillet. The ingredients were lampblack and fragrant yellow carnauba wax. For harder crayon we used more wax. When each batch was ready, we poured it into the flat tins that were then used to pack cigarettes in which strips of tin had been placed vertically at half-inch intervals. When the melted crayon cooled and hardened, the tin strips were easily removed and the sticks of crayon were ready to use.

I made a few lithographs with the Brown crayon, the most successful of them a portrait head of myself, drawn directly on the stone, not traced. Elmer Adler, the noted typographer and printer, director of Pynson Printers, bought a print of the lithograph for his collection of self-portraits of artists, and it appeared in an exhibition at the Whitney Museum of American Art.

For some time I had wanted to do an etched version of my lithograph of Don Becq's dancing class, and it came about in the fall of 1932. My mother had an artist friend, Roselle Oak, who painted and etched. She invited us to tea and asked me to bring some of my lithographs. She was a pleasant, matronly woman who had raised a family of three delightful children and managed to keep a considerable amount of work going.

After she had looked over my prints, I told her about my plans for making an etching, and she offered to help me transfer the drawing to a plate. And at our next meeting she showed me how to apply a liquid ground to the copper plate. The liquid was a bottled substance, brownish in color. Then she smoked the surface with a lighted wax taper.

"Now draw," she said. I traced my drawing on the prepared plate with a very sharp hard pencil, and when I lifted off the paper, I saw my bright copper line showing through the dark smoked surface.

"Funny," I said, "I thought you had to use a needle."

"Everyone does," she explained, "but not for etching. The acid does the biting for you. When you make a drypoint you use a sharp instrument called a burin. No acid." She added, however, that there were other processes, such as aquatint with drypoint, that combine both procedures.

I wanted a light shadow around the figures of the children, and she showed me how to put it on by touching the plate with a small piece of fine sandpaper.

The acid bath was waiting in an enameled pan. Mrs. Oak put on a pair of rubber gloves and put my plate in the bath. We watched it bubble. Then she touched it with a feather to make sure that acid penetrated all the lines of the drawing. When the plate was removed and cleaned with a solvent, I saw that a clean line had bitten through the plate and that the "sandpapering" had come through as a light halftone.

Mrs. Oak suggested that I have the plate steel-faced if I wanted to print a large edition. The steel facing would protect the line and keep it from blurring in subsequent printings. She gave me the address of Charles S. White, an excellent printer, who pulled several prints for me using a light silvery ink.

After the Weyhe Gallery had taken my lithograph of Katharine Cornell, Florence Bufano suggested that I take my prints to J.B. Neumann, the Viennese-born art dealer who was interested in seeing the work of new artists. J.B., as he was called, was a short, stocky man with a large head, quizzical eyebrows, slightly protruding eyes, and the smile of a delighted child. He selected a number of my prints, liking best the one of the llama I had done the day our lithography class went to the circus. Everyone else in the class had drawn acrobats and clowns, but the little animal in the menagerie had appealed to me.

"I cannot buy these," J.B. said, "but I will trade

them for some English eighteenth- and nineteenth-century prints. I'm sure you must be interested in the history of comic art." To my delight, he opened a box full of "tuppence colored, penny plain"* prints by Cruikshank, Dighton, Gillray, and Rowlandson. Here were works by the artists Ralph Barton had told me about, landmarks in the history of caricature, and I was being offered my choice. I tried not to be greedy and made my selection, and J.B. smiled his approval.

Neumann's gallery, the New Art Circle, was a showplace for the works of the German expressionists. There, for the first time, I saw the works of Max Beckmann, Otto Dix, George Grosz, and, most important to me, Paul Klee.

"You see," J.B. said about Klee, "he is more than a painter. He is an inventor. Now you, you should invent more, experiment. Use different media, make some collages! Use your imagination!"

But I was too preoccupied with finding the linear crux of one human being at a time to pay much attention to him. Later, however, I read Klee's *Pedagogical Sketchbook* and found his philosophy too obscure to understand. Nevertheless, if Klee's words were beyond me, I understood his works, which, in both scale and substance, are akin to caricature. And I shared his love of masks. I believe him to be one of the world's great artists.

*Also expressed as "penny plain, tuppence colored," this had no reference to the color of the coins themselves. Rather, the meaning had to do with the price of the print: if you wanted it plain, it cost a penny; but if you wanted it colored, it cost a tuppence.

The Mahatma

During the summer of 1932, I was in Woodstock again, painting in oil, doing lithographs, and drawing caricatures of some of the artists who lived or spent their summers there. Several of the caricatures found their way into *Creative Art*'s gossip column, written by Walter Gutman, who also wrote skillful articles on artists, became a painter himself, and edited a successful newsletter for an investment house. He was known as the Proust of Wall Street. Walter thought I had enough caricatures of artists, musicians, and other celebrities to make up a small exhibition, and he suggested that I show my work to Pegeen Sullivan, who was in charge of prints and drawings at the Macbeth Gallery.

Pegeen was a black-haired Irish beauty with a lilting voice. Walter claimed she knew more about graphic art than almost anyone else in the business. After she looked over the contents of my portfolio and brought them to Robert McIntyre, the director of the gallery, it was decided that a show of my work was to open the new street-floor annex of the gallery on East Fifty-seventh Street in the spring of 1933.

"You ought to do Henry McBride, the art critic of the *Sun*," Pegeen suggested, "and little Louis."

When I asked her who was little Louis, she said, "Louis Eilshemius, an old painter. He was knocked down by a taxi and he can't walk. He loves company. All the artists go to see him, and I'm sure he'd love to pose for you. Tell him you're having a show at Macbeth's and that I sent you."

Aline Fruhauf

Before his accident Louis Michel Eilshemius, an elderly, eccentric painter, had been the scourge of the galleries he visited. It was said that if a painting offended him enough he spat on it. If, on the other hand, it pleased him and if there were spectators present, he would go into a little dance. Henry McBride was one of the first of a small group of Eilshemius enthusiasts and kept him in the public's eye by publishing his letters in the *New York Sun*. The letters were written on stationery with the heading,

> *Mahatma. Dr. Louis M. Eilshemius, M.A., etc.*
> *Mightiest Mind and Wonder of the Worlds.*
> *Supreme Parnassian and Grand Transcendant*
> *Eagle of Art.*

Eilshemius was born in 1864 at Laurel Hill Manor, near Newark, New Jersey. The son of a wealthy Dutch importer, he was well educated, widely traveled, and had an academic training in art, abroad as well as in New York at the Art Students League. He painted in obscurity until he was discovered by Marcel Duchamp at the first exhibition of the Society of Independent Artists in 1917. In 1920, the Société Anonyme, founded by Duchamp, Katherine Dreier, and Man Ray, mounted the first one-man exhibition of his work. Subsequent exhibitions at New York's Valentine Gallery in 1926 and 1932 stimulated interest in the artist and resulted in feature stories in national magazines and the daily press. The paintings ranged from jewel-like watercolors and oils of poetic sunlit landscapes to dark, nightmarish pictures of duelists or of seminude females in which the predominant colors were a sooty Prussian blue and mustard yellow. A good number of

137

the smaller oils were on cardboard, and sometimes the artist surrounded them with "self–frames"* of mustard and gamboge accented with baroque curlicues.

Now that the artist was housebound, astute collectors were picking up his work, more often than not in a literal sense. The domestic who kept house for him and his brother never knew whether or not the painting under the arm of a departing visitor had been purchased or stolen. Half expecting to be viewed with suspicion when I called, I went to see the self-styled Mahatma early one afternoon. A short, plump woman with drab brown hair dragged into a topknot came to the door and eyed me with distrust.

"Who iss?" she asked sharply. Light from the street glinted on her tiny earrings. They were like the ones worn by the Slavic girls who came to our kitchen to attend Kati's soirees. I thought perhaps the woman would feel more kindly toward me if I spoke her own language, so, taking a wild guess as to what that might be, I summoned up the little Czech I remembered and wished her good-day.

"*Dobra Rana*," I said, making the *r*'s sound as sharp as blades of grass. The plain face lit up with a smile. I had guessed right. I said I had come to see Mr. Eilshemius, and she announced me by shouting upstairs, "Mr. Eilshemius-s-s! is somebody. A lady!"

The smell of the old house, a bouquet of long-departed pot roasts, unaired rooms, and gas, permeated the hall and carpet. A flickering feather of gas flame from one jet barely illuminated the stairway. The wallpaper was as dark as old leather.

From the landing I could see the artist's room. It was drab and cluttered with Victorian furniture. A marble mantel was stacked with unframed pic-

---

*Frames drawn or painted on the same material (paper or canvas) that the drawing or painting is on.

tures. A tiny, white-bearded man sat in a chair, his back to the window. He was babbling and shouting to himself but stopped when he saw me. Peering at me curiously, he said, "Don't touch me!" He unfolded his small, clawlike hands until they were parallel and shook them in a frenzied spasm.

"I had a terrible accident," he said. "A taxi ran over me. My leg got caught in the wheel. Round and round it went in the wheel. I'm in terrible pain. No one comes. Can't go anywhere, can't walk. Who are you?"

He brightened when I told him that I was a friend of Pegeen's and that she had suggested my doing his caricature for my show at Macbeth's.

Eilshemius's face had a childlike quality, a mixture of innocence and mischief. His faded blue eyes were alert and twinkling under dome-shaped lids that bore the faintest vestige of lashes, like a line drawn with a hard pencil. His nose was small and delicately arched; the nostrils were sharply cut and flared daintily. On his lap was an infant's receiving blanket, pale blue, patterned with little white rabbits. A nearby table held a fountain pen, some of the Mahatma stationery, and a glass of orange juice that looked as if it had been standing a long time. I made a few sketches, and then, fearing to tire him, I left, telling him I would be back.

During subsequent sittings, my subject held forth with a good deal of megalomaniac bombast. He was the world's greatest painter, composer, poet, and actor. He railed against "Picasso-basso" and the "Schmier of van Gogh," and then quite suddenly, he switched to a calm and rational manner of speaking. He was interested in the progress of the caricature, asked me who else I had done lately, and perked up when I told him his friend Henry McBride had posed for me. When I told him I had trouble drawing a dancer until I posed myself in front of a long mirror in just the right stance, his eyes lighted up. "That's what I used to do," he said. "And oh! how I used to dance."

Sometimes we spoke in French, and his personality would change again. He became relaxed, debonair, and witty. In his Gallic phase, he told me he enjoyed the company of attractive women and asked me to bring some of my better-looking friends in to see him. I brought Quaintance Eaton, Irma Selz, and the actress Blanche Yurka at different times. Usually he responded to the visitors with delight, but one day his mood was black. Hunched in his chair with wads of newspaper stuffed in his shirt, he complained of the cold and said his brother was keeping him a prisoner. Although this could hardly be construed as the truth, there had been, and still was, considerable antagonism between the brothers. Henry had long disapproved of as well as envied his brother's talent, his way with the ladies, and the fame that had brought scores of callers to pay homage to Louis. Once I caught a glimpse of Henry, a tall, red-faced man with snow-white hair and moustache. He looked in on us briefly, glowered, then stamped down the stairs muttering, "Goddam girls!" at every step until he reached the door. Louis pretended not to hear him but picked up his fountain pen and began doodling bathers by a waterfall on his Mahatma stationery.

The brothers, once wealthy, had little left but the house. Henry had an office downtown where supposedly he looked after the family finances. Louis was the actual breadwinner of the two. He sold his paintings to dealers and collectors. In an effort to display the jewels in appropriate settings, one gallery director went so far as to introduce a special Eilshemius frame, a heavy molding of greenish gold with simulated flyspecks tastefully applied.

Between two of the sittings, I sprained my ankle. During the recovery period, a letter from Louis, denouncing artists who painted nudes in unromantic interiors, appeared in Henry McBride's column. I wrote to Louis explaining why I couldn't come to draw and congratulating him on his fine

Aline Fruhauf

"Idyllium," pen sketch by Louis Eilshemius, opening letter to Aline Fruhauf, 1934.

letter in the *Sun*. His reply, on Mahatma stationery, was a pen-and-ink sketch of a nude, seated on a rock in a wooded landscape, enclosed in a doodled self-frame and labeled "Idyllium" (now in the Archives of American Art). Beneath the sketch, he wrote,

Dear Miss Fruhauf, Glad you enjoyed my letter anent nudes. Yes, I hate to see any in Kitchen chairs. I hope the other artists will take my hint to heart. The "Nymphs" reproduced in March Cre[ative] Art shows what I mean. Out of doors! Sorry you met with accident. I hope you are nearly O.K. by now. Will appreciate your

141

*visit on some coming day cette semaine. Au
plaisir und Auf Wiedersehen, Sincerely,
Louis M. Eilshemius.*

For the last sitting, Louis was comparatively
dressed up. He wore a jacket, and his tie, a gift
from one of his artist friends, was gray and violet
raw silk. The caricature was included in the exhibition at Macbeth's in the spring, and the following
year, it illustrated Harry Salpeter's article on
Eilshemius in *Esquire*, October 1934. Since I am
always somewhat apprehensive of my subjects'
reactions to my work and was especially so in this
case, I wrote Louis that it was to be used with the
article and that I hoped it wouldn't spoil our
friendship. He replied,

> *My dear Aline (Mrs. Vollmer), Greetings to you
> also. Glad your caricature of me will appear in
> Mguesine* [sic]. *Our friend Salpeter is to be con-
> gratulated for his success! Eh! sister, we'll be
> friends in spite of the caricature. My brother liked
> it at the time of Exhibit. All these six weeks or
> more I've been alone no visitors & I'm near
> raving & near collapse. And my pain is awful.
> Have new affair since 3 weeks ago, causing my
> being seated excruciating pain. No remedy—
> permanent. Right in my fame, I cannot enjoy it—
> can't move my body etc. C'est l'enfer—
> Höllenquälen! Au revoir Aline, Soon,
> Louis M. Eilshemius.*
> *P.S. After writing I made 3 line drawings. Well
> they were fine. You must have inspired better
> designs. Artists need* artists *to help them.
> Greetings to your hubby.*

When the drawing and article appeared, I brought
him a copy of *Esquire,* and he seemed pleased with
both works. He pointed to a stack of paintings on a
table in front of the fireplace and said, "See that
pile of pictures? Take any one you like." I selected
a charming summer landscape, eight inches
square, painted on my old favorite support,

Aline Fruhauf

Louis Eilshemius in *Esquire*, 1934. "Eh! sister, we'll be friends in spite of the caricature. My brother liked it at the time of Exhibit"—Eilshemius to Aline in the "Idyllium" letter.

shirtboard. When I got it home, I noticed a few brown spots that may have been tobacco juice; they came off easily with a little moistened cotton. Without further cleaning, I took it to be framed.

Shortly after my marriage in 1934, I brought my husband, Erwin Vollmer, to meet the artist. Greeting us with enthusiasm, Eilshemius said he wanted to give us a wedding present. It was a copy of some of his privately published piano pieces: "Six Musical Moods," which he inscribed "Wedding Bells for Aline Vollmer best wishes Louis Eilshemius 1934."

We moved out of New York for a while, then back to an apartment at 38 Grove Street in Green-

Making Faces

wich Village. Erwin was teaching biology at New York University. Our first daughter, Susan, was born on Christmas Eve, 1938. I didn't see Eilshemius again until a few days before his death in 1941.

One afternoon, the phone rang. It was our friend Dr. S. Theodore Weiss, then chief of the psychiatric ward at Bellevue Hospital, who called to tell me that Louis had been brought to the hospital. Henry Eilshemius had died two years ago, and whoever had been in attendance had deserted the younger brother, leaving him alone in the house. The people in the adjacent brownstone heard the old man screaming and banging on the wall. They called the police, who sent an ambulance, and, raving, starving, and half-frozen, Louis was taken to Bellevue and placed in the psychiatric ward.

"He couldn't have stood up if he'd tried," Dr. Weiss said. "The X-rays showed that the head of the femur, fractured at the time of his accident, had completed eroded. He has pneumonia. I put him in a private room. He can't last much longer, three, four days maybe, but I think he'd like to see you. Can you come down?"

When I got out of the elevator at the hospital, a pair of hooting orderlies were skipping down the corridor at top speed, wheeling between them a mercifully empty stretcher. When I asked them where the room was, they called out shrill directions as they sped past. I found the room, the door was open. Louis was propped up in bed, a shawl over his shoulders and a little pointed cap on his head. Despite extreme emaciation, his face still held its delicate charm. Forain could have made a beautiful drawing of him now. Gone were the quick, jerky movements and the boasting spiel. His eyes were as tranquil as an infant's.

"Bonjour Monsieur Eilshemius," I said, "do you remember me?"

"Bonjour," he answered, "yes, I remember you." I told him that Dr. Weiss had let me know he was here. He nodded. I wondered what I could say

144

to him, what would interest him without tiring him. I looked out the window at the cheerless street; against a background of dusty brick and cement, a few large snowflakes drifted down. I watched Louis silently for a few moments and said, "We have a little girl now, her name is Susie. She's just three years old. Someone is staying with her, but I'll have to leave soon."

He stared straight ahead, then looked at me, it seemed a long time. His voice was very gentle as he said, "You'd better go back to your baby, Aline. Good-bye." He died a few days later, December 29, 1941.

As soon as the news of his death became known, the price of his paintings began to soar. I went to see Pegeen.

"Let's go see some of the dealers," she said. "Maybe we can raise some money so little Louis won't have to have a pauper's burial." We went out on Fifty-seventh Street to fulfill our mission, but everywhere we went we were met with shrugs and flat refusals. It turned out, however, that relatives arranged a proper burial in Brooklyn's Greenwood Cemetery, and many of New York's most prominent artists paid him homage.

Twenty years later, when we were living in the Maryland suburbs of Washington, our little painting by Eilshemius, still one of our most cherished possessions, had never been cleaned and needed it badly. Knowing the risks involved in careless or improper methods of restoring oil paintings, I called on two old friends, Russell and Eleanor Quandt, for help. Russell, one of the finest restorers in the country, worked for the Corcoran Gallery of Art in Washington and the Abby Aldrich Rockefeller Collection in Williamsburg, and Eleanor, who helped him in research, was before their marriage the curator of American art at the Corcoran. Russell examined the painting under a high-powered microscope.

"There's no cracking, see for yourself," he said,

moving aside for me to look. Under the lens, the surface was furrowed like a ploughed field. He dipped a swab of cotton into a wax cleaning mixture and applied it to a small section of the painting; then he cleaned off the area with another swab moistened with mineral spirits. The cotton showed dark gray.

"Dirt," he said, "and smoke, maybe. No color is coming off. It's safe. The yellowish film is old varnish." Taking a third swab, he dipped it into pure isopropyl alcohol and wiped the same area. The alcohol dissolved the varnish, disclosing fresh clear color underneath. Russell gave me the name of the cleaning mixture and told me to follow the same procedure, working on only a small area at a time.

"Should I varnish the picture?" I asked.

"You can if you like," he said. "If you do, use the crystal clear varnish that comes in a spray can. It contains the same methacrylic resin I use to make my varnish."

When I took the picture out of its frame, I was glad to see that the framer had glued the shirtboard to a heavier support. As the cleaning process proceeded, the painting began to glow. It was as if I were seeing it for the first time. Against the pale cerulean sky, flecked with creamy clouds, a hawk wheels over a cliff crested with a feather of black pine. The red earth of the foreground is brushed with a delicate tapestry of ochre, gray-green, and cobalt blue. In the middle distance, a yellow-gray strip of sunlit river is bordered with misty blue-green palisades, and just behind them lie cool hills of a pale ultramarine. Near the lower corner, far left, in an area of gray turquoise, is a spired church, picked out in a minute impasto of gold ochre and whitened cobalt blue.

Ready for the final step, I put the painting on spread newspapers and sprayed on the varnish. Under the sheet of shining liquid the landscape shimmered for an instant, and the black feather of pine appeared to move as if touched by a light

breeze. I brushed away excess varnish with the
side of my hand and, when the picture was dry, I
put it back in its frame and hung it on the wall. It
was like a view from the window of a tower, very
early on a midsummer's morning. To assure its
preservation, I eventually gave it to the Phillips
Collection in Washington.

Aline Fruhauf

The sitting with Henry McBride took place in the
uncompromisingly public atmosphere of the lobby
of his midtown hotel, just west of Herald Square.
McBride was a tall, courtly man with white hair, an
oblong head, pendulous cheeks, a prim mouth,
and round blue eyes that combined a look of innocence and great caution. We sat near a window in
full view of passersby, inside and out. The session
was a pleasant one. But I found on reviewing my
notes at home that, although I had gotten his look
and his features, I was way off on proportions. I
told him of my difficulty, asked for, and received
the favor of another short sitting.

When we were once again comfortably settled in
our chairs in the hotel lobby, McBride complimented me on the probity of my approach to
caricature and hinted, with a twinkle, that other
artists who had done him were not so conscientious.

The finished product, like the brief contredanse
we had engaged in, had a polite elegance. Walter
Gutman published it in the December 1932 issue of
Creative Art, and the following March, it was, of
course, included in the exhibition at Macbeth's.
But early in the afternoon of the day the exhibition
opened, it mysteriously disappeared from the wall
near the window where it was visible from the
street. Pegeen, who had hung the show, was
distraught. Wringing her hands and moaning
softly when I came in, she turned to me and said,
"Aline-y, I just can't understand it. It was right
here," pointing to the empty space, "and then

Henry McBride in *Creative
Art*, December 1932.

147

ALINE
FRUHAUF

Harpo Marx in the *New York Evening Post*, 1929.

suddenly it was gone. What shall we say to Henry, if he comes in?"

"Don't worry," I said, "I kept a tracing. I'll go home, make another drawing, and bring it back in time for the opening."

It took me less than an hour, and when I rushed back into the gallery, triumphantly holding the new drawing, the staff cheered, and the show went on. The exhibition was a success. A lady came in and bought three caricatures at a clip: Jascha Heifetz in his Russian blouse with the red cross-stitching, Harpo Marx with flaming red hair, and Angna Enters in *Delsarte: With a Not Too Classical Nod to the Greeks* in a white costume with pale blue ribbons at the shoulders.

As for Henry, I was told that on his weekly rounds of the art galleries he took every opportunity to stop in front of Macbeth's window. After cautiously looking up and down the street to make sure no one was watching him, he adjusted his glasses and gazed at his picture long and searchingly, and then walked on. The caricature is also now in the Phillips Collection.

A Legal Twist

In the spring of 1934, Erwin and I were living in a one-and-a-half-room apartment on Jones Street across from the Walter Gutmans. I had accumulated enough caricatures of artists, dancers, and musicians to make up another show at Macbeth's. Pegeen told me that "Papa" Kelekian had been in to see it, liked what he saw, wanted me to do a caricature of him to add to his collection of likenesses of himself, and would be in the gallery the next afternoon. It was a command performance. Dikran Kelekian's own gallery was a sumptuous place, a treasure house for museums and lordly collectors, full of such antiquities as Genoese velvets, Flemish tapestries, fifth-century Coptic textile fragments reverently mounted on linen and framed under glass, Egyptian mummy portraits, and an occasional sarcophagus.

Kelekian's way of life was as luxurious and exciting as his exhibition rooms. He kept racehorses in Paris, and such well-known artists at Mary Cassatt and John Singer Sargent had been his friends. He had owned paintings by Courbet and Corot, Daumier, Delacroix, and Degas, Seurat and Cézanne, and he had encouraged and bought the works of such promising fledglings as Derain, Matisse, Picasso, and Rouault.

149

Pegeen introduced me. He was a tall, heavy man, who looked like a pasha who had momentarily forsaken his everyday cloth of gold for a London-tailored business suit. The color of *crème brulée* on the inside, he was solemn, stately, and bald, with a snow-white beard and moustache, and eyes like great Greek olives. A glittering watch chain traversed his waistcoat like the Super Chief crossing the Western plains at dusk.

Kelekian dwarfed the little gallery. When I backed away from him to get a better view, I bumped into my caricatures on the opposite wall. He returned my artist-to-subject scrutiny with a look of total appraisal. Then he reached into his pocket and took out a string of old amber worry beads and fingered them with slow, methodical clicks, a nerve-shattering obbligato to the worldly axioms he delivered in a voice that rumbled gently like far-off thunder.

"So (*click*), you are married (*click, click*). Marry someone (*click, click, click*)." Hardly suitable advice to a young bride, I thought. I plunged ahead with pencil and paper making one terrible drawing after another. After a while, the clicks accelerated. My model was growing impatient, so I called a halt to the sitting.

I worked and worked, and after several weeks of repeated failure I realized that Dikran Kelekian was one of the impossibles. I told Pegeen I was ready to give up, but she wouldn't hear of it.

"Papa will be disappointed," she said. "Besides, he's a very important figure in the art world and you should be represented in his collection."

I took the best of my drawings, colored it with opaque watercolor, and illuminated the Super Chief watch chain with "Oenslager gold." The finished picture looked like a Rajput portrait with a wry twist. Kelekian was silent when he looked at it, and his Greek-olive eyes were sorrowful as he wrote out my check. When I saw Pegeen again, I said I didn't think Kelekian liked the picture. She told me that "Papa" had indeed been wounded, but not for the usual reasons. "He expected a caricature," she said, "and you gave him a portrait."

Shortly after the second exhibition at Macbeth's, which was held in March of 1934, Berthold Neuer, the manager of the Knabe Piano Company on West Fifty-seventh Street, asked me to leave some caricatures of composers for display in his show window. "It might lead to something," he said. "Who knows? Someone might come in to look at a piano and end up by buying one of your caricatures." It seemed like a good idea. The Great Depression was at its height; the newspaper market for art work, with the exception of the *New York Times* and the *Tribune*, was practically nonexistent; and the demand for caricatures was at an all-time low. I bundled up some little drawings of Prokofiev, Ravel, and Schoenberg and left them with Neuer, who put them in the window to share honors with a concert grand.

A few days later, Neuer asked me to call Irving Wechsler, who operated a small gallery in Putnam's bookstore on Forty-eighth Street. "I like your drawings," Wechsler said. "Could you come in to the shop? I have an idea that I think might interest you."

I found him to be a most pleasant gentleman with pepper-and-salt hair and moustache and a matching tweed suit.

"I sell old prints," he said. "Most of my clients are lawyers. They have very little on their office walls but their diplomas and some nineteenth-century caricatures of English barristers by Ape and Spy. I think it's time somebody caricatured a few local judges, and if you would be interested in doing some on a speculative basis I could arrange for your drawings to be reproduced by a new offset process, called photo-gelatin. It's a very true reproduction. I'm sure we could sell the prints."

I told Wechsler I would let him know, and I discussed the project with my husband and with Reyner Samet, a young attorney who had recently

Frederick Crane, Chief Judge
of the New York Court of
Appeals, 1936.

married my cousin Carolyn. Both thought it was a
good idea, and Reyner gave me the names of six
New York judges well known to local lawyers.

I first wrote to Judge Frederick Crane, telling
him of my project and asking if he would pose for
me. He replied that he would let me know next

152

Judge Edward R. Finch, 1936.

time he would be coming down from Albany. He
posed in his chambers and wore his robe for the
occasion. He was an agreeable little man who
looked somewhat like the duchess's baby in *Alice
in Wonderland*.

With the first caricature well under way, I had a

key name—he had just been unanimously elected chief judge of the New York Court of Appeals—to drop in my letter-writing campaign. The next subject was Judge Frederic Kernochan, who let me draw him while the Criminal Court was in session. As the business of the court proceeded, he peered over his glasses and thoughtfully stroked his chin. He had the look of a handsome bulldog who had by some means or other come by rosy cheeks and a thick thatch of chestnut hair.

Judge Edward R. Finch was a lean pink-and-white aristocrat. He also posed in his robe in chambers. The robe fell in stiff metallic folds like those in the paintings by El Greco. His chair was high-backed and intricately carved. Rather than wasting valuable time in taking notes on the detail of the chair, I used a photograph of a seventeenth-century chair in a book on old furniture I had at home.

The Honorable James A. Foley let me come to Surrogate's Court to sketch. He was a solemn man with enormous hands, which he rubbed together. Behind him was a lushly carved figure of Justice, a sharp contrast to the austere figure on the bench.

Next, I visited the Appellate Court on Madison Square, where the presiding judge was a pale, smooth-faced, white-haired gentleman named Francis X. Martin. As soon as I was seated, a pair of guards hurried to my seat.

"This is the Appellate Division, Miss," whispered the first guard in a thick brogue.

"And there are no women allowed in here, ever," said the second.

I told them that I had obtained permission to draw the judge but that, since I didn't want to break any law, I would go quietly.

I called the judge's office; his secretary apologized for the slipup and told me that the guards would be informed the next time I came in. And when I went back they gave me a whispered welcome and warm smiles. After finishing my notes, I went to the door, and they stopped me

again. This time they wanted to see what I had
done. I told them I never showed anyone unfinished work, but they looked so unhappy that I
handed over the notebook. Together they studied
it very seriously, then handed it back in silence.

"Well?" I ventured.

"No comment," said the first guard.

"And I adhere to that," said the second.

The day I went to draw Judge Peter Schmuck
was cold and dreary. Rain, snow, and sleet pelted
from a pewter sky. Dressed for the weather, I came
to court early, as had the apple-cheeked judge. He
was seated on the bench looking over some papers,
and when he looked up and saw me, he nodded
briefly and went on with his reading. I found an
area with many empty chairs and thought how
nice it was to have so much room to spread out. I
put my umbrella and gloves on one chair, my hat
and coat on another, and by the time I had taken
the sketchbook from my briefcase, found a pencil,
put on my glasses, put the glasses case back in my
handbag, laid it down and removed my jacket, I
had used up three chairs and was sitting on a
fourth. Meanwhile, the judge had stopped reading
and was watching my preparations with interest.
When I was finally settled and had my pencil
poised to draw him, Judge Schmuck cleared his
throat and said, "Ah, you're sitting in the jury box.
But don't move. They can sit over there." A moment later, the jury filed in looking a little surprised
as the judge motioned them, one by one, to the
other side of the courtroom.

For the series, I used the watercolor technique
borrowed from Ralph Barton: Winsor and Newton's ivory black with a little vandyke brown.
Wechsler was pleased with the set and quoted a
line from Robert Burns's ode to an earlier
caricaturist, Sir Francis Grose: "A chiel's among ye
takin' notes."

"I've got another idea," he said. "A nice addition
to the series would be one of the United States
Supreme Court. You wouldn't have to go to

SUE

The Nine Old Men—The
United States Supreme Court
in 1936.

Washington; for one thing, they wouldn't let you
into the courtroom. No one is permitted to carry so
much as a pencil in there. You could work from a
photograph."

I agreed to give it a try and went to the New York
Public Library in search of a group photograph.
The chief of the Picture Collection, Romana Javitz,
a slender pale lady with the impassive, symmetrical
features and fluid lines of a porcelain Kwan-Yin
(goddess of mercy), found me a picture of the nine
sages. "Take it home and bring it back in four
days," she said.

This was the conservative Court inherited by the
Roosevelt administration when it took office the
year before, 1933, which was to frustrate many
New Deal economic recovery programs. I contemplated the faces of the nine old men and found
two that seemed vaguely familiar. Justice Louis D.
Brandeis bore a structural resemblance to Remo
Bufano, and Justice George Sutherland reminded
me a little of my Grandpa Fruhauf. When I finished

156

the group caricature, these two turned out to be
the best; at least, Justice Benjamin Cardozo, who
knew all the faces well, thought so. His cousin
Walter Hirsch, a New York attorney, bought a
print for him and sent me a copy of the letter
Cardozo sent in acknowledgment:

> *The picture is a "scream." Brandeis and*
> *Sutherland are, I think, the best. One never*
> *finds a caricature of oneself wholly satisfactory,*
> *yet the one of me isn't bad.*

The drawings were ready for the printer, but one
detail worried Wechsler.

"If you sign your right name," he said, "you
might be tracked down, hauled into court, and
sued for libel. It has happened in England. And
Daumier's caricature of Louis Philippe sent him to
jail for six months. I wouldn't like that to happen to
you. Couldn't you think of a nice short name like
Ape or Spy to put in one corner?"

I had not expected to go underground, but I was
willing to oblige. The most obvious *nom de pinceau* I
could think of was Sue. Not only was it a word
generally associated with the courtroom, but it
indicated the sex of the artist, as well. If I had to be
anonymous, I at least wanted everyone to know I
was a woman. I penciled in my alias only to find,
after the justices had been printed, that under
American law caricatures are not considered
grounds for libel. It was, of course, too late for
erasure, and I had a lot of explaining to do over the
years.

The prints were delivered to the gallery, but they
didn't sell. The depression was still upon us like a
black and lowering cloud, a time of breadlines, of
apple sellers, and of homeless men who built
shanties—Hoovervilles, they called them—by the
railroad tracks below Riverside Drive and in Central Park. I thought of the prints lying idle under
the counter at Putnam's and called Wechsler to say
I'd like to take a crack at selling them to New York

lawyers myself. We made an agreeable transaction and parted good friends.

My first customer was Philip Wittenberg, a well-known attorney and internationally famous authority on copyright and literary law, who liked pictures and collected them. He was an arresting figure, squarely built with a handsome head like an Etruscan terra cotta. His narrow blue eyes were both shrewd and sympathetic. He had a strong sense of the theatrical and a sharp wit. From the way he was looking at the prints, I could tell he was enjoying them.

"The New York judges are the best," he said, "but you'll sell more of the Supreme Court. What are you calling it?"

"*Baseball Team*," I said. "Nine men in uniform." After taking a complete set for his office, Wittenberg swiveled over to his phone and began calling up his friends, telling them of a new product that had just come on the market. The result was phenomenal. For two months I sold the prints to clients who ranged from young attorneys just starting their practice to older members of well-established firms who had at one time or another appeared before at least one of the six dignitaries. I was supplying a real demand, and it was a wonderful feeling. And everyone wanted a copy of the The *Baseball Team*.

The first day's haul bought a black leather carrying case, as large as a portfolio but as businesslike as a briefcase, and a black tweed jacket, a suede beret, and a white neckerchief. The costume was ever so slightly reminiscent of the garb of a Daumier *avocat*, but not enough so to be obvious—at least, no one ever mentioned it.

One day, like a balloon too long afloat, the selling spree came to a sudden and abrupt end. While waiting for an elevator in a Wall Street building honeycombed with law offices, I was stopped by a grim-looking charwoman armed with mop and pail. She might have stepped out of one of George Price's seamier cartoons in the *New*

Yorker. She looked at my beautiful portfolio-briefcase.

"Where's your peddler's license?" she sang out in E flat. I shook my head in complete surprise and said I didn't have one.

"I'll call the police!" she squealed. Her voice, in an eerie glissando, left E flat and assumed the piercing quality of a municipal siren. Brandishing her mop, she started after me. I turned and ran, spied an exit door, took to the stairs, and kept on going at a steady pace and never looked back.

On the journey down, some twenty-seven flights, I mused on the circumstances that had made me a fugitive from justice, actual or poetic. Could the law, unable to prosecute me for making funny pictures of its judges, finally get me on a charge of selling them without a license? If the charwoman and her corps of New York's Finest caught me on the next landing, could I get by with a small fine? And, were I found guilty of Heaven knew what felony, which of my up-to-now amiable lawyer clients could I call on to defend me? I had just about decided on Wittenberg when I found I had reached the ground floor, the lobby, the sunlit street, and safety.

After that encounter, something had gone out of the campaign, possibly because something had gone out of the campaigner. Nevertheless, I wrote some letters and sold sets of the prints to the law libraries of Duke, Harvard, and Yale universities.

In 1950, a chance visit to a Washington antique shop revived the sale of the prints and resulted in a warm friendship with the owner, Mary Gillis Skee. She was a spare, dynamic woman with flashing black eyes and a crisp manner. A magazine article about Washington dealers had dubbed her "the Red Queen of Georgetown." A former employee of the National Archives, she had an extraordinary memory and could reel off dates and whole portions of treatises as well as excerpts from letters of statesmen and the military. Of herself and her shop, she said,

I sell history and nostalgia. There are two kinds of antique shops, those with well-waxed furniture, polished brass and copper, orderly rows of china and glass, and mine. On the whole, I think my kind's better. People like to look around and discover things for themselves.

She had a way of making her antiques look even older. "Very simple," she said. "I just rub on a little dirt." A self-educated, native Washingtonian, she had great respect for the English language and knew how to use it with relish for the unhackneyed phrase. I saw her in action many times, once in public. She was being interviewed in the early days of television by a not-too-bright announcer. "Mrs. Skee," he asked, "how come you know so many big words?" She flashed him a look, took a deep breath, counted to ten, smiled sweetly, and said, "One of the privileges of being educated is the ability to use the dictionary."

My first entrance into her shop was announced by a mighty jangling of sleigh bells, which festooned the door. When the tumult subsided, she asked me if there was anything in particular I wanted. I answered with the old wandering shopper's cliché that I was just looking. I scanned the crowded shelves, tables, and chests, all laden with blue-and-white china, copper molds, old clocks, glass decanters, and other staples of the trade. Just beyond a small grove of brass candlesticks and some blue-and-orange Imari plates stood a specially built cabinet with a lift-down cover. It was full of old prints.

"I did some caricatures of judges in the thirties," I ventured to say. "I still have some of the reproductions."

"Bring them in," she suggested. "They're just the sort of thing I like to sell."

The next day I brought her a set, but she took only the print of the Supreme Court, which she thought would have a wider appeal in Washington than the individual caricatures of the New York judges, and we changed its title to *The Nine Old Men*, the popular reference to that particular Court. She taped one of the prints to the door where, yellowed by the strong sunlight and a little antique-shop dirt, it became an old print long before its time.

I was never fortunate enough to be in the shop when she was selling the print, but a mutual friend told me she had watched her on several occasions.

"Mary spread out her fingers," according to my friend, "pressed them on the table, leaned forward, and faced her customer. Then it was as if all the channels of her salesmanship were open, sweeping it through her person. To her the print was a kind of universal solvent, and everyone must have one, regardless of race, creed, or previous condition of servitude."

And Mary Skee sold and sold *The Nine Old Men* until she closed her shop forever.

Aline Fruhauf

Artists at Work

T he depression-born Federal Art Project of the 1930s has only recently been recognized as an important chapter in the history of American art. Not only did it provide the financial assistance much needed by artists, but—together with its sister projects for performing artists and writers, all under the Works Progress Administration—it also met most of the cultural needs and demands of the nation. Its meaning to the individuals it served, both artists and laymen, can only be measured by their individual testimonies.

To me, joining the Graphic Arts Division of the project meant that I could continue and develop my work as a lithographer. But more important was the fact that after working hours in the graphics workshop, I could meet with the other artists, sharing our tables, posing for one another, exchanging the fruits of our creative efforts, and discussing our technical problems. Friendships developed that lasted long after the project had ceased. The stimulus was there for me to begin my series, *Artists at Work*.

The first in the series was a lithograph of the distinguished dancer and choreographer Martha Graham. I had drawn her before, a hard-edged, full-length caricature for *Theatre Arts*, May 1930, that was also used in 1934 as the cover of the *Dance Observer*, the magazine founded and edited by her musical director, Louis Horst.

The setting for the lithograph was made to order for a black-and-white study: pale walls and drapes, a white porcelain vase on a black step stool, sharply patterned Navajo rugs, students in leotards of black and gray, and Martha herself in a broadly striped robe, her raven hair drawn back in a snood from her taut white face. Comic relief was supplied by Maedel, her black satin-skinned dachshund, who skittered about on the polished floor.

The next print in the series was of William Zorach, the sculptor, a man as monumental as his work. I drew him in his studio, posed in front of a bas-relief of dark wood, as he chipped away at one of his smaller works, a seated white marble cat.

I worked on the project from March to December 1936. After leaving it, I decided to go on with the series of artists and made a watercolor version of the Zorach, showing him in his red smock. I took it to show to Herman Baron, who ran the ACA Gallery on West Eighth Street. He liked the drawing.

"If you do some more artists, I can give you a show in March," he said.

We sat down together and made out a list of fourteen American artists, myself included. This was in October 1937, so there was time enough to do the work.

My husband was teaching biology at New York University in Washington Square, and we were living nearby on Grove Street, within walking distance of most of the studios of the artists on the list. After laying in a supply of paper, watercolors, and brushes, I began calling my prospective sitters for appointments.

The artists' studios, like Robert Edmond Jones's living room, reflected their tastes and personalities. Their paintings and the sundry bibelots they collected complemented one another. Lucile

William Zorach, Sculptor, by
Aline Fruhauf, 1937.

Aline Fruhauf, by William
Zorach, 1936.

Blanch's silver Persian, Miranda, had both the
color and texture of her mistress's hair, and Lucile's
house slippers repeated the rich rose-madder hue
of the cranberry glass spoon holder on the mantel,
a color that reappeared as an accent in her favorite
picture, a gouache she had made of a family of
acrobats while she was visiting the winter quarters
of John Ringling North's circus in Sarasota, Florida.

Across the hall from the Blanches—Lucile was
married to the artist Arnold Blanch—was the
apartment and studio of Stuart Davis and his
handsome wife, Roselle, who looked like Picasso's
studies of Fernande Olivier. Stuart, who was a jazz
enthusiast and whose paintings have been described as a kind of visual jazz, had studied with
Robert Henri and had done covers for *The Masses*
when he was nineteen. He exhibited in the famous
Armory Show of 1913. During the days of the
WPA, he was active in the American Artists' Congress and the Artists' Union, and he edited the
union's paper, *Art Front*.

Aline Fruhauf

Stuart Davis, 1937.

I made some drawings of him while he was sitting on the platform at one of the meetings of the congress, and when I entered his studio to draw him in his milieu, I was impressed by the orderly arrangement of the Petri dishes he used for his colors, of the little bouquet of brushes in a red jug, and by the general tidiness and beautiful use of the space he occupied. Like the brilliant abstract paintings on the wall, Stuart was immaculate, hard-edged, and dynamic. He was stockily built and of medium height, with a white, indoors complexion. He was strictly a city man and proud of it. His smooth, dark brown hair was combed straight back. He had a short neck, a blunt nose, and a large mouth with a prominent lower lip, which, at the time, was resolutely clamped on a little bulldog pipe. His brown gaze was sharp and alert, as if fixed on a target.

Just before I left the studio, I noticed a pile of little drawings on the top of a cabinet. They were abstract shapes, working drawings for parts of

165

Yasuo Kuniyoshi, 1937.

paintings to be assembled later. Each of his paintings was carefully conceived, and the last operation
was the joyful application of color.

Much of the painting by the Woodstock artists in
the early thirties was limited to landscapes of the
surrounding countryside. But when the artists
turned to still life, they painted carefully selected
objects from local antique shops and country
auctions. Outstanding among the still-life painters
was Yasuo Kuniyoshi, my next sitter, who at that
stage of his career gained a maximum effect with a
palette of few colors. To me, his pictures were the
most exciting of the period. They convinced me
that no home was complete without a white
ironstone compote or an iron weather vane in the
shape of a trotter. Eventually I was to find one of
each on Cape Cod.

My first caricature of Kuniyoshi appeared in *Creative Art*. Yas, as he was affectionately known to his friends, posed for it wearing his customary Woodstock garb: weathered khaki shirt and pants and an old hat pulled down over his eyes. Because of his well-defined jawline, small even features, and extremely noncommittal expression, he was easy to draw. In addition to the ink drawing, I made a lithograph in Arnold's printing shop, and Arnold pulled a few proofs.

Aline Fruhauf

When I visited Yas's Fourteenth Street studio, where he posed for his caricature in color, he looked as if he were standing in one of his own paintings. The background was an oyster-white wall against which stood a long table covered with a pale yellow cloth. To his right was the gray wicker rocking chair that appeared in so many of his paintings. Soft folds of a gray topcoat flung over the chair repeated the lines of a draped pitcher in a still life on the wall. Another painting featured a female figure in silvery grays with a background of Venetian red that looked as if it had been lightly brushed with cigar ash. Yas had a small, neat skull and hair like a cap of black feathers. He wore beautifully tailored trousers and vest of finely woven gray tweed, his shoes and shirt were a pale russet, and his tie and pipe were well-placed accents of black and Venetian red. They were the colors of his paintings.

"Too dark to paint today," he said. And eyeing the slate-colored square of sky that showed through the window, he held up a brush and said, "I'll pretend. Go ahead and draw." After a while, he gave my drawing a sidelong glance. "Don't work too long," he advised. "You'll spoil your impression. Anyway, I think you've got it."

At the Institute of Contemporary Arts in New York, the talented Peggy Bacon was autographing her latest book, *Off With Their Heads*, a collection of superb caricatures of New York celebrities in the worlds of art, literature, and politics. Ever since my teacher Grace Fuller had mentioned her as Par-

167

sons's prize pupil, I had sought out her work and admired the scampering, agitated line of her etchings and lithographs of people, children, and cats, and her penetrating, beautifully drawn caricatures in crayon and pastel.

An attractive woman, far different from the drab and unflattering self-caricature reproduced in the book, she wore a floor-length, black velvet sheath that set off her remarkably clear skin and round cornflower-blue eyes. Her thin nose, despite its faintly humorous, delicate outward sweep, gave her features a patrician grace, and her precise, pretty mouth was accurately punctuated at one corner by a beauty spot. Her fine brown hair was pinned in a prim bun at the back, and in front it rayed out in bangs, the hallmark of lady artists. Her profile, poise, and dress suggested Sargent's *Portrait of Madame X* in the Metropolitan Museum of Art. On the wall directly behind her, like a reflection in a small mirror, was her portrait by her husband, Alexander Brook, in which she wore the same black sheath. The background, I was happy to note, was a brilliant primrose yellow.

I bought a copy of *Off With Their Heads,* and when Peggy Bacon autographed it, I asked with some trepidation if she would pose for her caricature for my series. She agreed and asked me to call her in the morning.

The Brooks' apartment took over the entire floor of a brownstone in lower Manhattan. There were some lovely pieces of old furniture, and the decorative mood was Victorian with a light touch. All the colors were whitened; the browns were cocoa; the roses, raspberry ice cream; and there were sugar frostings, white lamps. Peggy sat on the sofa, I took out my pencil, and the sitting proceeded. The two caricaturists were deferential and polite, a little wary of each other. She was really very pretty. I wondered what kind of caricature she'd do of me. How odd it all was. We'd had the same teachers.

"Do you paint at all?" I asked.

"No," she replied, "my only work in color is in

pastel. But that little painting on the wall," she pointed to a picture of a little girl with a background of a city street, "is one I dictated. Alex painted it."

Over cups of tea, she talked about the *Goncourt Journals*, which I resolved to read as soon as possible; of the teachers we had shared, she pronounced Harry Baker "the handsomest man I've ever seen," Miller, "a dear and wonderful person," and Kuniyoshi, "a fine painter with beautiful taste." We also talked of Canton china, which she called "the most beautiful blue in the world," and of the vast quantities of drawings we had both made that ended up in the wastebasket.

She wore a handmade blouse of forget-me-not blue crepe, a black skirt, and black pumps. Her jewelry was Victorian—jet earrings and a brooch with a miniature portrait of a lady. For the artist-at-work detail, we went into a small room, whose gray walls had a rosy tint. There were white sash curtains and a couch with a rose-colored cover, ruffled at the bottom. A black kitten, with eyes like little green grapes, scurried down the hall, stopping in the doorway to look us over. Then Peggy put on a small apron of cherry-pink silk, sat down at her immaculate drawing table, and posed again.

Raphael Soyer was the old master of the contemporary school. A slight man with large brown eyes under dome-shaped lids, he had a scholarly air, especially when his silver-rimmed spectacles slipped halfway down his nose. His respect and compassion for humanity were evident in the way he painted. At the time I was drawing him, two live models lived in the studio: Walter Broe, an old man with a haunted face, and Barney, a drug addict with dead-white skin and a stumbling vacancy of expression. Raphael fed them and let them sleep in the studio. Periodically, the derelicts, homesick for the Bowery, disappeared for days at a time, only to return to the warmth and cheer of the studio and its gentle host.

Raphael liked the finished caricature and offered to exchange it for an oil portrait. I posed for two

Aline Fruhauf

Peggy Bacon, 1937.

169

Max Weber, 1937.

and chose the one in which I wore a gray jacket, figured blouse, black skirt, and my Daumier-avocat suede beret. In this formal addition to my narcissus corner, I looked like the tallow-skinned girls Raphael was painting at the time, and he had given me Soyer eyelids.

I sketched Max Weber as he spoke at various meetings and symposiums, and I got around the problem of supplying the modest-looking little man with a characteristic background by surrounding him with my versions, pastiches in watercolor, of a retrospective group of his paintings. His dealer at the time, J.B. Neumann, trotted out paintings from as far back as 1919 to one that had just come off the easel. As I copied them in pencil and wrote down detailed color notes, a curious thing happened; I found that I was getting right into the paintings, absorbing their spirit, content, and brushwork. Consequently, more emphasis in the final caricature was put on the paintings than on Weber himself, whose modest head and shoulders appeared in the lower, right-hand corner of the work as if he were the signature identifying the author of the works depicted on the wall above him.

Years later, in the 1950s, I saw Weber in the foyer of Paul Rosenberg's gallery where he was exhibiting. We had never met, and I didn't know if he had ever seen the caricature, so I was anonymous when I stopped to talk with him. He smiled, and I told him I had just seen his show and it was beautiful.

"You really think so? You don't think it's old hat?"

I assured him it wasn't, and suddenly we were talking about the by-products of being an artist and about how the discriminating eye, working round-the-clock, not only monitors the artist's work but also exerts its influence on the selection of even the humblest of household objects.

"Even a bowl for the kitchen!" he said, his eyes shining. "It's—it's like a religion!"

William Gropper, a political cartoonist, posed for me in his office at the *Daily Worker* while he was drawing his daily cartoon. He had unusual ways of doing halftones. One was to dip an old toothbrush in a bottle of ink and flick the bristles with a stick. It made an even spattering. "I'm crocheting," he explained.

Caricatures of Arnold Blanch, Adolf Dehn, Harry Gottlieb, Joe Jones, and Doris Lee, together with my self-caricature, completed the series of fourteen artists. The preview of the exhibition took place on the evening of March 27, 1938. I wore my basic black and tried to look as inconspicuous as possible. Erwin stood at my side, giving me tacit moral support as one by one the artists filed in, inspected their caricatures, and said nothing. It was like a funeral but quieter. Every now and then I detected a wan smile, only to find that it was directed at the caricature of someone other than its wearer.

Russel Wright of Neighborhood Playhouse

Aline Fruhauf

William Gropper, 1937, published in the *New Masses*, 1940.

171

Adolph Arthur Dehn, 1937.

172

Aline Fruhauf, "A Young
Lady Caricaturist," by
Adolph Dehn, unpublished
drawing, undated.

Aline Fruhauf, by Adolph
Dehn, in *Creative Art*, January
1933, under the caption
"Adolph Dehn Retaliates."

173

Jean Charlot, by Aline
Fruhauf, undated.

Aline Fruhauf, by Jean
Charlot, "For Aline Fruhauf
in admiration," unpublished
drawing, undated.

days, now a successful industrial designer, surprised me by coming by. He liked the show, especially the caricature of Lucile Blanch, which was
also a particular favorite of mine. Lucile was polite
about it. I had some favorable reviews in the press,
especially one from a young woman on the *World
Telegram,* Emily Genauer, who equated my work
with that in which "wit is combined with the
power of graphic expression." And my self-
caricature was sold to Charles H. Worcester, the
honorary president of the Art Institute of Chicago.
It was indeed flattering to learn that someone who
had never seen or heard of me bought the picture
on its artistic merits, and not because it was a good
likeness.

Peggy Bacon didn't come to the opening but
dropped in a few days later. She looked at all the
caricatures, and when she came to hers it was
almost as if it weren't there at all.

"I like the Soyer best," she said, giving me an
absolutely enchanting smile, and was off.

The World of Fashion

Susan, the first of our two
daughters, was born on December 24, 1938, a
lovely creature with big smoky eyes. My studio
doubled as the nursery, decorated in red, white,
and blue. Susie didn't seem to mind the smell of
turpentine, and as soon as she was able to manipulate the medium, she became an accomplished
finger painter.

Eugenie "Jonnie" Gershoy, the sculptor who
had done some delightful polychromed pieces
based on circus themes, as well as small figurines
of artists at work, and our mutual friend Lucile
Blanch were spending the winter in New Orleans.
As a present for me on the advent of Susie, they
fashioned a silken doll modeled on a famous
Creole beauty of the French Quarter. Her body
was made of creamy-rose crepe de chine, her
features were embroidered, and her auburn hair
was a towering coiffure of wool yarn. Over her
long, lemon-colored skirt of watered silk, she wore
a belted silk jacket patterned in red, green, violet,
and gold on silver. I still had the amber beads I
wore as a child, and the string was just long
enough to make a double strand for Toinette.

During short but happy summer vacations with
Susie and Erwin on a farm in Pennsylvania, the

influence of *le Douanier* Rousseau took over from that of Kenneth Hayes Miller, and with a palette loaded with viridian, cobalt, and ultramarine, I painted the lush farmland of Bucks County—painstaking renderings of old barns, covered bridges, and the New Hope Railway Station before it was relocated as a museum exhibit in the Bucks County Historical Society.

The *Artists at Work* were stacked against the wall in the studio-nursery when Arshile Gorky came by to see them.

"These are paintings in miniature," he said. "You should do them bigger, in oil. Then you'd really have something."

Good advice, perhaps, but instead of following it, I embarked on a new series of caricatures. The Nazi occupation of France had turned public interest from the fashion designers of Paris to those of New York, and the New York designers became the subject of the series.

I began with Muriel King, who had been selected by the enterprising Dorothy Shaver of Lord & Taylor as one of the outstanding creators of evening gowns and dinner suits. Miss King was a statuesque brunette with very white skin and short black curls. She had been a student of John Sloan's, and she showed me some excellent watercolors she had done of a garden. "Sloan told me I could be a painter if I wanted to," she said, and then went to change into a gown she had designed for herself to show off her garnets.

It was a magnificent long gown of changeable taffeta, the color of lightly broiled tomatoes, just the right contrast for the necklace of clustered wine-dark stones. Her black curls were crested with a tiny bow of black velvet ribbon. The walls of the small sitting room were brown, grained like wood but in large, regular, S-shaped whorls that looked like great waves of marcelled hair and gave the room a surreal feeling of great depth and movement. Miss King leaned against a coffee-colored fireplace whose mantel held conch shells

Aline Fruhauf

Muriel King, 1939.

and sea fans; their colors, pink, cream, and orange, were repeated in a large still life above them. It was a stunning setting for a formal portrait, and I half wished I had followed Gorky's advice and started a portrait in oils.

When I got home, I found I had concentrated too much on the décor and had no idea of how I was to solve the problem of the head. Jonnie Gershoy dropped in to see Susie and found me drawing like mad and leaning scraps of paper on various surfaces—wood, marble, glass—hoping the texture under the paper might somehow free the line and help me to achieve the combination that would

177

abstract the face of Muriel King. The wastebaskets were full of all kinds of discarded paper: old envelopes, magazine wrappers, and bits of coated stock torn from advertisements in the *New Yorker*.

"None of these talks!" I exclaimed.

Of all my artist friends, Jonnie understood the problems I constantly wrestled with in pursuit of caricature. They were also hers. She picked up one of the sketches at random.

"Wait a minute," she said, "I know that face from somewhere, a tall girl, very black hair. Now I have it. She sat next to me in the Sloan class."

"Was it Muriel King?" I asked, jumping with excitement.

"That was her name. You see, you had it all the time."

I drew a body to fit the head, articulated the rest of the composition, and finished the "formal" portrait in a couple of days.

When my old friend and teacher Belle Boas came to visit Susie, she also inspected my newest works—an almost primitive landscape of Fetzers' Farm in New Hope and the caricature of Muriel King.

"It would seem," she said, "that to have done the one, you would have had to do the other."

It was true. The drawing gave construction and design to the painting, and the painting enriched the quality of line in the drawing.

My next subject was Mr. John, whose millinery establishment combined the atmosphere of a Third Avenue antique shop with that of the showroom of a theatrical costumer. A huge and ancient spread eagle of carved and gilded wood hung over the street door, and on the wall opposite the elevator in the lobby, four or five Civil War forage caps and officers' capes hung from a row of coathooks. When the elevator door opened to the shop, which took up an entire floor, I was greeted by a suit of armor garlanded with fake gardenias. Placed around the enormous room were a number of white flowerpots holding clothes trees made of brass tubing. Bright-colored handbags hung from their branches. More brass tubing, looped like a facetious pen line, fenced off areas of the shop and outlined birdcage booths where glamorous customers, looking as much as possible like Greta Garbo, half closed their heavy eyelids and swung their long page boys as they tried on marvelous broad-brimmed hats. A good-looking young man in a dove-colored jacket was showing a customer a cigarette holder.

"Gold," he said softly, "and bamboo." I thought it was Mr. John and began moseying toward him with my sketching materials. Just then, the real Mr. John appeared. He was short, dark, cherubic, with hair thinning on top but worn long in back, just trickling over the big, loose collar of his white shirt. The black-and-white herringbone of his tweed jacket was much larger than ordinary. It must have been specially woven. The handkerchief in his pocket and his tie were matching red silk.

I introduced myself as the artist who had called for an appointment and asked if it would be all right to walk around him and sketch from all angles. Saying that would be fine, he then placed a deep-crowned hat on another mask-faced beauty and turned to chat with Thyra Samter Winslow, the short-story writer, who was cradling a tiny, shivering toy dog with eyes like a many-times-magnified insect's. As I looked around, I noticed that the hats not only modified the rude jokes time had played on the faces of the older customers, but also dramatized what beauty was left. Thyra Winslow's ravaged face, now shadowed by a magnificent concoction of geranium velvet, had taken on the haggard beauty of a music-hall singer as seen by Toulouse-Lautrec.

Tom Brigance, another of the designers singled out for excellence by Lord & Taylor's Dorothy Shaver, specialized in sports clothes and bathing suits. He was small, dark, and intense, with bright black eyes. There was nothing indefinite about his features. They were easily captured on paper.

Tom Brigance, 1939.

Having no need for a sitting, I followed him around the workroom at a speed necessary to keep up with him, making notes on the clothes he had created.

"I'll bet everything you do," he said at one point, "whether it's cooking or drawing, you do with the same fury. And I'm sure your baby looks just like you, black hair, black eyes, and screams all day."

"No," I assured him, "Susie has hazel eyes, reddish hair, and a placid disposition."

The women's garment industry, of necessity, keeps a tight surveillance on originality, and it was surprising that I met with little opposition as I roamed from workroom to workroom, sketching as I went. Only once was my presence challenged. In the studio of Clare Potter, who created elegant sports clothes for the wholesale trade, the manufacturer saw me taking careful notes on Mrs. Potter's spring collection and exploded. It seemed nothing could convince him that I wasn't a copyist and that cheap replicas of "Clarepotter" originals would not be appearing next morning in every store on Fourteenth Street. But somehow Mrs. Potter managed to make it clear that I was there to draw her, not the models, and I stayed on.

Clare Potter was slim and attractive, and I drew her as she was adjusting the hem of a pale blue jersey dress fitted on a headless mannequin. She wore a spinach-green knit blouse and a red wool skirt, crossbarred in wide squares with thick black lines edged in yellow, and her jewelry was a choker of thick tubular coral beads, the kind worn by Dutch girls when garbed in their national costumes.

The little black dress as designed by Nettie Rosenstein has a unique place in American fashion history. Examples of this style can even be found in the Smithsonian Institution's costume collection. My sitting with their originator took place in the Chinese-modern living room of her spacious apartment on Central Park West. Mrs. Rosenstein was a slight, very gentle woman with pale ivory skin, large dark eyes, a small mouth, and a long

thin nose that was a little off center. A distinguished figure in a room of subtle colors, she was
dressed in a high-necked, long-sleeved gown of
coral-red crepe, draped like the garment of a T'ang
figurine. Her jewels were several strands of small
Oriental pearls and one great emerald set in a
bracelet. She wore her dark hair in three upswept
lacquered curls in front, and the bun in the back
was stuck with a small tortoise shell comb. She
settled herself on a pale blue brocade sofa, one
slippered foot and a triangle of ivory silk barely
showing. On the wall behind her, flanking a
Chinese painting, were a pair of smoky-mirror
Venetian sconces. The textured Chinese rug was
the color of cream of mushroom soup. A boulle
coffee table displayed a single tea bowl, delicate as
a blossom.

For her caricature, I used the angle of her nose as
the main diagonal of the composition, so that the
nose added a charming dissonance, keeping the
picture from being over bland. But, in 1940, when
Vogue was to reproduce eight of the drawings of
designers, Beatrice Mathieu, a sometime fashion
writer for the *New Yorker* and a public relations
expert familiar with all the gossip of Seventh
Avenue, told me that Nettie Rosenstein had a new
nose.

"You better hurry and change your drawing,"
she urged.

I raced to the Condé Nast office to see Dr. Agha,
the art director. Luckily the drawing had not yet
gone to the engraver's. And that evening, I was
met at her door by a new personality, gay and
vivacious, wearing a little black dress. Gone was
my beautiful diagonal. In its place was something
else, cute, I supposed, as a button. I applied plastic
surgery to the paper face and rushed it, *dernier nez*
and all, back to Dr. Agha.

The eight caricatures appeared in full color in the
issue of October 15, 1940. There on facing pages
were my renderings of Nettie Rosenstein, Tom
Brigance, Germaine Monteil, Mr. John, Valentina,

Richard Koret, Clare Potter, and Helen Cookman. Shortly after they were published, Alexander Liberman, one of the Condé Nast editors, called to tell me that a young man was clipping my caricatures from copies of *Vogue*, gluing them to little wooden boxes, lacquering them, and offering them for sale to the individual designers. I was flabbergasted.

"Do you know anything about this?" he asked.

"Certainly not," I said. "All I can say is, if you find him, make him stop."

I never learned the identity of this young man whose career had crossed mine, and I never saw the results of his enterprise.

During this period of involvement in the world of fashion, all the clothes consciousness I had assimilated since my first day in kindergarten rose to the surface. The dress designers looked at my clothes as if they were examining tissue through a microscope. I knew the look well. My father had it. To avoid the all-encompassing stare that began with the hat or lack of it and went to the shoe tips, I dressed as inconspicuously as possible and keyed my garb to the type of clothing my designer-sitters were noted for, hoping in this way to achieve a chameleonic anonymity. If I wore a hat, it was the black wool cap my Aunt Lena had crocheted for me, the texture of which was so close to that of my own hair that it was barely discernible except, of course, to the milliners.

Pola Stout, designer of woolens, appraised the tweed of my suit, as did Helen Cookman, the originator of the Lady Chesterfield. For Clare Potter, I wore a jersey dress under my jacket. Valentina, on the other hand, called for restrained elegance. I still had the basic black crepe I had worn at the opening of my *Artists at Work* show. My old French teacher, Mme. Renaud, would have approved the color, cut, and workmanship. But I misjudged Valentina. Although she was also wearing black, it was a tailored suit topped by a hard little sailor hat of bottle-green hatter's plush.

Aline Fruhauf

Valentina, 1939.

Valentina was famous for the spectacular gowns she designed for such ladies of the stage as Katharine Cornell and Lynn Fontanne, and she herself shared the aura of the theatre. Slim and blonde, she had great greenish eyes framed in sweeping lashes. I had previously sketched her for *Top Notes*, one of a series of interesting people in the audience. She then wore a gown of draped white crepe and a Juliet cap of gold cord, and her hair was coiled over each ear like flaxen Danish pastries. Gold chains encircled her graceful neck, and when I heard her speak Russian, I was sure

183

she must be either an exiled grand duchess or a première ballerine.

On the spring afternoon she sat to me in the entresol of her house, where sconces with crystal prisms glittered like icicles on the cool gray walls. She crossed her long legs and placed a ledger in her lap, fabric samples pinned to its yellow pages. She lit a cigarette in a long white holder and, with a regal gesture, signaled me to begin. The fruitwood marquise, covered in lilac silk, was the only seat in the room. I looked vainly for a chair, but there was none. I looked down to the floor. It was a horribly familiar pinky gray that brought back the memory of myself as a little girl in a white dress, my face puckered and reddened like a baked apple, my mouth squared and ready to cry, on my first day at kindergarten. I put down my notebook and pencils, spread the skirt of my best black silk, flexed my left knee, and gently slid to the floor. I had made a perfect landing, without tears. Then I began to draw.

Later, Aline Bernstein's costumes and settings illuminated many Broadway productions. And her most recent contribution to the history of dress was the founding of the Costume Institute, a museum collection which is now part of the Metropolitan Museum of Art. I had made some sketches of her on shipboard years ago. Although they were unsuccessful and immediately discarded, they had some value as first sittings for the caricatures I was about to make. Mrs. Bernstein was not overfond of caricatures per se, but she cast her lot with me, knowing I had a series to complete for a show that would include the drawings that had appeared in *Vogue*.

The Bernsteins' living room in their apartment on Central Park West was warm and friendly, glowing with beautiful colors and with furniture chosen with affection. As usual, I was ahead of time for our appointment. I heard the sounds of the elevator, then of the opening of a door, and a plump, pink-cheeked woman in black came in with a pair of dachshunds. She unleashed the dogs, took off her hat and coat, and sat down to talk to me as if no time had elapsed since our last meeting. She showed me her portrait by Robert Henri. Since I had last seen her, she had written several books and had appeared as a principal character in the romans à clef of Thomas Wolfe's. As I drew I couldn't help thinking of Mrs. Esther Jack who, in an older white-haired version, was facing me. I was drawing the character in a book as well as a woman with whom I had worked long ago in a little theatre. Thinking that I would follow a career in stage design, she had once advised me to get a book on the history of costume, Camille Piton's *Le Costume civil en France*.

"What happened to you and stage design?" she asked.

"Well," I answered, "I did that caricature of Paula Trueman, and I've been drawing them ever since, and here I am drawing yours!"   We talked about our families. She showed me a picture of her new son-in-law, and I showed her one of Susie. She looked at my face and said, "You like her?" I nodded, beaming.

"Let's go into the room where I work," she said, and I followed her into a small austere chamber with a narrow bed covered with an ancient fabric softly colored like carnelians. Over her drawing table, a T-square and triangle hung like devotional symbols, and tacked on the wall was a working drawing of a woman's costume. The drawing table held an array of small sable brushes and neatly sharpened pencils, and an open box of watercolors showed little squares of paint shining like uncut jewels.

Before we returned to the living room, Aline Bernstein put on a beige smock and posed in a French provincial chair the color and texture of old amber.

"You know," she said, "I think if I had my life to live over again, I would have done things differently. And sometimes I think it might be fun to live in an all-modern house, with all-modern furniture."

I noticed how much older and heavier she had become. Yet the face within the face that looked out at me was still that of the very lovely child she must have been.

A former member of the Condé Nast Publications, Henrietta Malkiel, introduced me to Beatrice Mathieu, who was enthusiastic about my series and very helpful in suggesting additions to it. Bea was always beautifully turned out, and like a great many smart women she hated to wear hats. But she was a publicist, and one of her clients, Sally Victor, persuaded her to do so.

"I'll make you one," said Sally Victor, "that will make you look as if you didn't have one at all."

The result was a skillfully wrought, black felt pillbox. Black fishnet had been stretched over it, and from a short distance, it looked like an extension of her hair, and it was vastly becoming.

Another of Bea's clients was Germaine Monteil, who later forsook fashion design for the cosmetic business. As *Vogue* described her, she was dark-haired and tiny, she loved skiing and dancing, and she was famous for "her young, limber lines, for being the first to do tailored evening suits." Bea, as she had done with Sally Victor, made the appointment for our sitting. It was a tense moment. Madame was busy cutting and draping a precious white fabric on a live model, and the air was charged with suspense. Suddenly she stopped and cried out, "No, no! I cannot, I cannot!" and laid down her scissors, dismissed the model, and with a "How do you want me?" placed a cigarette between her lips and sat down. Lowering her eyes, she picked up a pad and pencil and began making notes.

The Monteil working costume was simple, comfortable, and fetching: a beige cotton over-dress, buttoned at the side, with short sleeves and a full skirt. Underneath it was a starched white dickey with a pussycat bow at the throat. Her tiny

shoes were red kid Oxford ties with wedge soles,
the first of a line of play shoes designed by Joyce.
Madame was beautifully made up and nicely
perfumed.

A sheer white dress with balloon sleeves and a
wide gold kid belt hung against a velvet curtain the
color of mushroom gills. A model slithered in
wearing a long chartreuse evening gown with long
tight sleeves and a bare midriff. I sketched the
Monteil creations, thanked Madame for posing,
and went home to give Susie her supper and start
the Friday night spaghetti.

Jessie Franklin Turner was the grand old lady of
the tea gown. I expected her to pose in flowing
velvet or trailing chiffon. But, like Valentina, she
surprised me by wearing a tailored suit, and her
short white hair was covered with a pale silk turban.

Susie, now four years old, was attending nursery
school and a dancing class. Her dance teacher,
Polly Korchen, told me that two of her artist
friends, Eleanor Lust and Jimmy Ernst, were
starting a new art gallery, the Norlyst Gallery, and
were interested in my caricatures. After coming to
see my work, they set a date for a show that would
feature the designer series but also include some of
the New York judges and other works. The exhibition was scheduled to run from June 15 to July 6,
1943. A week before it opened, they called in
another artist as coexhibitor. She was Paula
Lawrence, a comedienne who was scoring a hit in a
musical called *Something for the Boys*. Her specialty
was wire-sculptured caricature.

It was wartime. Erwin was scheduled to go to
Pensacola for indoctrination into the Navy. The
opening took place a few days before he left.
Members of Paula Lawrence's cast arrived along
with droves of newspaper people, sportswriters,
and radio broadcasters. Among the old familiar
faces were those of my old friend of newspaper
days Irving Hoffman, the Bufanos, and Ruth and
Philip Wittenberg. Deems Taylor arrived with a

Lilly Daché, 1942.   Fira Benenson, 1942.

pretty radio actress, and J.B. Neumann came with
Dikran Kelekian. Sparked by our Baltimore Tea
Punch—a concoction of black tea, dark rum, and
lemons—and Paula Lawrence's ready-mixed
Manhattans, the decibels rose to an almost deafen-
ing pitch.

My mother and grandmother were both there.
Mr. John came in. When I introduced him, he
bowed low over Grandma Anna's hand and kissed
it "with a loud smack," she said. Later I noticed he
was wearing his hair a new way, brushed forward
in crescents.

"Darling," he said, "I love mine. Beautiful color.
If you'll change the hair to Napoleonic, I'll buy it."

Deems Taylor introduced me to his pretty girl-
friend, looked around at the caricatures, grinned,
and said, "You've improved."

Charmion von Wiegand, an attractive painter,
introduced me to her teacher, Piet Mondrian, an

artist who really reduced things to their lowest terms. All I could think of as I viewed his long oval face was a pecan on which had been limned the merest suggestion of features, a vertical down the middle and two horizontals, one at the eye level, one at the mouth.

As the crowds milled around, I watched one modiste, with what Max Beerbohm would have called "a propulsive profile," eyeing first her caricature, and then the revised one of Nettie Rosenstein. The look she turned on me was one of total nonrecognition. Photographs that appeared later showed her with a considerably altered nose. The face of American design was changing.

My round-toed, ankle-strapped, wartime shoes, unrationed because they were made of some truly inferior reptile, began to hurt, and my red, impulse-bought dress with black buttons the size of silver dollars seemed somewhat overdone; it would have infuriated Frank Alvah Parsons, and Frank Crowninshield would have accused me of trying to "knock 'em dead." Only my black skull cap, crocheted by Aunt Lena, seemed right. Paula Lawrence, gorgeously made up in cream and rose with inch-long eyelashes, wore a marvelous gown, half black, half chartreuse, and a hat that she described as having hot and cold running horses.

The photographers arrived: Al Soberman, a laboratory technician in the biology department at Brooklyn College, and two of his friends. Their equipment was impressive. Al, nicknamed Sabini, posed Paula and me beaming at each other in front of our respective works. Again and again, as the flashbulbs went off, we were told to wet our lips, and we said "cheese" until our jaws ached.

When he had finished with us, Sabini assumed a new guise. He took off his coat and tie, unbuttoned his collar, slanted heavenward the animated tadpoles that were his eyebrows, and delicately dilating his nostrils in an expression of exquisite boredom, he walked around the gallery inspecting the exhibits. As he approached me, he whispered,

"Introduce me to your directress as the promising Mexican painter Manuel Sabini."

I took him over to Eleanor Lust, and soon they were engaged in earnest conversation. I heard her ask him where his paintings could be seen, and he answered her with a flurry of handplay, a mighty heaving of plump shoulders, and helpless expostulations in shattering English. She was notably impressed.

"Who is he?" she asked me when he had moved off. "How long have you known him? Where are his paintings?"

Fortunately, I didn't have to answer. I was interrupted just in time by Mondrian, who complimented me on my work. When the show was over, I asked Sabini, now fully dressed and without his photographic equipment, whether he had brought enough film for all the pictures he had taken.

"Film?" he asked innocently. "What film?"

I might have known.

The next morning I picked up the caricature of Mr. John, and with a now-practiced hand, I changed his hair style with an HB Venus pencil and Winsor and Newton's ivory black. When I got it back to the gallery in the afternoon, I found a harassed Jimmy Ernst, noticeably upset, holding his hand over his heart. There had been an incident.

"Jessie Franklin Turner came in," he said, "incognito. But, of course, I recognized her from your caricature. She wore a gray suit and a wide-brimmed gray felt hat, like a Confederate general's, and she was carrying an enormous handbag, like a knapsack. She stormed over to her picture, said that she was a friend of Mrs. Turner's and that Mrs. T. would be outraged to see this monstrous thing. She demanded to know the price, took out a roll of bills, peeled off the exact amount, and handed it to me. Then she yanked the picture off the wall and, before I could say anything, she stuck it under her arm and marched downstairs. Oh,

Aline! Is this the way it's going to be?" Fortunately, there were no further incidents, and the show went well. I was sure that Mrs. Turner had destroyed her picture, but it turned up thirty-three years later, in 1976, in an antique shop in upper New York State. Mr. John bought his revised caricature, and Richard Koret, who designed handbags, and Rosalia Zampano, who did tailored clothes and sportswear, bought theirs. Germaine Monteil had bought hers earlier but lent it to the exhibition. The remaining fifteen caricatures of designers were rented by Rosalia Zampano for a month. And writing in the *Morning Telegraph,* George Freedley, the founder and director of the Theatre Collection of the New York Public Library, called my caricatures "mental cocktails."

Soon after the exhibition closed, Elizabeth Hawes agreed to sit to me. Polly Korchen arranged for her to see my work, and she arrived with her little boy Gavrik, who was about Susie's age. Susie took him into the studio-nursery, and while they played with the dollhouse, we had our first sitting.

I was curious about this woman, who could write a book called *Fashion is Spinach* and, at the same time, carry on a successful dressmaking establishment. The clothes she designed had the timeless quality of works of art and were made of excellent fabrics. Her customers wore her dresses and coats for years. She was a small, dark, magnetic woman, with a high forehead and a beautifully curled bang over her left eyebrow.

She was married to Joseph Losey, the film director, and the next sitting took place in their Victorian house, a few blocks from our apartment in the Village. She had been vacuuming her high-ceilinged living room, which was elegant with blood-red velvet draperies, crystal chandelier, and contemporary furniture, and she was appropriately dressed in dust-colored pants and shirt, and suede shoes. Gavrik, sandy haired and wearing huge spectacles, came in and sat on a sofa. He was wearing corduroy overalls and a striped T-shirt. I

191

drew him, too. There was little conversation but a good sense of rapport. Mother and son posed together with respect.

I finished the drawing to my satisfaction but took it to Polly for her opinion. She pronounced it "very good" and thought it was cause for celebration. We went to the Jumble Shop on Eighth Street and had a drink. Miss Hawes liked it, too, and bought it.

In November of 1943, Elizabeth Hawes became the chairman of the Committee for the Care of Young Children in Wartime, and her latest book, *Why Women Cry, or Wenches with Wrenches*, dealt with the problems of wartime mothers. To promote the book, her publishers asked certain artists to depict the different types of women described in it. Their works were to be sold at auction for the benefit of the committee. The magazine *Pic*, in its issue of February 15, 1944, devoted a full page to reproductions of the artists' drawings: William Steig's *Equal Righter*, William Gropper's *Contented Cow*, Emlen Etting's *Lady*, Arbit Blatas's *Career Woman* (a portrait of the actress Sylvia Sidney), James Thurber's *Forgotten Female*; and, as if to humiliate me, my sympathetic caricature of Elizabeth Hawes and Gavrik, lent by Miss Hawes to represent her as the author of the book, was reproduced with the caption *She-Wolf*—the successful, ruthless businesswoman who makes more than $3,600 a year. I wrote an angry letter to the editor but the damage had been done.

The caricature of Elizabeth Hawes completed the series of twenty-one designers. In addition to those mentioned above, the series included caricatures of Fira Benenson, Lilly Daché, Louise Barnes Gallagher, Oman Kiam, Peggy Morris, and Herman Patrick Tappé.

Omar Kiam, 1942.

Spider's Web

After completing the series of designers, I sought respite from caricature once again by painting in oils. And the Norlyst Gallery gave me another show the following spring, 1944. It included landscapes, city views, and some figure paintings. Then Susie and I pulled up stakes and went to California to join Erwin, who was stationed in San Diego. Summer, however, was scarcely over when we were back on the East Coast, living in the Maryland suburbs of Washington. Erwin had been transferred to the Naval Medical Research Institute at Bethesda, Maryland.

Once settled, I scanned the Washington area telephone directories for the names of old friends. Prentiss Taylor, my fellow-student lithographer, was living in nearby Virginia. He was teaching art, making prints, and had become a leading spirit in local art organizations. In no time at all, he arranged an exhibition of my caricatures at the central branch of the District of Columbia Public Library.

Belle Boas, too, had left New York, where she had been teaching a course for future art instructors at Teachers College, and was the new director of education at the Baltimore Museum of Art. She invited me to have lunch with her and the staff of the museum. There I met Adelyn Breeskin, then acting director of the museum, and Vivian Baylin, Belle's trusted and competent assistant.

Belle showed almost no signs of aging. She was still teaching little children to draw and paint. At the time there was no room in the museum for the children to work.

"But, Aline," she said, and her low voice held a mounting excitement, "we go out into the galleries, spread papers on the beautifully polished floors, and I give them paint and brushes and water. They take to art like candy!" Her eyes crinkled up, and her face shone with happiness.

I had brought along some of the *Artists at Work*. Mrs. Breeskin liked them and arranged to exhibit them at the museum in January of 1946.

They were shown again, two years later, at the Watkins Gallery of the American University in Washington, and for the first time I was unable to attend the opening of one of my exhibitions. On that day, January 15, 1948, Susie was sending out postcards announcing the arrival of her little sister, Deborah Ann, who for the first few weeks of her life lived up to Tom Brigance's supposition of what a child of mine would be like.

Belle wrote that her assistant was now Mrs. David Lichtenstein, living in Washington.

"I've given her your address. I know you two will get along."

The friendship sponsored by the gentle woman we both loved proved to be a happy one. As the result of my activity as art chairman of the Chevy Chase Elementary School PTA, Vivian Lichtenstein became the first to teach an after-school art program in Montgomery County. Today, I like to think that the classes we began, which still go on, are a lasting tribune to the memory of Belle Boas.

Two years after leaving New York, I was shamelessly homesick for the frenzied bustle of that city and for the colorful people of the theatre, music, art, and fashion worlds I had loved to draw.

Making Faces

As compensation, I sought out curious houses and landscapes and applied to them the same reduction to lowest terms I had previously applied to humans.

On a cold day in January of 1946, I got off the Friendship Heights streetcar, drawn as if by a magnet to the yellow house on R Street in Georgetown. Every time I had previously passed that house, coming from or headed back to Maryland, I had craned my neck, almost to the point of dislocation, to get one more glimpse of it. It was a

The Yellow House, 1959.

huge house, built in 1854, and was like the houses Charles Addams drew for the *New Yorker*. On a little rust-colored hill flecked with snow it loomed, three tall stories of Victorian elegance. Two flights of steps—the first was of red brick, the second, of wood painted a battleship gray—led up to its porch. The white scallops of fretwork that adorned its yellow facade came to a climax over the doorway in an emblazonment of carved stalactites.

I went across the street to the Georgetown branch of the public library and got permission to stand at a window on the second floor to sketch the house. Georgetown is full of landmark houses, some of which have been lacquered into a Christmas-card quaintness by the addition of shiny black trim. Ornate cast-iron garden furniture or carriage lamps flanked their doorways. This house, however, had no such tacked-on decorator touches. Its tiled mansard roof, as somberly irides-cent as the feathers of a dark pigeon, was the inverted peach-basket hat of a dowager of distin-guished lineage to whom fashion was not only superfluous but highly undesirable. Its long win-dows were draped in creamy-white Austrian curtains resembling rows and rows of drooping eyelids that might fly open at any moment to reveal countless gelid eyes.

I finished the sketch, took the streetcar back home, and began work on a painting of the house.

Twelve years later, in 1958, I decided to do a lithograph of the painting, and before I finished the drawing on the stone I heard that the house was to be sold. This, I thought, was the perfect time to see it up close. When I climbed the two sets of steps, it was like walking into my own painting. Soon, I was standing under the wooden stalactites. I rang the bell, and an attractive, white-haired lady came to the door.

"Good afternoon," I said faintly, "I have been painting and drawing your house off and on for twelve years. I hear it is now for sale. May I see the inside?"

"Please come in," she said with a smile.

I half expected to see a Mary Petty maid flitting about in a gilded, rosy-silk interior, but the décor was dark and sedate, and we were alone. I noticed a terra-cotta bust of a long-haired gentleman near the window.

"That's Davy Crockett," I was told. "And if you think it's a fake, you're wrong; the fake's over here." On the other side of the room, to my surprise, was its duplicate. I was then taken on a tour of the house.

On leaving and thanking my hostess, I said the house had meant a great deal to me.

"It's very sweet of you to say that," she said. "I call it Wuthering Heights."

When the lithograph was finished, I took a proof to my new-found friend.

"I've got something for you, too," she said somewhat mysteriously. "It's a painting on a cobweb."

She brought out a small picture in a walnut frame: a portrait, slightly larger than a miniature, of a blonde woman in a sixteenth-century black dress with a small white ruff at the neck and a cap of dark blue velvet sewn with pearls and sapphires. She wore a heavy gold necklace set with larger jewels. The shear silk of the cobweb had given way at one corner, and when the picture was handled, the tear shivered ominously under the glass. The rest of the picture seemed to be held together by paint alone.

"Mary, Queen of Scots, after Holbein," was my uneducated guess at the portrait's identity. But when I examined the work more closely I found an inscription very low on the mat that read "Philippine Welser, 1527–1580," and on the back of the frame there was a printed label with the name Fr. Unterberger, Innsbruck, and the information, in English, French, and German, that the portrait was painted on a spider's web.

My curiosity was piqued. It didn't take long to

learn that Philippine Welser was a member of the

influential German family that rivaled the Fuggers *Aline Fruhauf*
and the Medici, that she was famous for her beauty
and learning, and that she had secretly married the
Archduke Ferdinand, the second son of Emperor
Ferdinand I. It look longer to learn that Franz
Unterberger of Innsbruck was an antique dealer,
who, during the last quarter of the nineteenth
century, employed a number of church artists to
copy paintings on cobwebs, and that the original of
the cobweb painting was a posthumous portrait of
Philippine that hung in the castle of Matzen in the
Tyrol.

During the course of my research on this esoteric
use of cobwebs, which ran from the Smithsonian
Institution and the Library of Congress in
Washington to the New York Public Library and
the Museum of Natural History in New York,
Edgar Breitenbach, the chief of the Division of
Prints and Photographs at the Library of Congress,
told me that he knew one of the Welser descen-
dants, the Baron Hubert von Welser.

"He has completely restored the old family
castle, Neunhof, at Nuremberg," he added. "It's a
charming place, authentic in every detail, even to
the plumbing. If you send him a photograph of the
portrait, he may be able to throw some light on the
subject."

I sent the photograph to the baron and with it a
photograph of my painting of the yellow Victorian
mansion, its provenance. The mansion and cobweb
portrait, after all, were contemporary artistic
endeavors. The baron, with apologies for his
"horrible English," professed to find my painting
"much better (if at all a comparison is allowed)"
than the cobweb. But the cobweb, he wrote, was
"a remarkable and seldom [sic] representative of a
quite peculiar way of thinking and painting of the
years about 1860 or some years later."

His letter, dated February 19, 1961, was a long
one. He wrote that the iconography of his "Aunty
Philippine" was now the object of research in
which he was very interested. "But not so with

199

cobwebs and spiders," he was quick to add, "though we have a lot of them on walls and ceilings, but all being no product of human art." It was from this letter that I learned of the portrait of Philippine in the castle at Matzen. The baron owned a copy of it in oil on wood and had once seen in a jeweler's shop at Innsbruck a copy in enamel, "real Limosin-work, to pin it on one's hat." He believed they had all been copied from the frontispiece of a biography of Philippine by Wendelin Boeheim published at Innsbruck about 1890, a copy of which he sent to me under separate cover.

If my sources were reliable, the use of cobwebs as a support for painting in oil or watercolor had quite a history. According to a dispatch from Prague published in the *Washington Post* on March 16, 1924, Count Czernin had acquired a painting on a spider's web alleged to have been made in 1530, and mention was made of another sixteenth-century example, which turned up in 1854, attributed to one Andres Solari del Gebbo. From articles by Ina Cassirer (*Natural History*, April 1956) and by Karl Toldt (*Der Schlern*, 1953) I learned that during the eighteenth century in Bruneck, a small town in the South Tyrol, a church painter named Elias Prunner made a painting on a cobweb, and his most famous pupil, Johann Burgmann, substituted the sturdier silk of the Austrian spotted moth, *Hyponomeuta evonymella Linnaeus*, for the spider's web. In May, the cherry trees in this part of Austria were invaded by this species of tent caterpillar, whose silk veiling is so dense it can be snipped from the trees in swatches sometimes as long as two feet. In 1765, the Empress Maria Theresa, in Innsbruck to celebrate the marriage of her son Leopold to the Infanta of Spain, was so fascinated by Burgmann's work that she bought his entire output and commissioned others to be sent on to Vienna.

Georg Prunner, a relative of Elias's, was an engraver. He found that he could stretch the fine

silk on tiny inked copper plates and actually succeeded in printing miniature engravings on the
fine stuff. Other works on caterpillar silk by artists
of this period were delicate brush drawings in ink.
The finished pictures were placed between plates
of glass, set in cardboard mats decorated on both
sides with gold lace, and hung in windows.

Burgmann and other painters used watercolor
slightly thickened with opaque white. Sometimes
nuts were added to the water to add some oil to the
paint. After the silk was stretched on a cardboard
mat, it was first sized with diluted milk and then
the paint was applied with tiny brushes reputedly
made of the pinfeathers of a woodcock.

After Burgmann's death in 1825, the art of cobweb painting died out. Some fifty years later, it
was revived at Innsbruck by Unterberger and by
another enterprising art dealer named Czuchna,
who hired church artists to copy the genre paintings of the Munich school by such artists as Rudolf
Epp and Franz von Defregger. The largest cobweb
painting I was to see was a copy, five by seven
inches, of a painting by the latter, privately owned
in Laurel, Maryland. It showed a Tyrolean family
with their dog, and it came from the shop of Franz
Unterberger.

The *Christian Science Monitor* on July 20, 1952,
carried the story of a Viennese artist named
Justinian Szodan, who had recently exhibited
forty-eight paintings on spider webs. They were
what was left of the dedicated work of a lifetime;
twelve of his paintings had perished in the bomb-
ings of the Second World War. And, oddly enough,
two other contemporary practitioners of this art,
which flourished in Austria, turned up in this
hemisphere: Mrs. James Blunt Clopton, a matron
from Huntsville, Alabama; and Mrs. Stella Campin
of Randolph, Iowa. Not surprisingly, each of the
two ladies thought she was the only spider-web
painter in the world.

The last bit of information on web painting came
in the form of a long-awaited letter from the art

historian Eugen von Phillipovich of Copenhagen. It was a recapitulation of information I already had, with references to the articles in *Natural History*, the *Christian Science Monitor*, and *Der Schlern*. My next step was the obvious one. I had to do my own cobweb painting and contribute something contemporary to the archives of this uncommon field of endeavor. To round things out, the adventure that began with one of my own paintings should end with another. I decided to do a self-caricature on a spider's web.

It was late in the summer. No caterpillar silk was available. I had to fall back on that of the spider, the support used by Mesdames Clopton and Campin. Finding a web was not easy. There were a few isolated gray networks, draped like bunting, in the corners of the garage, but no matter how carefully I handled them, they collapsed into sticky strands. A neighbor volunteered the one in his window well. It was the funnel-shaped construction of the *Agelena labyrinthica*, and it appeared to be dense enough to hold paint. Before detaching it, I made a small cardboard mat and poured some Elmer's glue around the edges of the opening. Then, holding the mat under the web, I snipped a section of it with medium-sized scissors, and with some deft finger work and maybe some magic, I was able to secure it. After a breathless journey from the garden into the house and upstairs to my drawing table, I put the mat over a box cover so that the stretched web would be supported and yet, with grateful acknowledgment to Mrs. Campin, would have free circulation of air. I decided to use the Prunner-Burgmann watercolor method as described by Mrs. Cassirer and Dr. Toldt instead of the oil technique practiced by the ladies of Alabama and Iowa. With a small sable brush, I dribbled pinpoints of milk across the square of web, tipping the mat so that the fluid covered the surface. A large hole appeared at the bottom of the square, but the rest was holding. The surface looked like membrane-thin tracing paper. I stippled on some opaque white and, as the web seemed to be holding, I plunged ahead and then finished the work with a cerulean-blue background.

When the paint had dried, I decided to fix the hole. Back at the window well, with scissors, cardboard, and glue, I snipped what remained of the ravaged web. Laying a small piece of the web on the back of my picture, I sized it front and back with more of the milk. It stuck. I had accomplished what is probably the first self-caricature of an artist painted on a spider's web.

Art and Music
in Washington

An exhibition of my caricatures, to be called "Art in Washington," was scheduled to be held at the Whyte Gallery, Washington, in 1950. It was to include caricatures of the artists and other leading personalities of the Washington art scene. It was arranged by Franz Bader, who, with his artist-wife Toni, had come to Washington from Vienna in 1939 after Hitler's troops occupied Austria. Joining forces with James Whyte, a prominent bookseller, Bader became the general manager of the Whyte Gallery, and as the scheduled exhibition testified, he devoted much energy to promoting the works of Washington artists.

Prentiss Taylor was my first subject for the series. And he presented the old problem I faced in sketching old friends and close relatives: so many intermittent images from over the years confounded the mind and, hence, the pencil. My image of the black-haired, rosy-complected youth of the lithography class at the Art Students League in the 1930s imposed itself on the much heavier, urbane gentleman who, with his thinning gray hair, resembled a genial tonsured monk. Prentiss was the president of the Washington Artists Guild, a world traveler, superb host, photographer,

Aline Fruhauf

Prentiss Taylor, 1949.

connoisseur of fine prints, gourmet cook, and herbalist. The postcards he sent to his friends from every corner of the globe were written in such a minute hand that more than ordinary patient study was required to decipher their well-turned Prentissian phrases. And his files of newspaper clippings on art subjects and of exhibition catalogues rivaled those of a richly stocked art reference library.

Prentiss posed at his easel in the attic-studio of the house he shared with his widowed mother in Arlington, Virginia. Like the series of American designers and the one of New York artists, this new series was planned to portray its subjects "at

David Edward Finley, 1949.

home" in the surroundings most intimately associated with them. And, also like the earlier
series, it was to be executed in color, chiefly watercolor.

When I went to the National Gallery of Art to
sketch its director, David E. Finley, I found him all
prepared to be caricatured. He had at hand to
show to me a little engraving by that eminent
seventeenth-century master of the grotesque,
Jacques Callot. The sitting was brief; I got him right
away. The eye was large and low in the profile. In
the finished picture, I posed him standing by
Goya's portrait of the Marquesa de Pontejos. I had
no reason for this, except that I liked the picture
and the marquesa reminded me of my sculptor

friend Eugenie Gershoy. I hadn't done a caricature of a famous painting since the Mona Lisa, and the idea of juxtaposing the little man and the tall and delicate lady in pale silks amused me. I later discovered, however, that Goya was not one of Finley's favorite painters.

"Of all the paintings in the gallery," he is alleged to have said, "why did she pick that one!"

If David Finley was the easiest to caricature of all the sitters in the diversified group that made up this series, Alice Roosevelt Longworth was the most difficult but the most entertaining. She lived on Massachusetts Avenue, just around the corner from the Whyte Bookshop and Gallery, and she was a loyal friend and patron of both the book and art departments of the lively establishment run by James Whyte and the Baders. Her affectation of flat-crowned, wide-brimmed hats—felt in winter, straw in summer—symbolized her presence at the theatre, at lectures in the National Gallery, at Senate hearings, and at horse shows. One of Washington's most literate hostesses, she had, in her own words, viewed the Washington scene with a detached malevolence. And as with all personalities with tart and glittering wit, a great many remarks were falsely attributed to her.

"Among other things," she claimed, "I never said that Tom Dewey looked like the little man on a wedding cake."

It was 1949, and Harry Truman's victory over Dewey was still the talk of the town.

Franz Bader thought that Mrs. Longworth would be a fetching addition to the series even though she was not an artist or a museum director. After he told her about the proposed exhibition, she agreed to sit to me. I called for an appointment. Her voice over the phone was well modulated and husky, with a clipped international-set accent ideally suited to the high comedies of Noel Coward or S.N. Behrman.

At the appointed time, two in the afternoon, a maid showed me up the stairs to a first-floor living room of the four-storied town house, which was cream colored, inside and out. The way was hung with the skins of wild animals, souvenirs of her father's African expeditions, and with a set of Joseph Pennell's lithographs of the building of the Panama Canal, souvenirs of his presidency. As my sitter and hostess had not yet appeared, I had time to take in the room where she received her guests. There were many pictures on the walls, including some purple and crimson costume drawings by Leon Bakst for Diaghilev's Russian Ballet, a water-color of the south portico of the White House by John Singer Sargent, and a tiny still life by Bernice Cross, one of the Washington artists in my series, which depicted a pansy and a fern in a goblet and whose colors were purple, gold, green, crimson, and brown. Prominently displayed was a devastating caricature by C.D. Batchelor of Eleanor and Franklin Roosevelt entitled "All this and Truman too!" I began to make sketches of the furniture and to take color notes: claret velvet love seat, red-and-white striped satin armchair, a faded rosy-flowered chintz sofa with a mustard cushion, a brass clock (which showed that I had been there half an hour), and brass fretwork candlesticks, probably Chinese. Despite the time, I went on with the inventory: green hassock with wrought-iron legs, black tole woodbin, and regulation fireplace accessories. After an hour had passed, I gave my phone number to the maid and left.

As soon as I reached home, the phone rang. The voice, this time, was rich and fruity with apologies. Alice Longworth had forgotten all about the sitting. "Would I forgive her?" and "Would I come to lunch the following Thursday?"

Ushered upstairs again, past the animal skins and the Panama Canal, I sat in the far corner of the room, pencil in hand, just as I used to sit in the second row of a darkened theatre waiting for the curtain to go up on Act I.

There was a hush. From the top of the stairs, the lithe figure of the lady with a clear, sharp profile and gray hair made her entrance. Her smile was enchanting. The thin line of her mouth, with its slightly projecting lower lip, seemed to have been put there with a pen dipped in red ink. Her eyes were a crystalline blue. She wore a dark rose-colored suit with a belted jacket, a dark brown or plum-colored blouse that set off her pearls, and low-heeled, brown suede shoes with tips and straps of brown kid, and she carried a boxlike handbag of black suede. Her appearance effected an extraordinary visual happening: all the colors in the room seemed suddenly to hang together as in an interior painted by Vuillard. She came toward me, hand extended, talking rapidly, and I found myself riposting with unexpected agility as I had with Sam Behrman.

Seated on the striped chair, she gave me her undivided attention, and I tried unsuccessfully to capture her mobile features, the quick smile in the middle of a sentence, and the change in the alignment of her features when she tossed her head. It was like trying to abstract quicksilver, and I fell into the trap of trying to draw and talk at the same time.

"Nobody can do me," she chuckled wickedly, watching me struggle with obvious enjoyment.

"What about that sculptor who did the portrait bust of you that's in the Smithsonian?" I ventured.

"Poor man," she said brightly, "he committed suicide."

Lunch was announced, and we went down to the dining room. It was a very good lunch: eggs Benedict with plenty of hollandaise sauce, bright green sprays of broccoli, and a bottle of Lancer's.

"Don't open a fresh bottle," she cautioned the maid. "There's plenty left in the other one."

But she was too late. I tasted it and said it was a lovely wine.

"Yes, isn't it. Arthur Krock brought it."

After lunch, we resumed the sitting. I covered up my work, explaining that my rough sketches were just that.

"I have no curiosity," she assured me and, eyes sparkling, asked for a sheet of paper. Taking a pencil, she began to draw me. Now I was the curious one and, as I craned my neck to look, she slapped her hand over the drawing.

"Nobody's allowed to see mine either!"

As I made one more try, she called my attention to the Batchelor caricature of Eleanor and Franklin. I had become aware of the family resemblance between the two female cousins and mentioned it.

"She came out before I did, you know," and drawing herself into an erect sitting position and patting her flat midriff, she added, "Wouldn't you think she'd take better care of her figure. Would you like to see my imitation of her?"

She slumped down, and then, with both hands, she tugged at the skin of her throat, pulling it upward in multiple folds, and lowered her chin into the folds, smiled a toothy smile, crinkled her eyes, and raised her clasped hands, producing an uncanny, in-the-flesh caricature of Eleanor Roosevelt. I made a quick sketch, thanked my hostess, and prepared to leave.

The show was over, and the curtain line, uttered gaily at the head of the stairs, was "Drop in again, when you're slumming."

I worked on the caricature up to the very last minute, filling wastebaskets full of drawings that didn't look anything like Alice Longworth. The details of the room, however, were catalogue perfect, and I did an excellent job on her legs and feet. But the only drawing that in any way approached her was the quick sketch of her burlesque of her cousin Eleanor, and that, like the sketch she made of me, must forever remain a secret.

The show opened as scheduled on March 11, 1950. Twenty-two caricatures made up the series, which included, in addition to those already mentioned, such personalities as Duncan Phillips, the founder and director of the Phillips Collection; Jacob Kainen, painter and printmaker, who was also the curator of the division of graphic arts of the

Aline Fruhauf

Duncan Phillips, 1949.

Smithsonian's U.S. National Museum; Eleanor
Quandt, former curator at the Corcoran Gallery of
Art; the painter Sarah Baker; and the sculptor
William Calfee. The show then went on to the
Baltimore Museum, where it was on view during
the month of June.

   Six years later, Day Thorpe, the music critic of
the *Washington Evening Star*, saw some offset prints
I had made of my caricatures of Gershwin, Ravel,
Stravinsky, and Rachmaninoff and suggested that
I do a series of Washington musicians. With the aid
of Patrick Hayes, Washington's foremost concert
manager, who not only supplied the names but
voluntarily acted as my impresario, I soon had a
long list of composers, soloists, choir directors,
and other participants in the musical life of
Washington. At the time, I was experimenting
with the ancient art of encaustic painting, so beautifully practiced by the Faiyumic portraitists of the

211

second century A.D. Egypt, in which pigments are mixed with beeswax. I decided to attempt the new series in this fascinating medium.

I was first attracted to wax as a medium when, as a child, I visited Dennison's store on lower Fifth Avenue. Besides purveying party favors and crepe paper of every imaginable hue, Dennison's was doing a thriving business in sealing wax, not only for use in sealing letters and documents, but also in decorating glass and pottery vases, and in fashioning beads. There was a workshop in the center of the store, where customers could learn to heat the wax over an alcohol lamp and manipulate it. The wax came in all colors, including gold, silver, copper, and a transparent red amber that looked and smelled like Pears soap and was highly inflammable.

I soon joined the multitude of my generation of amateur craftsmen who took to covering vase after vase from the shelves of Woolworth's, a venture into arts and crafts that followed my pillbox and coat hanger period. I swapped the vases with my schoolmates for the little white metal charms given away as premiums by the Mirror candy stores and for the carved ivory bibelots found in many of the Japanese shops on upper Broadway. They made welcome gifts. The vases had an art nouveau elegance; even the color combinations were Whistlerian—rose and silver, blue and gold, peacock blue and green—although I had never heard of Whistler. My last and most successful one was a long-necked, Chinese-looking vase, about four inches high, vermilion melting into black. I gave it to the Bartons for their gold-walled living room.

My next venture with melted wax was the "fudge party" Konrad Cramer and I had at Woodstock to make lithographic crayons. And I still have pleasant memories of the delicate fragrance of the yellow carnauba wax as it sizzled in the frying pan heated by a blowtorch.

We were in New York for the Christmas holidays in 1955 to visit the children's grandmothers and

the many friends we had left behind when the
Second World War separated us from our
hometown. I was attracted to the Faiyumic portraits on mummy cases at the Metropolitan
Museum. There probably is no artist alive today
who does not have more than a sneaking admiration for the immortality of these eighteen-hundred-
year-old faces, still softly glowing in their earth
colors, impasto-accented in black and white, and
illumined in gold.

My old friend Bumpei Usui, painter, framer, and
collector of pre-Columbian art, told me that his
wife, Frances Pratt, had done some successful
encaustic paintings. When I asked him for details
of the technique, his explanation was indeed
cryptic.

"Hot wax and color, you heat it on a stove, then
burn it in," was his laconic reply. But he was kind
enough to add, "Come to the studio tomorrow
night; we'll show you how."

Frances, slim, blue-eyed, and elegant with her
hair worn in bangs, welcomed us to the studio,
which was hung with cages of brilliantly colored
birds. She got out the electric palette she had
designed, an aluminum box with a heating element
inside, recessed wells for the paint, and a flat area
for mixing the colors. She then handed me a brush,
a small square of Masonite prepared with gesso, a
few sticks of commercially produced encaustic
paint, and a small cup of turpentine. She switched
on the current, and the palette began to heat up.

"Go ahead, paint," she said.

I took a deep breath and dipped, mixed, and
painted the old refrain, my self-caricature. When I
finished, Frances produced an infrared lamp.

"Look away," she warned me. "It's bad for the
eyes. Always wear dark glasses when you use the
infrared."

She then passed the lamp over the surface of the
picture, saying "That's to burn it in to seal it. Now
let it cool, but don't touch it. It'll take a few days to
harden. The damar varnish in the paint is the

hardening agent, and it will continue to harden for years."

Back at home, I prepared to start my series of Washington musicians by sizing a number of Masonite panels with five thin coats of gesso, using a modern recipe that combined sheet gelatin and whiting. And having acquired one of the Pratt-designed aluminum palettes and some sticks of encaustic paint that I assumed adhered to the same formula as those used by Frances, I set out to work.

My first efforts were failures. I painted too thinly. The weather, too, had something to do with it. On damp days, the paint slid around on the gessoed panels, ignoring the brush. Moreover, I used red conté crayon to outline my drawings, and then reinforced the line with lead pencil. The lead combined with the heated paint and ruined the colors. Buying a thick silver wire from a jeweler's supplier and sharpening one end with sandpaper, I tried to solve the problem by drawing in silverpoint. It worked nicely. The line was a silvery gray and left no color.

After completing the twenty-four works of the series, I found, much to my chagrin, that not enough damar varnish had been added to the mixture of beeswax and dry color in the commercially produced sticks of encaustic paint I had used. Far from having the hardest, most durable surface known to the painter's craft, the pictures were scratchable; even worse, their painted surfaces could be eradicated forever by the swipe of a rag soaked in turpentine. Usui told me that this would not be the case if I made my own paint, but I had become allergic to the fumes of the hot pigment that filled the house with the delicious smell of melting beeswax. My only hope was in the passage of time. If the works survived the hazards of their first few years, perhaps, like the Faiyumic portraits, their immortality would be assured.

The largest painting of the series was of the Budapest String Quartet, twenty by twenty-four inches. All the others were a uniform fourteen by ten. I made arrangements to sketch the quartet at rehearsal in the auditorium of the Library of Congress. One didn't sketch at their concerts. The cult of the quartet's devotees, to whom the concerts were a sacred rite, had supersonic hearing and extrasensory perception and could tell if I was even thinking of taking a pencil out of my purse to make notes on my program. Their electrifying glares warned me not to start scribbling and commanded me to sit back and listen to the music.

Aline Fruhauf

The members of the quartet—Joseph Roisman, first violinist; Alexander "Sasha" Schneider, second violinist; Mischa Schneider, cellist; and Boris Kroyt, violist; known to some as Alexander's Catgut Four—were no longer from Budapest although the ensemble originated there. They traveled the world over, made their recordings in New York, and were in residence at the Library of Congress every spring and fall, where they performed on Thursday and Friday nights under the patronage of Gertrude Clarke Whittall. At the rehearsal I sat eight rows from the stage. Now and then, the musicians interrupted their playing with animated talk in Russian, their native tongue. During one particularly lively exchange, Mischa Schneider, Sasha's brother, called out to me,

"You, up there. You talk Russian?"

When I assured him that I didn't, he muttered, "Dat's good," and the four-way conversation was resumed with considerable laughter and eye rolling in my direction.

The Mischa Schneiders and their two boys also lived in the Maryland suburbs, and I saw them frequently on the street or at the Farm Women's Market. One morning, after a concert in Washington that had been misconducted, so to speak, by an out-of-town cellist, I met Mischa coming out of a shop. I told him I had seen him at the catastrophe and asked him if he could explain why so many cellists aspire to be conductors. After giving the matter some thought, he said,

The Budapest String Quartet,
1957.

"Cello is a very difficult instrument and . . . ," finishing the sentence with an eloquent shrug.

In doing their composite portrait-caricature, I used my thumbnail to scratch through the paint to the ground of gesso for the white accents, and for the blacks, I used a pen dipped in India ink. Frances had told me that ink could be burned in along with the paint, so I repeatedly passed the infrared lamp over the surface.

One of the encaustics was a double portrait of Werner Lywen, first violinist of the National Symphony Orchestra, and Richard Dirksen, music director of the Washington Cathedral. The harpsichord used by Dirksen was the beautiful Dolmetsch that had first belonged to Day Thorpe and later to harpsichordist Ralph Kirkpatrick. It was a lovely thing to look at as well as to listen to, painted park-bench green with an inch-wide stripe

Aline Fruhauf

Paul Hume, 1957.

of gleaming gold. Somehow I couldn't submit my
rendering of that fine instrument to mere
"Oenslager gold." I sent to New York for what was
called "shell gold," a gold tablet the size and shape
of a kidney bean imbedded in a blue plastic disk. It
was made of pure gold dust, held together with
gum arabic, and could be used like watercolor. I
gave the pictured harpsichord its gold stripe and,
after it dried, burnished it, Renaissance style, with
a wedge-shaped piece of polished agate. It worked

217

so well that when the time came to portray Sylvia Meyer, the harpist of the National Symphony, I was able to give her a harp of pure gold.

Paul Hume, the music critic of the *Washington Post*, another of my sitters, had inadvertently entered the annals of political history in 1947 when he severely criticized the singing of a president's daughter. Harry S. Truman's acid reply to Hume's critique of his daughter Margaret's concert at Constitution Hall had become a historical document. Hume, a well-trained tenor himself, frequently performed in the series of concerts sponsored by the Phillips Collection. It was in his role as critic, however, that I sketched him, seated in his accustomed place, the last row of the oak-paneled music room of the Phillips Collection.

Richard Bales, composer, and director of the National Gallery's orchestra, was one of the more engaging sitters. His research into American music had produced three patriotic cantatas: *The American Revolution, The Union*, and *The Confederacy*. The last named included the rousing minstrel song, "The Yellow Rose of Texas." In my caricature of him conducting among the lush foliage and giant ferns of the gallery's East Garden Court where his concerts were held, I gave him a boutonniere appropriate to the song.

Among the other sitters were Howard Mitchell, conductor of the National Symphony; Paul Callaway, organist and conductor; Robert Evett, composer; Russell Woollen, organist and pianist; and, of course, Patrick Hayes and his wife, the pianist Evelyn Swarthout.

Under the title supplied by Erwin, "The Face of Music in Washington," the series went on exhibition in the art gallery of the Dupont Theatre, opening on November 12, 1957, and scheduled to continue through December 23. My mother came down from New York for the late-afternoon opening on the twelfth. Susie was away at college, but Debbie was there, dressed in a pale blue frock and a matching ribbon in her long black hair. Erwin

Aline Fruhauf

Richard Bales, 1957.

stood by me, a tower of strength. My exhibitions—
before, after, and during—were now an old story
to him. Pat Hayes's rosy face was a reassuring
sight. He had been generous with his time and
service, and through his Sunday radio broadcasts,
he had stimulated so much interest in the exhibition that it was extended through the following
March. And Mrs. Hayes looked stunning. Her
cameo features and pale gold hair were set off by a
slim sheath of black sequins. Most of the music
people showed up, and there were no incidents. A
box of flowers arrived from my colleagues Sarah
Baker and Prentiss Taylor. Nestled in the green
paper was a dainty little corsage of yellow roses
and lily of the valley. I sniffed the bouquet, but
there was no odor. The flowers were wax.

   In November 1958, the series went on exhibition
at the Baltimore Museum.

219

Return to Stone

After two years of working in encaustic, I was ready for another wax medium, my old love, lithography. Prentiss, who was now the president of the Society of Washington Printmakers, suggested that I get in touch with George Miller, whose workshop on West Twenty-second Street in New York had been the stronghold of printmakers for more than thirty-five years. A master printer, Miller had turned out lithographs for such well-known artists as George Bellows, William Gropper, Childe Hassam, Louis Lozowick, Lynd Ward, and, of course, Prentiss himself. I wrote to Miller asking him to send me a stone, and it was when the stone arrived, well wrapped and crated, that I started the lithographic version of the yellow house in Georgetown. Miller ran off an edition of the print for me. Then I decided to splurge and asked him to send me several stones so that I could experiment *à la mode de Lautrec*.

I devoured the stones, using sketches I had made at a symposium held at the Institute of Contemporary Arts in which the composers Roy Harris, Walter Piston, and Aaron Copland, and the great teacher who had taught them all, Nadia Boulanger, were the participants. Nothing much came of this lithographic bacchanal but a feeling of exhilaration. I had been tracing my drawings for too long a time and needed the freedom of a fresh start.

There was a bone-smooth, sixty-pound stone in the house and a fresh supply of crayons, neatly packaged like licorice candies in their little boxes. For subject, I turned once again to the Budapest Quartet. But after I drew in the players, I found my composition weak and lacking in lustre, and the worked-over areas were harsh and sooty in texture. I covered the stone with a paper towel and went off to a lecture by Edith Hamilton at the Institute of Contemporary Arts.

Miss Hamilton, a renowned classical scholar who preferred to be called a student, had just been made honorary citizen of Athens. She was ninety years old—a spare, arresting-looking woman with white hair, a proud nose, heavy brows, and snapping dark eyes. She wore a sweeping gown of cornflower-blue satin and affected a lorgnette.

As I sketched, I made notes on the lecture on one side of my pad. Rivalry between the United States and the Soviet Union for the conquest of outer space had just begun, and Miss Hamilton urged "education for its own sake, not merely to get ahead of the Russians, but to enrich life and outlaw boredom. No one within walking distance of a library," she proclaimed, "need ever be bored."

The institute was founded in 1947 "to present the best in all the contemporary arts." Nevertheless, Edith Hamilton was sharply critical of modern art, literature, and poetry. As I looked around the audience, I could see that some of my artist friends were reacting according to their aesthetic principles. Some bristled with audible outrage while others applauded vigorously and waggled their heads in earnest approval. Although she was a slight woman, Miss Hamilton's gestures were commanding, and to me, at least, she personified the cold, clear light of reason.

At a party after the lecture, I met a friend of Miss

Aline Fruhauf

221

Hamilton's who asked to see my sketches. She thought I had caught something of her spirit. When I explained that I had a caricature in mind, possibly a lithograph, she told me that Feliks Topolski had done a very good one for *Vogue*. I admired the masterly draughtsmanship of that Polish-born British artist, who regularly published his own *Chronicle* in London, and began thinking of what his version might be like. But I was glad I had never seen it; it might have affected my own effort.

The next morning I took some of my cherished Whatman watercolor paper, and with *sumi* ink and a Japanese brush I did a few Edith Hamiltons in the Oriental style with a free-arm movement to loosen my line. Then I uncovered the Budapest stone. One look convinced me that it had to be blacked out. Lacking distilled water to dilute the ink, I took the chance that the newly fallen snow was free of chlorine and fluoride, put some in a saucer, poured in some ink, and spread the mixture over the stone. The result was not a pitch-black ground, but the quartet was annihilated; only a provocative shimmer of their half-hidden music stands remained. With one of my *sumi*-ink drawings as a guide, I drew in the figure with red conté crayon and scratched out the lighter areas with a razor blade. As if by magic the image of a Delphic sibyl emerged. And for once I had sense enough to stop. I taped a paper towel over the stone, turned the stone over, and drew a head of Schoenberg on the other side.

When I went to New York for the proving, George Miller, who distrusted the use of liquid tusche, didn't think the stone would print. "But I etched it," he said. His son Burr was more hopeful. He pulled a proof, and aside from narrowing the background at each side, the drawing needed no correction.

When I make a good print of anyone I admire, I like to give the subject a proof. I was a long time in doing it in this case—two years, in fact. Remembering Edith Hamilton's attitude toward modern art, I felt she might not be complimented. Besides, she was a very old lady. Her old friend Huntington Cairns, however, suggested that I call her longtime companion, Doris Reid, who told me Miss Hamilton was curious to see the print and asked that I come to tea. Since I like to get home early enough in the afternoon to rest and prepare dinner for the family in a somewhat leisurely manner, I asked for a morning appointment, and it was arranged.

The vestibule of the Hamilton residence on Massachusetts Avenue, near the Canadian Embassy, was painted in the flat basalt black of ancient Greek vases, and there was a frieze of classical figures near the ceiling. Doris Reid, a pleasant, businesslike woman with short gray hair, ushered me into a living room bright with chintz, a painting or two, and a view of the garden. Miss Hamilton came in. She had been reading the galley proofs of her twenty-eight introductions to the complete works of Plato. She had aged much in two years and seemed smaller and more fragile than when I heard her lecture. She wore a gray-and-black silk dress with a velvet collar and a choker of large white beads, which, like her hearing aid, seemed much too heavy for her. I felt awkward and presumptuous and wondered what on earth had possessed me to interrupt this delicate old lady in the midst of her work. I thought of my little grandmother Anna, who, at the age of ninety-eight, said to me, "When I feel myself slipping, I recite Virgil."

Miss Hamilton, however, showed no signs of slipping. Her voice was firm and clear, and she was in perfect command.

"I apologize for not shaking hands," was her greeting. "I'm suffering from shingles, and for my deafness, which is particularly bad today. I'm grateful that my hearing rather than my sight has been affected; I can still read Plato."

Miss Reid, whose low, resonant voice was more audible to Miss Hamilton than mine, acted as

Aline Fruhauf

223

interpreter, and my message delivered in her clear, decisive tones didn't sound as unreasonable as I thought it would: "She says she waited two years to give you this print, which is intended as a tribute. She was encouraged to go ahead with it when she heard that Feliks Topolski had done one of you. She hopes you will accept the print, but will understand if you don't."

At the mention of Topolski, Miss Hamilton shuddered slightly. Then, with a wry smile and in the little girl's voice old ladies sometimes affect, she said, "I like it better than the Topolski," and asked, "How did you come to do it?" I replied that I had drawn her while attending her lecture.

"I can't imagine how just seeing me on a platform lecturing could have such an effect."

I assured her that her impact had been considerable, and the questioning continued. "Do you think that someone who did not know me, having seen this, would recognize me in a crowd?"

"That would depend on the person," I replied, and she seemed satisfied. Leaning toward me with a penetrating look, she then asked, "What is it you do?" When I said I was a caricaturist, she again queried me, "Does this in any way affect your attitude toward people? Do you see them in exaggerated form?" And I had to admit that I had no answer.

After posing for some random sketches, she excused herself and went back to her Plato. I had had a lesson in Socratic dialogue.

When Aldous Huxley came to Washington to lecture at the Institute of Contemporary Arts in November of 1960, I wanted to draw him. Remembering Boardman Robinson's advice never to draw anyone with a preconceived idea, when I attended the prelecture press conference at the home of Robert Richman, the founder and president of the institute, I tried to forget Max Beerbohm's caricature of the young Huxley with its boyish features and corkscrew legs.

I reached the Richman residence in Georgetown

early. I wanted to see Huxley make his entrance. After I waited a few minutes, in he came with Mrs. Richman. Tall, stooped, and gray, he reminded me of an elegant piece of driftwood, an image that completely obliterated Max's from my mind. The only note of color was a bright yellow flower in his lapel, a late blooming chrysanthemum. He and Mrs. Richman had been walking across the street in the gardens of Dumbarton Oaks, where many were still in bloom. I was introduced, and Huxley sat down, his baroque figure making an interesting contrast to the straight lines of the settee. His eyes were large, the color of pale chalcedony, and they were unfocusing. His nose was almost aquiline, and his skin was taut over high cheekbones. Full lips and eyelids suggested a Cambodian Buddha, and I imagined him wearing a Nehru hat or a turban.

"A long time ago," I reminded him, "I wrote you a letter enclosing a lot of little caricatures of the characters in *Those Barren Leaves*." He thought a minute, recalling the letter, and then we continued where our correspondence had left off. I told him that I had just finished reading S.N. Behrman's *Portrait of Max* and wondered if he had found Max as enchanting and exquisite as Behrman had. "Rather an old bore," said Huxley. "Took him twenty-five minutes to tell a story."

The reporters came in. Mrs. Richman introduced everybody, and Huxley rearranged his long legs and waited for the questions.

Why did he pick southern California as a place to live? "I like it. I need a warm climate." How did the students at M.I.T. react to his lectures? "With the new emphasis on the scientific idyll, the cactus instead of the rose, they are profoundly concerned with how they, as individuals, fit in. They take an ethical point of view. It's a good sign." Did he have any suggestions regarding new methods of educa-tion? "Many things are lying in wait: the training of imagination, autosuggestion, yoga. We must see how many things can be fitted in for an increase in

Aldous Huxley, 1960.

226

awareness." Can you tell us something about mescaline and synthetic mushroom? "They have the same effect—the transfiguration of the external world. Mystical experiences are enlightening and explain many things in art."

The interview was over. Huxley saw us to the door. Strong light from the street brought his features into sharp relief and set the lapel flower ablaze with color as pure and brilliant as chrome yellow squeezed from a tube of paint. I thought of Madame Ginoux, the remarkable portrait that had rocketed me into my yellow period, which led me to Huxley's writings. I wondered if this meeting with Huxley would have ever taken place if Gauguin had not been with van Gogh at Arles in November 1888.

My two encounters with Igor Stravinsky took place at press conferences in hotel rooms, the first in New York in 1934, the second in Washington in 1960. He was a small man with broad shoulders, a slim waist, and a propulsive profile. At first his long, ovoid head suggested an Aztec carving; then it became a blanched almond. Curious, how the nut asserts itself in my association with faces. Donald Friede, the publisher, was also an almond, but a sugar-coated one, and Mondrian, a pecan.

At the first meeting, Stravinsky's hair was brownish and beautifully groomed, I was sure, with a pair of military brushes. He was well turned out in gray flannels, a chocolate-brown cardigan, a gray striped shirt with a white collar, and a brown foulard tie with copper dots. And his image was punctuated by a large onyx ring on his right hand, pointed black shoes, and a cigarette in a long black holder. I made a brush drawing for *Musical America*, and when I went to the office to pick it up after it had been published, I found that one of my anonymous collectors had gotten there first. I made another drawing in watercolor and exhibited it in a group show at the ACA Gallery.

Twenty years later, I drew him conducting a concert at Dumbarton Oaks and added a new observation to my "nut-alikes": the back of his head was a filbert.

In 1960 he came back to Washington to supervise the production and to conduct the performances of his first opera, *Le Rossignol* (1909–14), and for the second time, twenty-six years after the first, I attended his press conference. It was held a few days before Christmas, the coldest day of the winter, and it was cold in the drafty hotel lobby, which had been decorated in an attempt at cozy elegance. The green walls were hung with gilt-framed mirrors, and there were tufted, pseudo-Victorian taupe settees, little round tables covered with floor-length cloths of taupe felt, vases of wax roses, artificial Christmas trees, and candles whose flames were tiny electric bulbs that glowed without warmth. Every time the revolving door opened, a chill blast from the street sent me huddling deeper into my coat. The mirrors not only reflected the green walls with conscientious candor, but suffused everything else in the lobby with a curious underseas half-light. I saw my reflection and shuddered. More than anything in the world, I wanted a cup of strong hot tea.

Soon one of the blasts heralded a little man with a familiar profile accompanied by a taller man who, I assumed, was his co-conductor and Boswell, Robert Craft. I had a fleeting memory of Toulouse-Lautrec's large painting *At the Moulin Rouge* (Art Institute of Chicago), in which Lautrec had painted himself leaving the café with his tall cousin. Oddly enough, the composition of the picture was completed, lower right, by the figure of a woman whose face, like mine, was bathed in green light. Stravinsky and Craft entered the elevator, and any further projection of my thought was interrupted by the entrance of reporters and music critics. The petite and pretty public relations woman for the Washington Opera Society began handing out press releases, warning us that Craft had said we better have some questions ready or all we'll get will be a travelogue. A telephone call to the lobby

Aline Fruhauf

Igor Feodorovich Stravinsky, 1934.

informed us that Stravinsky was ready to see the press.

When we reached his suite, Stravinsky was drinking tea. He apologized, saying that he had been rehearsing and was very thirsty. He was wearing a neatly pressed, gray, double-breasted suit with a matching cashmere pullover, a white shirt, slim gray silk tie, and the onyx ring. His beautifully brushed hair and the mere trace of a moustache were almost white.

"Ladies and gentlemen," he greeted us, "sit

down as best you can; we have not much chairs here." The man from the *Washington Post* was the first to speak. In the loud, distinct tones some people reserve for children, the deaf, and foreigners, he said, "You are looking very *well*, Mr. Stravinsky, *better* than when I saw you in New York ." And with equal emphasis, Stravinsky replied, "We are looking *wonderful* until we begin to look *badly*." "That's long enough," said the man from the *Post*.

No questions were forthcoming so, as predicted, Stravinsky went into orbit: "It always begins, they ask me, When were you born? I say, Long ago. I have been traveling by air. Lima, Buenos Aires. No jets, only from Rio. Wonderful. Imagine, eight hours, Brasília to New York. Mexico? Good orchestra. Lima and Bogotá, very provincial. Glad to make it here. I don't like performances of my work without my personal touch. Best conductor? Myself. I know what I'm doing. I don't know what others do."

"Where are you going next?" Stravinsky was asked. "I have to go home, to compose. I go to Santa Fe in July. I am working on a cantata for TV, a biblical subject, Noé, to be narrated and danced. Balanchine, New York City Center Ballet. Robert Graff will conduct, not Robert Craft, no."

The questioning continued. "Mr. Stravinsky, some of your great works are approaching a half-century anniversary. Could you tell us some of your impressions of fifty years ago?"

"Facts I can guarantee," he replied, "not impressions. Maybe interpretation. Modified tempi only. A little faster now. The time we live in is different. Sometimes my music is wrongly printed. A quarter note with a tail means one-eighth. Tail doesn't appear, so it is one-quarter, twice as slow. Absurd!"

Asked about art in Russia, he said, "They are very conservative in art, 150 years late. It is a very old country for music. It is impossible to speak to them. They are not free to speak. Shostakovich is trembling all his life. One can have no relations with such people. The artists are not technicians. God bless America!"

"But have you heard any of the new artists?" he was asked.

"No, I do not go."

"Then how do you know?"

He waved his hand impatiently and said, "They have no technique." It was final. He finished his tea.

The man from the *News* said brightly, "I see you've gotten used to tea bags." In reply, Stravinsky opened his beautifully cut mouth exposing beautifully even white teeth in an expressionless grin and made no comment.

"How about performances of your work in the Soviet Union?" he was asked.

"They are very embarrassed about it. Leonard Bernstein did a very fine performance of my work there. And now, before you go, I would like to introduce Mrs. Stravinsky." A blonde, fashionably dressed in black silk and pearls, came to the door and smiled expansively. "Eager," as she called him, poured himself a generous slug of Scotch and drank it. The interview was over.

On leaving, all I could think to say was, "I've been making drawings of you since 1934."

"Nice," he replied, "You must have quite a collection."

In the spring of 1966, Lord David Cecil, Goldsmiths' Professor of English literature at Oxford and author of the definitive biography of Sir Max Beerbohm, came to Washington to lecture on painters of the romantic English school. Hoping to meet someone who had been so close to the writer and caricaturist I admired so much, I wrote Lord David asking if he would pose for a caricature and talk to me about Max. He called me, and we made an appointment for a sitting.

For a first look, a long view as it were, I went to the first of his lectures at the National Gallery. He seemed withdrawn and pedantic on the platform.

But face to face in the apartment where he and Lady Cecil were staying during the six-week series of lectures, he was animated and outgoing, radiating good will and a quality I can only describe as innocence. He was not very tall, his face was pink, his nose was the upswept kind with a slightly bulbous tip, and his hair, which was parted on the side of his high forehead, was the exact color and apparent texture of cigar ash. He was in his shirtsleeves, and his small bow tie was slightly askew. The informality of his appearance and manner put me at ease at once, and I started to draw and talk at the same time.

"I can give you only half an hour," he said. "I have an appointment."

I began to sketch a three-quarter view and said, "I can't rely on memory alone. Contrary to Max's golden rule, I have to draw from life. And at this moment I can almost feel Max looking over my shoulder, shaking his head and saying, 'That is not the way to do it.' "

"Well, no one ever did anything quite like Max," said Lord David. "Have you read his essay on caricature?"

"Yes, by heart," I replied. "Would you mind moving your head a little to the right?" He obliged and continued to talk.

"Of course, I was terribly pleased and flattered when word came from Elisabeth that I had been chosen to write Max's biography."

Elisabeth Jungmann had been companion-secretary to Gerhart Hauptmann and, after the death of Max's first wife, Florence, to Max. She became Lady Beerbohm just before his death.

"It must have been quite a change for her, from Hauptmann to Max," I said as I walked around to get his profile.

"Yes, and if he hadn't been so charming she wouldn't have gone to him." Then he added, "Max was a happy man. And they [his two wives] were both nice women. The one I liked best, though, is Dora. The little nun. His sister."

"I've been greatly influenced by Max," I said, "all my life."

"So was I, in the beginning."

"The only one," I went on, "I've ever met who didn't share my enthusiasm for Max was Aldous Huxley."

"Well, they weren't interested in the same thing," and apparently confusing Aldous with his brother Julian, Lord David added, "how many sea urchins were developed in a year, for example. I knew Aldous Huxley. He was the first to be interested in my writing when I was a schoolboy. Somerset Maugham was very critical of Max. And very jealous. There they were, one at one end of the Riviera, poor but happy; the other at the other end, very rich and perfectly miserable. Max was a better writer than Maugham."

He settled himself in his chair and continued, "Max had a manner, an elegance of speech, very much of the Oscar Wilde period. I remember one time at luncheon, the elder Lady Cunard was mentioned. Someone asked, 'How is Lady Cunard?' 'Just the same,' was the answer. And Max said, 'Oh, I am so sorry to hear that.'"

In his biography of Max, Lord David described Lady Cunard as "an exotic American whose conversation was full of embarrassing audacities. George Moore," he added, "might call her his dear lady of dreams, but they were not the kind of dreams Max enjoyed."

The half hour was almost over. We talked about our families, and Lord David said, "We have a daughter in college, and our son is an actor in the theatre at Salisbury. And now I want to introduce my wife." A small, attractive woman entered the room. "I wanted to come in before," she said, "but you were so busy!"

I began to pick up my things and asked Lord David to autograph my copy of his biography of Max. As he signed it, he apologized for having to rush away and said if I needed him to pose again to phone him.

Aline Fruhauf

233

Sosakuhanga

A year or so after I had done the "wax recording" of Richard Bales, the conductor of the National Gallery's orchestra, I found among my notes a ballpoint drawing of him that had the elongated characteristics of a work by Sharaku, the eighteenth-century actor-caricaturist. It would be an interesting experiment, I thought, to make a woodcut in the Japanese style, a pastiche of a Sharaku.

Sharaku was my favorite Japanese printmaker. I felt a strong kinship with his artfully transposed impressions of the Kabuki stage. Woodcuts of Sharaku's time were the work of many hands. Clever craftsmen transferred the artists' drawings to wooden blocks, carved a separate block for each color, and then aligned the superimposed printings to achieve an ultimate design. No such technical collaboration exists today, at least not in this country, so when I learned that Keiko Hiratsuka Moore was teaching a twelve-hundred-year-old technique called *Sosakuhanga*, a method in which drawing, cutting, and printing were all done by one artist, I went to see her to ask if she thought I could transfer my drawing to a block and print it. Keiko, a soft-voiced, flowerlike young woman, said yes, it was possible, so I signed up for some lessons.

The wood used in Keiko's studio was not the traditional cherry but satin-smooth silver magnolia, obtainable only in Japan. Up to then, no satisfactory American equivalent had been found. After I had made a tracing of my drawing on rice paper, Keiko told me to go over it with ink. Then she pasted it to a small block with a mixture of rice flour and water. With tiny sharp tools, first a knife and then a chisel, she showed me how to cut away each side of the line until it stood forth in sharp relief. Although my hands were clumsy, as soon as I cut into the wood I knew I was in love again. But it was taking so long. "You'll see," Keiko said comfortingly, "soon the knife will be like your brush."

While I worked and Keiko corrected me, her mother, a small woman with shining teeth and hair skinned back and skewered in a knot, bustled about uttering prayerful little cries of encouragement and moans of real pain when I sliced through a precious line. For years she had watched her famous printmaker-husband and was familiar with every step of the process. Small Thalia Moore, one year old and very beautiful, was in the next room napping. Her grandmother ran in to have a look at her, and then suddenly reappeared with a lacquer tray, small cups of steaming tea, and a plate of rice cakes. Printmaking was hungry work and I disgraced myself wolfing down the delicate fare. I felt gross and oversized compared to these exquisite women with their centuries-old traditions and manners.

At last one day the block was finished. "Now we're ready to print!" Keiko said, and she began the preparations. She produced a round tin of ink that looked like shoe-blacking, a stiff-bristled brush, a saucer for the ink, another for sesame oil, a little stick of bamboo, sheets of cream-colored Okawara paper, bits of newspaper, and a bāren. The bāren is a disk, covered with bamboo leaf, with a flexible handle of bamboo that can be grasped in a closed fist. She mixed some ink in one saucer and dipped the brush in it. With a scrubbing motion, she worked the ink onto the first face I had carved out of wood. Then she applied a few drops of oil to the bāren with the bamboo stick. "That's to keep the bamboo-leaf covering from drying out and splitting. Many Japanese printmakers pass the bāren through their hair to supply the necessary oil." When I ran my hand through my own dry mop, I realized I would have to use the sesame oil. She laid a piece of the Okawara paper, dampened to the exact degree of moisture, over the inked block. If it had been too wet, the ink would have blotted and smudged; if it had been too dry, the paper would have stuck to the block. Then she put a piece of the newspaper over the Okawara, grasped the bāren, and, with a circular motion, rubbed it over the newspaper, which absorbed any ink that might come through from the back of the Okawara and thus prevented the bāren from getting ink on it. When it seemed that enough ink had been applied to the Okawara, Keiko removed the newspaper and applied a block of wood to the center of the Okawara. Holding the block firmly with her left hand, she carefully peeled off the top of the Okawara to see how it was printing, then carefully did the same thing with the bottom half.

"Not enough ink," she said and applied more, first at the top half, then at the bottom, all the while holding the block of wood in place so that the paper wouldn't slip and spoil the impression. Several applications of ink are sometimes required. At last, she peeled off a perfect print. We all cheered and, with a broad smile on her face, Mrs. Hiratsuka went to the kitchen to prepare tea.

"Do you have a little signature or monogram to make a stamp?" Keiko asked. I remembered that years ago Deems Taylor had dashed off a *han* for me. I hadn't used it since I painted it on my Fourth Dimension, embroidered it inside the pocket of a coat, and used it as a copper monogram on a brown shagreen cigarette case I had made in Paris. I cut a quarter-inch version into a block of magnolia

wood. *Shuniku*, the vermilion paste seal-ink that
came in a red lacquer box, required some skill in
application. Keiko told me to put it near a lamp
until it was warm, and then place the paper to be
stamped over a folded piece of soft cloth, dip the
stamp in the ink just long enough to get an even
supply, and then stamp the paper. After a few
tries, I was able to get a clean impression. I signed
one print and gave it to Bales as a Christmas
present.

To go with the *han* he had designed for me so
long ago, I decided to do a Japanese-style woodcut
of Deems Taylor, my ex-boss on *Musical America*. I
had done a caricature of him for *Vanity Fair* many
years ago, but it was lost in 1936 when the
magazine was absorbed by *Vogue*. I thought I could
do another from memory. My visual image of
Deems had been reinforced twice since he had
posed for me—the first time when he came to my
designers' show in 1943, the second when I saw
him at the dedication of the George Gershwin
manuscripts at the Library of Congress in 1953. He
looked the same. Lean bald men with firm jaw-
lines, deep cheek creases, and glasses seldom
change much. At the library, we chatted a while,
congratulated each other on still being alive, and,
on parting, he said with a grin, "Good-bye, see you
in another twenty years!"

In his essay "The Spirit of Caricature," Max
Beerbohm gives an imaginary address to a mythical
school of caricature:

> *The perfect caricature is not a mere snapshot. It*
> *is the outcome of study; it is the epitome of its*
> *subject's surface, the presentment (once and for*
> *all) of his most characteristic pose, gesture, ex-*
> *pression. Therefore I should not advise any*
> *young caricaturist (however quickly perceptive)*
> *to rely on one sight of his subject. On the other*
> *hand, let him not make too long a delay, in-*
> *asmuch as too great familiarity blunts impres-*
> *sions. There is another golden rule, which, if he*

*be worth anything at all, he will know without
being told: he must never draw from the
model. . . . It is only in recollection of his
subject that the unconscious process of exaggerat-
ing begins to work. Let him allow this process
to run its course, leisurely, to his fingertips.
Then, not till then, may he clutch his pencil.*

Every time I read this passage, I realize that I have
been breaking the golden rule for years. Memory,
however, did play its part in the Deems Taylor
caricature, which I proceeded to transfer to a block
directly, without pasting on a tracing. Lapsing into
Western ways, after several mishaps with too-wet
paper and too-fluid ink, I lapsed even further,
forsaking the bāren for my smooth wedge-shaped
piece of agate, and going over, whole hog, to
printers ink, which has an oil base.

The image of Deems Taylor on the wood looked
like a leprechaun in a mackintosh, but the print
gave him the decided air of a gentleman of Japan,
or at least of Titipu. I sent him a proof, stamped
with the *han,* and his reply came in a few days:

> *The print arrived as I returned from the opening
> of the revival of* Peter Ibbetson, *and both events
> together made me feel as if I were back in the
> thirties, at the beginning of things again.*
>
> *It's one of the cutest caricatures I've seen in a
> long time, and I'm very glad you "got around" to
> doing it.*

One day, on an errand at the Library of Congress, I passed by the Coolidge Auditorium. The
doors were open, and there on the platform, as if
they were waiting for the musicians, stood the four
chairs of the Budapest String Quartet. I made a
quick sketch, and when I got home I transferred it
to a block of magnolia wood. At the time, I was in
for a long siege of dental work, a process
euphemistically known as rehabilitation that
required vast reserves of stamina from patient and
practitioner alike. Morning appointments some-

Deems Taylor, 1960.

times lasted until early afternoon. Irwin Freitag, my Friday dentist, told me I could bring drawing materials to the office because there would be long periods of inactivity while we waited for the Novacaine to take effect. I asked him if I could bring my woodcut tools and, not knowing precisely what was to follow, he said, "By all means."

Soon I was settled in the chair, pleasantly lulled by the drug but conscious enough to chip away at the large white spaces around the Budapest's chairs on the block. My neatly arranged tools were well out of the way of the set used by the dentist, but under my chair was a growing pile of shavings. Dr. Freitag, a meticulous man, spied the pile in horror. I apologized for messing up his office but reminded him that he had told me to bring my homework. His assistant came to the rescue by putting a large paper bag under the chair to catch the studio debris. Order was restored, and we took turns plying our respective crafts, filling the air with the merry sounds of alternate chipping and drilling.

Only after I pulled my first proof of the Budapest Quartet did I realize that, in my latest effort to reduce them to lowest terms, the gentlemen had disappeared altogether. Keiko helped me pull some prints. I called the woodcut *Musical Chairs*, and the first proof occupies a prominent place on the wall of Dr. Freitag's waiting room.

Un-ichi Hiratsuka, Keiko's famous father, came to Washington to join his wife, daughter, and her family, bringing with him a supply of the lovely satinlike wood. New shipments took months to come from Tokyo, and Hiratsuka was on constant lookout for an American equivalent, but with no success. On one of my trips to New York, Bumpei Usui, a never-failing source of information, told me that the closest thing to the wood of the magnolia was that of the tulip poplar. Back in Chevy Chase, I happened to mention this bit of information to my friend, the writer and illustrator, Marion Holland. "I think I can get you some little pieces,"

Maurice Ravel, 1976 wood-cut, from the drawing in the *Musical Courier*, 1928.

she said. "There's a cabinetmaker in Leesburg, who told me that tulip was used to make the in-sides of bureau drawers in old chests. I'll ask him if he has any to spare the next time I'm down there."

The little squares of thin wood Marion brought me were beautifully seasoned. They looked like butter and had the same respect for a precious line as their Japanese relative. I made a little print of the Temple of Apollo at Pompeii and gave it to Marion to give to the cabinetmaker. He had never heard of a woodcut, but he put it on the wall of his work-shop as a curiosity.

With the same supply of wood, I made a wood-cut of my drawing of Ravel.

In lumberyards, the wood of the tulip tree is known as yellow poplar. Not all lumberyards stock it, but I found one in Georgetown that did. Keiko and I got some for her father, who was so pleased with the way the wood cut and printed that, in gratitude for the information supplied by his countryman Usui, he made me a little color print of the blossom of the tulip tree. And when Usui framed the print, the episode of the wood of the magnolia family came full circle.

The print of Ravel launched me on a whole new series of prints: woodcuts of musicians. I found not only that cutting the image in wood preserved the linear flow of the drawings in pen and ink, but that the resistance of the wood, however slight, to the cutting tools added a new dimension to it. Making no attempt to reproduce the pen line itself, I trans-lated it into the terms of the new medium, which called for a larger format. And in place of the fine line of the pen, the cut away from the line, which left it in relief, added a new strength to both the delineation and the characterization of the subject.

For the new series, I turned to my early drawings or, when they were lost, to their reproductions of Béla Bartók (*Musical America*, December 24, 1927), Pablo Casals (*Musical America*, January 21, 1928), Aaron Copland, George Gershwin, Sergei Prokofiev (*Musical Courier*, February 1, 1929),

Arnold Schoenberg, 1977 woodcut, from the drawing in *Musical America*, November 1933.

Sergei Rachmaninoff, 1977 woodcut, from the drawing in *Musical America*, 1934.

Sergei Rachmaninoff (*Musical America*, December 19, 1934), Arnold Schoenberg (*Musical America*, November 29, 1933), and Igor Stravinsky (*Musical America*, April 10, 1935).

I also translated my drawings of Martha Graham (*Dance Observer*, May 1934); of the Chinese actor of female roles, Mei Lan-fang (*Top Notes*, March 1, 1930), who performed with his troupe in New York in 1930; of Aldous Huxley, as he appeared seated

Igor Stravinsky, 1967.

at his press conference; and of the distinguished attorney Clarence Darrow, whom I met at Montreux, Switzerland, where we were staying in the same hotel in 1929.

Twenty-one years after I attempted a caricature of Alice Longworth, I saw her as she walked away from her house on Massachusetts Avenue to her waiting car. I was en route to the bus stop in front of her house and stood well back to get a good look without her seeing me. Her back view was just as

unmistakably hers and was decidedly worth drawing. Eventually I made a pen-and-ink drawing of
it, and later a woodcut. A print of the woodcut was
included in the annual exhibition of the Society of
Washington Printmakers in December 1971. It
came to her attention, and I was told that she was
gleefully autographing prints of it around town. I,
too, wanted one, so I called her to say I would be
happy to exchange autographed prints with her.

"That's terribly amusing," came her melodious
voice over the telephone. We settled on an early
afternoon appointment. She was the same breezy
little woman I remembered, and she had aged but
little. After we had each signed our respective
prints, she offered to take me home. The car was
waiting. I gave the chauffeur directions, and when
we were seated Mrs. Longworth turned to me,
saying, "This is fun! We can have a ride and a talk."

I looked at the chiseled profile on my right and
marveled at her good bones. There were no rings
on her fingers, but she wore a narrow strip of
copper on her wrist, the type made in England and
the talisman of many athletes and aging females.
Laughing, I held out my bracelet, a version
fashioned of twisted copper wire by Taos Indians.
"Of course," she said with a shrug, "It's pure
nonsense, but I wear it anyhow. Everyone has
arthritis; no one calls it rheumatism anymore. Eat
lots of honey; that's very good for arthritis."

Recalling a newspaper article , I asked her if she
could still sit in the full lotus position. In reply, she

Aline Fruhauf

Martha Graham, 1976 wood-
cut, from a drawing in the
Dance Observer, 1934.

243

Making Faces crossed her right knee over until her right ankle touched her left thigh and then pulled her left foot close to her right thigh. "I sit this way," she said. "Very comfortable for long rides by car."

"It's strange," I said, "I've spent my lifetime making faces, and *Making Faces* will be the title of my book. And now the book ends, not with a face, but with a back. Yours. The woodcut. The tail-piece."

"That's a very good title! How did you think of it?" she asked.

"It's not mine, actually. Do you remember Blanche Yurka, who played Hamlet's mother in the John Barrymore production?"

"Yes, I remember, of course."

Blanche, I told her, was doing some plays at the Maverick Theatre at Woodstock, and I was trying to make a drawing of her for display in the lobby. I drew and drew; one drawing after another hit the floor. I groaned in anguish, and Blanche looked at me, and in the wonderful rich contralto she used for Shakespeare and Ibsen, she intoned, "I thought it was supposed to be fun. If you suffer so, why do you do it? But there you sit, making faces."

Aline Fruhauf

Mrs. Longworth Facing
Dupont Circle, 1971.

INDEX

247

Sergei Prokofiev

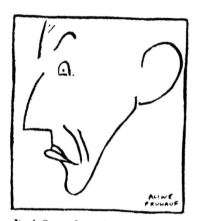

Noel Coward, author and one of the three stars of "Design for Living" at the Ethel Barrymore Theater.

ALINE
FRUHAUF

Fay Wray

Herblock

N

AARON COPLAND, COMPOSER, WHO IS GIVING A SERIES OF LECTURES AT THE NEW SCHOOL OF SOCIAL RESEARCH, 465 WEST 23RD STREET, NEW YORK

ALINE
FRUHAUF

HELEN HAYES, at Present Giving So Fine and Moving a Performance at Maxine Elliott's, as She Appears to Aline Fruhauf.

Eugene O'Neill